*The Heavens Declare*

# The Heavens Declare

*Natural Theology and the Legacy of Karl Barth*

Rodney Holder

Templeton Press

Templeton Press
300 Conshohocken State Road, Suite 550
West Conshohocken, PA 19428
www.templetonpress.org



Library of Congress Cataloging-in-Publication Data

Holder, Rodney D.
The heavens declare : natural theology and the legacy of Karl Barth / Rodney D. Holder.
p. cm.
Includes bibliographical references (p. ) and index.
ISBN 978-1-59947-396-3 (pbk. : alk. paper)
1. Natural theology. I. Title.
BL183.H65 2012
210—dc23
2011036870

Designed and typeset by Gopa & Ted2, Inc.
Printed in the United States of America

12 13 14 15 16 17 10 9 8 7 6 5 4 3 2 1

In memory of my uncle and godfather,
Peter Drinkwater (1930–2011),
who inspired and encouraged me
from my youth onwards

# Contents

# Preface

THE GREAT twentieth-century Protestant theologian Karl Barth has left a legacy of suspicion with regard to the project of natural theology, that is, the seeking of evidence for God's existence in the ordered structure of the world. However, contemporary scientific advances and the flourishing modern dialogue between science and religion, as well as the attacks on theology from the so-called "new atheists," who deny that there is any evidence for religious belief, have made it important to revisit the role of natural theology. This book does that through engagement with the thought of major theologians who have responded to Barth in ways more or less sympathetic to his position.

My own interest in this topic stems from my long-standing involvement in the relationship between science and religion. In particular, in my academic work in recent years—especially in my book *God, the Multiverse, and Everything*—I have focused on a modern version of an argument toward God from nature. My theological training, combined with a great interest in Germany, where I have lived and worked as chaplain of the English Church in Heidelberg, has brought me in touch with the thought of Barth and other great figures in German theology. Barth is a theologian I admire immensely, both because he maintains an orthodoxy which I share and because his theology was so important for the opposition of the Confessing Church in Germany to the Nazi regime. Dietrich Bonhoeffer, a disciple of Barth, is even more of a hero of mine, as someone who paid with his life for his role in the anti-Nazi conspiracy. Hence, for some time I have been questioning how to reconcile my work in natural theology with the theological concerns of these historic figures.

Of the other theologians whose thought I engage with in the book, Alister McGrath deserves special mention because I had the privilege of being taught by him at Wycliffe Hall, Oxford. Moreover, he has advised and encouraged me in this book project, despite the fact that it might result in a critique of his own work. Like all of the theologians studied here, McGrath is a theologian I admire and one whose fundamental orthodoxy and concern for the centrality of Jesus Christ I share.

It will be apparent that my own outlook has been heavily influenced by John Polkinghorne and Richard Swinburne, whom I mention frequently in the book. However, I do not devote separate chapters to them, since the main focus is on the place of natural theology within systematic theology, rather than the science–theology dialogue or the philosophy of religion. Hence, I consider instead, and in addition to those already named, the very different ways in which systematic theologians Wolfhart Pannenberg and Thomas Torrance have engaged with the sciences.

In the last few years, I have written articles for several journals devoted to the individual theologians studied in *The Heavens Declare*. These articles have been brought together, and substantially enhanced with further material, in order to produce this book. I am grateful to the following for permission to use the articles listed:

- The Gospel Coalition: Rodney D. Holder, "Karl Barth and the Legitimacy of Natural Theology," *Themelios* 26, no. 3 (2001): 22–37 (formerly published by the Religious and Theological Studies Fellowship of the Universities and Colleges Christian Fellowship).
- Taylor and Francis Ltd.: Rodney D. Holder, "Modern Science and the Interpretation of Genesis: Can We Learn from Dietrich Bonhoeffer?" *Theology and Science* 6, no. 2 (2008): 213–31; and Rodney D. Holder, "Thomas Torrance: 'Retreat to Commitment' or a New Place for Natural Theology?" *Theology and Science* 7, no. 3 (2009): 275–96.
- John Wiley and Sons: Rodney D. Holder, "Science and Reli-

gion in the Theology of Dietrich Bonhoeffer," *Zygon* 44, no. 1 (2009): 115–32.

- Petr Sláma (editor, Protestant Theological Faculty of Charles University in Prague): Rodney D. Holder, "Creation and the Sciences in the Theology of Wolfhart Pannenberg," *Communio Viatorum* 49, no 2 (2007): 210–53.

I am grateful for the helpful comments of anonymous referees of the above. Others to whom I owe a debt of gratitude include the following: Denis Alexander, director of the Faraday Institute, who has supported the project throughout; Polly Stanton, the Institute's administrator, who helped with the permissions; and Rebecca Beale, who carried out a most useful literature survey for me on Thomas Torrance. I am most grateful to Natalie Silver, managing editor at Templeton Press, and the rest of the publishing team, for seeing the work through to completion. I am also most indebted to the John Templeton Foundation for financial support of the project. Finally, my wife, Shirley, has been, as ever, the most wonderful support, enabler, and encourager.

*The Heavens Declare*

CHAPTER ONE

# The Enterprise of Natural Theology

## *Historical Overview*

NATURAL THEOLOGY is generally understood to concern the knowledge of God available to all human beings without recourse to special revelation, although, as we shall see in later chapters, some modern theologians wish to define it differently. John Macquarrie gives a typical definition: "Natural theology is the knowledge of God (and perhaps also of related topics, such as the immortality of the soul) accessible to all rational human beings without recourse to any special or supposedly supernatural revelation."[1] It is an area of intellectual inquiry with a long if checkered history, dating back at least to the era of classical Greek thought. Within Christian theology the expression *theologia naturalis* was coined by St. Augustine.

Natural theology found classic expression in the works of St. Anselm and, supremely, in the "Five Ways" of St. Thomas Aquinas presented in the *Summa Theologiae* (hereafter, *ST*). These are all variations on the notion of "First Cause." We see change in the world so there must be an unchanged changer. There must be a stopping point to the regress of causes, and even if there is an infinite backward chain of causes, there must be a first cause of the chain itself. The world and everything in it is contingent, so there must be a necessary being to explain why anything contingent exists. Things in the world exhibit the qualities of truth, goodness, and nobility to varying degrees, so there must be a being that is the truest, best, and noblest of all and which causes the being, goodness, and any other perfection of everything else. Things in the world are ordered for a purpose or goal, and that requires an orderer (this is the teleological or "design" argument that features in differing guises in much subsequent discussion). Aquinas ends each of his Ways by stating "and this we call God" (*ST*, 1a. 2, 3).

Before expounding the Five Ways, Aquinas makes an important distinction that is relevant to much of the discussion of this book: "The truths about God which St. Paul says we can know by our natural powers of reasoning—that God exists, for example—are not numbered among the articles of faith, but are presupposed to them" (*ST*, 1a. 2, 2). Arguing that effects only demonstrate the existence of prior causes, and not their essence, he states more explicitly, "God's effects, therefore, can serve to demonstrate that God exists, even though they cannot help us to know him comprehensively for what he is." My own claim for what natural theology can deliver is very much in line with this, though even more limited in eschewing the words "demonstrate" (*demonstrare*) and "prove" (*probare*), which Aquinas uses.

With the rise of modern science in the sixteenth and seventeenth centuries, natural theology started to take a different form, appealing to particular structures within the natural order, rather than order per se, as exhibiting the signs of design. This was the physico-theology of such figures as Boyle, Hooke, and John Ray—indeed, of many of the early founders of the Royal Society. For example, the intricate detail of the eye of a fly shown under a microscope, and illustrated in Hooke's *Micrographia*, far outshone that of a human artifact such as a nail, which showed rough edges. However, arguments of this kind were often combined with an appeal to more general features, too, such as the lawlike behavior of the natural world that the sciences were uncovering. The early Boyle Lectures gave expression to much natural theology at the beginning of the eighteenth century.

The fortunes of natural theology fluctuated with the advent of the Enlightenment. At first, natural theology was elevated because the alternative way of knowing God, through revelation and therefore through external authority, was deemed suspect: the Enlightenment also saw the advent of biblical criticism. But theologically there was a considerable danger in utilizing natural theological arguments to the neglect of revelation, since this seemed to point only to the need for a deistic conception of God, rather than the Trinitarian theistic conception of orthodox Christian faith—particularly as the universe came to be seen as a clockwork mechanism.

Enlightenment philosophers Immanuel Kant and David Hume attacked natural theology vigorously. Kant said that we can only experience phenomena; we cannot experience "noumena," things "as they are in themselves." And we impose order on the phenomena via the structures of our minds. It is human mind–imposed order rather than real order that we can know nothing about. It is thus not "God-imposed" order, so the design argument of natural theology is apparently undermined. However, scientists in particular find, contrary to Kant, that the empirical reality of the world does seem to force itself on us. Prime examples would be the totally counterintuitive phenomena described by quantum theory, and the four-dimensional curved space-time of general relativity. Indeed, as we shall have cause to reiterate, Kant has been shown to be in error in claiming the necessity of describing the world through Euclidean geometry because this is embedded in the structure of our minds.

Hume made a number of criticisms of natural theology, particularly the argument from design.[2] For example, he pointed to the lack of analogy between mechanical artifacts pointing to a human designer and natural phenomena supposedly pointing to God. A house points to an architect or builder because we have many instances of existing houses. Natural phenomena are not like houses in that respect, and one needs a very close analogy to make the inference to design. To transfer an inference about parts of the universe exhibiting design to the whole doing so would be disproportionate: there is no similarity between a house and a universe![3] Moreover, since a cause ought to be proportioned to its effect, one cannot infer an infinite deity from anything finite. And then, why infer one god as the creator and not several deities, if the analogy is with a house or ship that was built by many men?[4]

Perhaps a better analogy for the universe, says Hume, is an animal. God would then be its soul (curiously an idea that some modern theologians have actually favored, though it certainly departs from classical orthodoxy's maintenance of the distinction between the creator and the universe).[5] The animal analogy also leads him to a different idea for the cause of the universe, namely generation; an ostrich lays an egg in the sand to produce another ostrich, and so on. Intelligence and design do not at any rate constitute the only option.[6]

Hume's arguments have been very influential, with many scholars today believing he dealt the death blow to the argument from design. Historically that seems not to be the case, since natural theology, even in its physico-theological form, continued flourishing well into the first half of the eighteenth century. Indeed the high point was William Paley's 1802 volume, *Natural Theology*.[7] However, even this was not the end, with important contributions coming in the *Bridgewater Treatises* of the 1830s. These publications resulted from the will of the late Earl of Bridgewater, who had left £8,000 at the disposal of the president of the Royal Society, to pay those selected to "write, print and publish one thousand copies of a work *On the Power, Wisdom, and Goodness of God as Manifested in the Creation*."

One of the most significant of these later writers, and a *Bridgewater Treatise* author, was William Whewell. Whewell coined the term "scientist" for the person who had previously been known as a "natural philosopher" or "man of science." Whewell's 1833 *Bridgewater Treatise* was titled *Astronomy and General Physics Considered with Reference to Natural Theology*, and in the dedication he made an important distinction. The aim was to show religious believers "how admirably every advance in our knowledge of the universe harmonizes with the belief of a most wise and good God." He noted, however, how much more important was revelation, which was required "for the purpose of reforming men's lives, of purifying and elevating their characters, of preparing them for a more exalted state of being."[8] Here we have an example of natural theology that accords more with the concept as expounded by Thomas Torrance and Alister McGrath, whom I discuss in later chapters, of supporting existing religious belief, as well as the recognition of its relatively minor status in comparison with revelation. John Hedley Brooke also thinks that the function of much natural theology is not exclusively to "prove the existence of God" for unbelievers, but to fulfill various roles within the community of faith, such as encouraging a "sense of awe and wonder" in believers.[9] It is interesting that Darwin used a quotation from Whewell's *Bridgewater Treatise* to face the title page of *The Origin of Species*: "But with regard to the material world, we can at least go so far as this—we can perceive that events are brought about not by insulated interpositions of Divine power, exerted in each particular case, but by the establishment of general laws."[10]

Notwithstanding the importance of contributions such as that of Whewell, Paley's famous image of himself crossing a heath and finding a watch has undoubtedly abided as the paradigm of natural theological reasoning. On examination the watch seems intricately put together for a purpose, to tell the hour of day, and if the parts were differently shaped or differently arranged from how they are, then the watch would have failed in its purpose. The natural conclusion to draw is that the watch had a maker who designed it for its purpose. Of course, Paley's ultimate point is that "every indication of contrivance, every manifestation of design, which existed in the watch, exists in the works of nature; with the difference, on the side of nature, of being greater and more, and that in a degree which exceeds all computation."[11]

Paley's argument is more subtle than is often given credit for nowadays. Thus he has clearly considered various objections to the argument, some of which remind one of Hume—for example, whether the imperfection or malfunctioning of the watch should affect our conclusion that it was designed. The answer is no, because the original intention could still be discerned. A particularly interesting question is whether the existence of the watch would be accounted for if we were told that it was one out of a large number of possible combinations of material forms. That kind of argument is sometimes advanced today in order to deny that the fine-tuning of the universe requires explanation. Paley dismisses it as not something "any man in his senses" would think.[12] I have argued that it fails in the fine-tuning case both because there is special significance in the configuration of the universe we observe and because, in fact, we have a good explanation for this particular configuration.[13]

Another objection Paley considers is whether it would make any difference to the argument if one found that the watch could generate other watches. In the first place, that would enhance the impression of design, not lessen it, he says, because it is evidence of even greater contrivance. Second, while a watch might generate another watch, it is not the maker in the same sense as a carpenter is the maker of a chair. It is not the source of order and purpose in the new watch, which must still be sought from an overall designer. Paley writes, "There cannot be design without a designer; contrivance without a contriver; order without choice; arrangement, without anything capable of arranging; subserviency and relation to a purpose, without that which could intend a purpose. . . ."[14] Even if our watch was produced by a preceding watch, that would not explain the contrivance of watches and their fitness for purpose. This seems to me to answer a point raised by Richard Dawkins, namely that evolution explains the appearance of design, and of purpose, in the natural world. Paley was therefore "wrong, gloriously and utterly wrong," according to Dawkins.[15] What Dawkins fails to realize is that the process of evolution needs a designer: a backward sequence of causes does not explain the existence of the sequence itself nor why it is productive of design and purpose. The remark of Charles Kingsley that it is even cleverer of God to "make things make themselves" than to create them all separately seems to be in line with what Paley says here.

Paley is widely discredited nowadays, precisely because it is thought that Darwin showed how evolution could produce the appearance of design without a designer. Of course, Paley did not take account of the possible mutation of species, and thus the evolution from simple beginnings of the immense and complex diversity of life we see today. However, as noted above, he was astute enough to consider whether a process of generation could substitute for design, and concluded that design was still required. It seems to me that that point is still valid, and in accord not only with the way such figures as Kingsley, Frederick Temple, and Aubrey Moore enthused about evolution, but also how Darwin himself described it in the closing pages of *The Origin of Species*: "To my mind it accords better with what we know of the laws impressed on matter by the Creator, that the production and extinction of the past and present inhabitants of the world should have been due to secondary causes, like those determining the birth and death of the individual."[16] And again: "There is grandeur in this view of life, with its several powers, having been originally breathed into a few forms or into one; and that, whilst this planet has gone cycling on according to the fixed law of gravity, from so simple a beginning endless forms most beautiful and most wonderful have been, and are being, evolved."[17]

Paley's thought also ranged wider than the design or "contrivance" of particulars within the natural world, such as the individual organs of animals, which are indeed explained by evolution even if evolution itself requires an explanation. Thus he also considered the design of the laws of nature. In particular he realized that the stability of planetary orbits is owed to the inverse square law of gravitation. Other laws would have resulted in the planets either spiraling into the sun or flying away from it. When the very narrow range in which the law must fall for preservation of the system is compared with the infinite range of possibilities, the only reasonable conclusion to draw, says Paley, is that a "designing mind" is responsible for the choice.[18] To my mind this is the best of Paley's arguments, and it is one that has lasted. It has been resurrected in the modern discussion of anthropic fine-tuning with the added nuance that only if there are three (out of infinitely many possible) spatial dimensions is there an inverse square law and hence a stable solar system.[19] But the focus on the design of physical law, rather than the design of individual features separately, is most significant here, since individual features might come about through the operation of laws.

Despite Paley's acknowledgment that there may be deficiencies in design, a problem is that he paints a picture of such a harmonious and "happy world" that the problem of suffering is almost trivialized: "In a spring noon, or a summer evening, on whichever side I turn my eyes, myriads of happy beings crowd upon my view."[20] What John Polkinghorne refers to as the "shadow side" of nature[21] needs seriously to be addressed in any cumulative argument for the existence of a loving God. Indeed, although Darwin had been content to adopt Paley's view when wandering in the meadows around Cambridge, he found the pain and suffering in nature hard to reconcile with God's providential design. He made this clear in a letter to his friend and supporter, the Harvard botanist and Christian believer Asa Gray. He pointed to the ichneumon wasp, which plants its eggs in its host, with the result that the newly hatched young eat the host from the inside: "I cannot persuade myself that a beneficent and omnipotent God would have designedly created the Ichneumonidae with the express intention of their feeding within the living bodies of Caterpillars."[22] Tennyson was soon writing in a similar vein of "nature, red in tooth and claw." This is indeed a problem, and needs a treatise in its own right, so I can do no more than make a few brief remarks at this point.

In the modern science-religion debate, a number of lines of argument have been suggested in which science is seen as helpful to theodicy rather than otherwise. John Polkinghorne has advanced a "free process" defense of natural evil to parallel the free-will defense to human-caused evil.[23] Polkinghorne, Arthur Peacocke, and others have suggested that it may only be by a process of allowing nature to explore possibilities, through the interplay of chance and necessity over eons of time, that rational, free creatures like ourselves could arise in the universe. Earthquakes, animal predation, death, and disease may be necessary if we are to be here to think and argue about such matters at all. Other theodicies such as John Hick's notion that the world is a "vale of soul-making,"[24] an environment in which human beings can learn what it means to love, also have their place in the modern debate. My own view is that all of these have something to offer. Most important perhaps, the Christian faith makes the unique claim that God himself has entered into this world in the person of Jesus Christ and suffered in it and for it, an idea explored particularly in the writings of Jürgen Moltmann. As Dietrich Bonhoeffer, one of the theologians considered in this book, puts it, "only the suffering God can help."[25] God is at any rate not the remote experimenter in the sky but knows what suffering is like from the inside. Furthermore, the claim that there is an eternity of bliss to follow the present dispensation can form an important ingredient in an overall theodicy.

## *Natural Theology Today*

In recent years, natural theology has undergone something of a renaissance. I believe that John Polkinghorne's modest proposal for a revived natural theology has great merit.[26] Polkinghorne sees the comprehensibility of the universe—indeed the very possibility of doing science at all—and the specialness of the universe as described by the anthropic fine-tuning as suggestive of a Creator. However, he believes that such a natural theology is also limited in not seeking to rival scientific explanations for the detailed processes of the world. Polkinghorne thinks that this modern form of natural theology answers the criticism of Hume regarding the anthropomorphic nature of the analogies of the old physico-theology, such as likening the design of the world to that of a ship. Polkinghorne writes, "If the true gift of the Creator is bringing into being a world endowed with the kind of intrinsic potentiality that we have been discussing, that is an act very different from any human crafting of existing material."[27] On the other hand, natural theology is limited theologically: "Its restricted insights can only be a part of the intellectual quest of theological inquiry. At best it could only, by itself, lead to the impersonal conception of the Cosmic Architect or the Great Mathematician."[28] I agree with Polkinghorne here. Natural theology can lead one to a limited conception of God but not to the full understanding of the God of Nicene orthodoxy.

The work of Richard Swinburne, who has restated the classical arguments of natural theology in probabilistic terms, especially in his classic text *The Existence of God*, is also of immense importance.[29] I find myself deeply impressed by Swinburne's work. The notion of "inference to the best explanation" has been developed by philosophers such as Peter Lipton to provide criteria for theory choice in science, and it has been applied to theology by Swinburne's predecessor in the Nolloth Professorship of the Philosophy of Religion at Oxford, Basil Mitchell. Swinburne's development of Bayesian confirmation theory presents a formalization of this notion bringing similar criteria to bear, the most especially relevant for theology being simplicity. Swinburne utilizes the Bayesian probability framework to mount a cumulative case for the existence of God, taking into account the cosmological and teleological arguments, together with arguments from consciousness, morality, providence, history, miracles, and (for Swinburne, the decisive argument) religious experience. He also considers the problem of evil as a possible counterargument.

I myself have found the anthropic arguments coming from modern cosmology particularly striking and persuasive, so much so that I have written a book expounding the thesis that the universe's fine-tuning is best explained theistically, and in particular offers a better explanation than a "multiverse."[30] This is a teleological argument that Swinburne himself presents in *The Existence of God* and elsewhere.[31] Of particular concern to Swinburne is the requirement that the universe permit the existence of human bodies.[32] Other philosophers who have advanced the fine-tuning argument include Robin Collins and William Lane Craig.

Arguments for the existence of God that arise out of modern cosmology constitute an important element of modern natural theology. They are, I believe, of great value for apologetics. They offer significant opportunities for theologians to engage with science, and indeed form an important aspect of the flourishing dialogue going on today between theology and the sciences. But a fundamental question needs to be faced. Is this approach to knowledge of God actually valid? Here I do not mean whether particular arguments are successful or not—this is clearly a matter for debate depending on particular formulations—but something much deeper and more basic. Is this an approach that Christians ought to pursue? Can it lead to genuine knowledge of God? Or is it just idolatry, substituting human endeavor for God's only true revelation of himself in the Christ of Scripture?

Following St. Thomas, Roman Catholic theology has always recognized the importance of natural theology. Thus the First Vatican Council condemns those who deny that God as Creator and Lord can be known by the "certain natural light of human reason."[33] However, there is a strong strand of Protestant theology that totally rejects this whole approach. The great pioneer of this rejection among Protestant theologians is Karl Barth, for whom natural theology is presumptuous and apologetics illegitimate.

In this book I examine Barth's theology and ask whether his rejection of natural theology is justified. The reader will not be surprised to learn from the above that I believe Barth's stance to be too extreme. However, my problem is that I share Barth's fundamental theological outlook—his focus on Jesus Christ as God's supreme revelation, and his Trinitarian orthodoxy. His challenge is devastating if it is true, as he claims, that to engage in natural theology is to deny these more fundamental truths. I aim, therefore, not just to critique Barth but to discern how one might hold the tension between a modest natural theology and the centrality of Christ. In the following pages I engage in dialogue with Barth and with a select group of significant theological successors to Barth who have responded to his approach in various ways, both sympathetically and critically. The aim is to face the concerns raised about natural theology and to take advantage of any theological opportunities presented by these theologians, all of whom I approach with respect and admiration.

Barth's challenge came as a reaction to the failures of nineteenth-century liberal Protestantism, which he saw as having succumbed to the Enlightenment's hubristic elevation of human reason and corresponding rejection of revelation, and it informed the struggle of the Confessing Church in Germany against Nazism. Yet natural theology is surely vital for the science-faith dialogue, and for the task of countering the arguments of the "new atheism." Is there any kind of *praeparatio evangelica* given by the natural world as investigated by science, or does the natural world only say something to us about God if we already have a belief in God from somewhere else (revelation)?

In seeking to answer this question, I begin by reexamining Barth's argument, especially noting the importance of its context in 1930s Germany. I follow this up by examining how Barth's position has been critiqued and developed by others. The different reactions and approaches of Dietrich Bonhoeffer and Wolfhart Pannenberg in German Protestant theology are examined. I show that, despite strong leanings toward Barth, Bonhoeffer nevertheless begins a critique of his erstwhile mentor and offers intriguing possibilities for natural theology. Pannenberg is the most positive of the theologians studied, since he is concerned both with public evidence for theological claims and direct engagement with the natural sciences.

The historical-critical engagement continues with two notable British participants in the science-religion dialogue, Thomas Torrance and Alister McGrath. Torrance is clearly in the Barthian tradition, having been largely responsible for introducing Barth to the English-speaking world, and I see McGrath, who has written a biography of Torrance, as taking on the mantle of Torrance. However, both these theologians are more nuanced regarding natural theology, and are positively engaged with the sciences.

The book concludes by defending an overall position that takes account of the theological concerns of those studied as well as others engaged positively in natural theology, such as Polkinghorne and Swinburne. Broadly speaking, I intend to show how it might be possible to hold together the notion of revelation (Barth's primary emphasis) while employing reason and empirical evidence, including that from the sciences, in the justification of belief. Indeed, one of my main points is that some kind of natural theology is required to evaluate any claim to revelation anyway, rendering the distinction between revealed and natural theology rather blurred. I also argue that the distinction is blurred even further if one accepts that the limited knowledge of God available in creation is God-given, just as is our knowledge of God in Christ.

CHAPTER TWO

# Karl Barth
## Natural Theology Challenged

IN THIS CHAPTER I examine Karl Barth's celebrated criticisms of natural theology in some detail. I describe how Barth broke onto the theological scene, bringing a necessary and revitalizing corrective to nineteenth-century liberalism. I examine the interwar context in which Barth worked and his famous disputes with Adolf von Harnack and Emil Brunner. Central to Barth's theology is the self-revelation of God in Christ as attested in Holy Scripture. I argue, however, that Scripture itself commends a limited natural theology, and this formed part of the proclamation of the early church. While remaining deeply impressed by Barth's Christocentrism, I argue that Barth's approach leads ultimately to an irrationalism that deprives Christians of an important means of commending the faith in a pluralist society.

Karl Barth was born in Basel in Switzerland on May 10, 1886.[1] He studied theology at the universities of Bern, Berlin, Tübingen, and Marburg. His teachers included Harnack and Hermann Gunkel at Berlin, and Wilhelm Hermann at Marburg. At this time Barth heard Harnack, the doyen of liberal Protestant theology, "with unbounded enthusiasm,"[2] and he was profoundly impressed by Hermann, whose teaching led him first to question how far theological liberalism should be allowed to go. "I soaked Hermann in through all my pores," he says, and most crucially, "Although Herrmann was surrounded by so much Kant and Schleiermacher, the decisive thing for him was the christocentric impulse, and I learnt that from him."[3]

From 1911 to 1921 Barth served as pastor of Safenwil, an industrial and agricultural village in the Swiss canton of Aargau. As we shall see, here while working in pastoral ministry he was driven to rethink and challenge all that he had been taught, and to set off in an entirely different direction. He took the theological world by storm with his revolutionary commentary on Romans, *Römerbrief*, produced during this period (first edition 1919, substantially revised second edition published in 1922). The second edition of this work marked the beginning of a new movement, variously known as "dialectical theology" or "theology of crisis," characterized by the denial of any "point of contact" for God's grace in sinful human nature or culture, and the consequent "dialectic" between God's supreme judgment of "No" to humanity in the cross and his gracious "Yes" in the resurrection.

In the 1920s Barth took up university chairs at Göttingen (1921–1925) and Münster (1925–1930). During this period he attempted to move his theology forward with the first volume of *Christliche Dogmatik* (1927), though he deemed that project unsatisfactory, replacing it later with the *Kirchliche Dogmatik*. In 1930 he was appointed professor of systematic theology at Bonn and in 1931 published *Fides Quaerens Intellectum*, a study of the theology of St. Anselm of Canterbury. In Anselm he found that theology does not have to justify itself through criteria external to itself, a central tenet of Barth that we shall have cause to question, but which informs his theology from now on. For Barth, faith (*fides*) is the "knowledge and affirmation of the word of Christ" and it is this that theology is seeking to understand (*quaerens intellectum*)—that is, theology starts from a prior commitment.[4]

In 1932 Barth published the first volume of his monumental four-volume (though really fourteen very substantial part-volumes) *Kirchliche Dogmatik* (*Church Dogmatics*), with volume IV/4 left incomplete at his death in 1968. In this immensely significant work, he gives expression to his finally clearly perceived conviction that "Christian doctrine, if it is to merit its name, and if it is to build up the Christian church in the world as it needs to be built up, has to be exclusively and consistently the doctrine of Jesus Christ."[5] However, with Hitler coming to power in 1933 Barth found himself in the forefront of the church struggle against Nazism, and was the author of the 1934 Barmen Theological Declaration of the Confessing Church (see later).

In 1935 Barth was dismissed from the University of Bonn because he asked for the oath of allegiance to Hitler to be modified so as to reflect his prior "responsibilities as an Evangelical Christian."[6] In court he read out a passage from Plato's *Apology* of Socrates: "Men of Athens, I respect and love you, but I shall obey the god rather than you"[7]—an interesting citing of a pagan author in the light of Barth's rejection of any natural knowledge of God.

Barth returned to Switzerland to take up a specially offered chair at the University of Basel, a post he held until his retirement. After the war he lectured widely and published extensively, from *Dogmatics in Outline* (1947), comprising lectures on the creed delivered in Bonn just after the war, to *Evangelical Theology* (1962), produced in the year of his retirement. But *Church Dogmatics*, completed during this period, remains Barth's monumental achievement and supreme contribution to twentieth-century theology.

## *The Theology of Karl Barth*

Karl Barth undoubtedly stands as a towering figure over twentieth-century theology. Thomas Torrance argues that Barth was "the most powerfully biblical and evangelical theologian of our age," and that he ranks with the very greatest theologians of all time—including Athanasius, Augustine, Luther, and Calvin.[8] John Webster likewise writes: "Barth is the most important Protestant theologian since Schleiermacher, and the extraordinary descriptive depth of his depiction of the Christian faith puts him in the company of a handful of thinkers in the classical Christian tradition."[9] Therefore, only with the greatest respect and trepidation do I venture to engage with what Barth says about natural theology.

Barth's starting point is his desire to deny all knowledge of God apart from God's own gracious revelation of himself. God reveals himself in Christ, and this revelation is made known to us in Scripture. By God's grace alone (*sola gratia*) can we know him: we cannot know him by our own efforts. This divine revelation is a miracle. In contrast, "natural theology is the doctrine of a union of man with God existing outside God's revelation in Jesus Christ."[10] Furthermore, "as the content of proclamation and theology it can have no place at all. It can be treated only as non-existent. In this sense, therefore, it must be excised without mercy" (*CD*, II/1.170). And Barth sees no difference between different forms of natural theology. The latest German manifestation should give no cause for casting of stones in the light of a history of compromise between natural and revealed knowledge of God in preceding centuries (see *CD*, II/1.174).[11]

As noted by Alister McGrath, Barth's initial target is not in fact natural theology but religion itself,[12] though much the same strictures apply to both. Barth contrasts "religion," which he sees as concerning man's own striving for God, with "theology," which is man's response to God's self-revelation. He writes, "The event of God's revelation has to be understood and expounded as it is attested to the Church of Jesus Christ by Holy Scripture."[13] Barth's shattering indictment is that in contrast to this, "religion is unbelief" (*CD*, I/2.297–325).[14] Religion is man trying to do for himself what only God can do for him. It is man justifying himself rather than through faith accepting justification by the grace of God.

Barth would affirm that God has revealed himself both in history and in creation, but all argument should be from God to the world, not the other way around. Let us look at these aspects of God's revelation in Barth's thought, beginning with history.

First, Barth does not deny that events recorded in Scripture objectively happened. Supremely, Barth affirms the resurrection of Jesus from the dead as an objective event. However, he denies the value of seeking historical evidence in support of this claim. While the resurrection is indeed an objective event, we must not seek "proof" for its occurrence. It is to be accepted by faith.

Barth viewed the nineteenth-century battles about the historical Jesus as futile and irrelevant. He also thought that reliance on history made the ordinary Christian beholden to the expert. It may be that he was reacting to the negative assessment of history in the Enlightenment; for example, Gotthold Ephraim Lessing envisaged an "ugly, broad ditch"[15] separating the contingent truths of history from the necessary truths of reason. The message of the famous parable of the rings in Lessing's *Nathan der Weise* is that we belong contingently, by historical accident, to one religion or another, and it is not decidable at this stage of history which is the "true" religion; that will emerge through the manifestation of moral virtue at some future date—that is, in experience. Indeed the only recommendation is that practitioners of religions foster moral virtue, which will ultimately be the deciding factor.

For Barth this is to deny the meaning of revelation as understood by the Lutheran Church to which Lessing still gave allegiance: "Within history, in which there are the various religions, and in which there is also a Lutheran Church, there are only human pre-decisions, and human affirmation of this or that historical possibility. But there is no encounter with God decisively intervening from outside or above, and demanding faith as man's final decision to obey; no revelation in the sense in which the Lutheran Church had understood it before the eighteenth century."[16] And in the end, does this not make God redundant? Barth writes, "Did Lessing really even count upon God's final word concerning the dramas and drama of human history, after having in principle cut God off from every word previous to the last word spoken, or to be spoken, within this history? Is it not a fact that Lessing's man is self-sufficient, and has no need of God in any event?" (*PT*, 250).

A further significant factor is that, when historical research on the Bible was actually done in the nineteenth century, its import was largely negative. The most famous example is probably David Friedrich Strauss's *Life of Jesus* (1835). Strauss regarded the Gospels as so imbued with myth (the Fourth Gospel above all) that it is virtually impossible to recover any historical core of the life of Jesus at all. The miracles that Jesus performs and the ontological claims about his person made in the tradition—that he is God-man—are ruled out of court. The religious genius, or God-consciousness of Jesus, was deemed, at least in the first edition of *Life of Jesus*, not to be unique. In a new version of *Life of Jesus* published in 1864, Strauss pointed to an ideal of moral perfection and God-consciousness exemplified by

Christ, but even then, this is something that humanity as a whole can develop further. Later still, Jesus was described as a "spiritual fanatic."

Barth presents a number of challenges to Strauss. For example, he writes as follows:

> Is it not a fact that the New Testament records are useless as "sources" of a pragmatically comprehensible picture of a man and of a life? For it is from the very first word that they seek to be something quite different, namely testimonies to a "superhuman being," corresponding feature by feature to the prophecies of the Old Testament, a being whose image must defy all historical reconstruction.
>
> Is it not a fact that a "historical Jesus" established behind the so-called sources, and therefore quite independently of the witness of the New Testament, can only be comprehended as such if we remove those predicates of his which are essential to this witness: his consciousness of himself as the Messiah of Israel and as God's eternal Son, his proclamation of the kingdom of God and expectation that he would come again, and his resurrection from the dead? Is it not a fact that the sentimental, moralizing description of character which is indispensable to the establishment of this figure has nothing at all to do with the faith of the Apostles? ("Strauss," in *PT*, 551)

Furthermore, the goal of historical research can only be a relative Christ, a Christ "who could on no account be the Word that became flesh, executing God's judgment upon us and challenging us ourselves to make a decision."

Barth says that Strauss did for history what Ludwig Feuerbach had done for psychology in arguing that God is a projection from our minds. His verdict is scathing: "Proper theology begins just at the point where the difficulties disclosed by Strauss and Feuerbach are seen and then laughed at" ("Strauss," in *PT*, 551).

On the other hand, rather than being laughed at, perhaps the Enlightenment analysis should be challenged on its own grounds of rationality.

It seems to me that the fault is glaring: if one starts from naturalistic presuppositions, naturalistic conclusions follow. As I argue in chapter 6 when discussing Alister McGrath's approach to natural theology, this is precisely what Feuerbach did.

Similarly, in the realm of historical research, it may well be that the negative import was a result of the methods employed, and, contra Lessing, it may also be the case that certain historical events can have universal validity. Generally, following the Enlightenment, historical Jesus research made no allowance for the supernatural. This was the case with Strauss. It was also the case, for example, with Ernst Troeltsch, who enunciated the principle of analogy, whereby past events are deemed by fiat to be similar to present events. Thus, miraculous events in biblical times were ruled out because there was no analogy with present events. Such methods are bound to lead to a nonsupernatural Jesus because they start from premises that rule out the supernatural. But this need not be so, and more open-minded premises might well lead to other conclusions, as is evidenced by more recent trends in historical Jesus research. Moreover, it has been argued that evidence from testimony can in principle make it probable that a miraculous event occurred, and that Hume's famous argument against miracles, from which much of the subsequent antimiraculous prejudice came, is fundamentally flawed.[17]

In the case of the resurrection, we do, of course, have evidence in the form of eyewitness accounts. Barth would deny that these could even in principle provide "proof" that the resurrection occurred because the accounts themselves come from faith, and therefore from a particular perspective. What he fails to realize is that this is true of any reporting of evidence. This fact does not mean that we cannot examine the evidence for its reliability and make a judgment. Evidence of testimony enhances the prior probability that an event occurred. The problem with relying on faith alone is the danger that our beliefs become purely subjective—a result very far from Barth's intention. One cannot escape the need for the exercise of reason, and if Christianity makes historical claims, it seems only right to subject these to the tools of reason.

Barth's position regarding natural theology is consistent with his views about history. When he discusses the doctrine of creation, he does so by expounding Genesis 1 and 2. He makes no reference to scientific views about creation, for while he thought at first that this might be necessary, he later saw "that there can be no scientific problems, objections or aids in relation to what Holy Scripture and the Christian Church understand by the divine work of creation."[18] Science and the Christian doctrine are completely separate and nonoverlapping; they are about different things, but theology is primary: "There is free scope for natural science beyond what theology describes as the work of the Creator" (*CD*, III/1.x).

For Barth, that God is Creator is just as much a matter of revelation as everything else in the creed:

> The doctrine of the creation no less than the whole remaining content of Christian confession is an article of faith, i.e., the rendering of a knowledge which no man has procured for himself or ever will. (*CD*, III/1.3)[19]
>
> We are not nearer to believing in God the Creator, than we are to believing that Jesus Christ was conceived by the Holy Ghost and born of the Virgin Mary.[20]

The doctrine of creation is an article of faith, according to Barth, because we understand the creation as God's work and not vice versa, so we have to understand God as Creator first. Science might tell us about the development of the creation over millions of years, but continuation is "quite a different thing from this sheer beginning, with which the concept of creation and the Creator has to do" (*DO*, 51). I would argue that the distinctions are not quite so sharp as this. The doctrine of creation embraces "continuation" in that God sustains the universe and its laws in being. There seems to me to be a genuine overlap of concern here, since the big bang theory has something to say about the beginning, and revelation something to say about God's creating and sustaining activity. Moreover, some cosmological models deny that the world has a temporal origin (for example, the Hawking-Hartle model removes the "specialness" of the first moment, and some inflationary cosmologies posit no beginning in time), so talk of "sheer beginning" may be something of a hostage to fortune. It is ontological origin that is important for Christian doctrine—why is there something rather than nothing?—rather than temporal origin.

Wolfhart Pannenberg, whom we shall discuss in more detail in chapter 4, comments on Barth's lack of engagement with the sciences at this point:

> The most remarkable example of the theological retreat from a discussion of the scientific description of nature was Karl Barth, who in the preface of his doctrine of creation in his *Church Dogmatics* decided that in principle a theological doctrine of creation should not concern itself with scientific descriptions and results.[21]

One problem with this approach is that Barth denies the believer any external means of correcting faith—for example, a naïve belief in the creation of the world in a literal six days should be abandoned on the basis of modern science. Barth is not so unsophisticated as to accept such a simplistic reading, but any Barthians inclined to do so would not let science have any say in the matter.

Pannenberg is keen, again as we shall see in more detail, that Christian truth be seen as public truth. This was evident most clearly in Pannenberg's early work in his insistence that the resurrection of Christ in particular was a publicly accessible historical event. This view contrasts strongly with that of Bultmann, on the one hand, who saw the resurrection as happening in the private world of the experience of the disciples, and of Barth on the other, who, following Martin Kähler's thesis that the content of faith is *übergeschichtlich* (suprahistorical), went on to interpret the incarnation as "*Urgeschichte*"—"prehistory," but equally inaccessible to public knowledge via historical research.[22] Anticipating what is to come, we can say that Pannenberg promises to be a far more useful ally than Barth against the likes of Richard Dawkins, who contrasts science and theology precisely at this point—science being publicly checkable and religion glorying in its freedom from any kind of empirical evidence. To Dawkins, faith "means blind trust, in the absence of evidence, even in the teeth of evidence."[23]

Another area in which scientific or philosophical arguments might impinge on theology concerns the reality of the world. Most scientists are realists, because their experience of doing science leads them in this direction, though realism has been questioned by some philosophers, most recently by those of a postmodern bent. However, Barth, for whom the key is the incarnation, does not invoke such scientific or philosophical arguments. We can be sure that the creation is real simply because God has become a creature. Because God has become man in Jesus Christ, the existence of creation can no longer be doubted (*DO*, 53). It seems to me, however, that God's faithfulness is seen in creation in other ways, too. The operation of scientific laws, especially their regularity, is evidence for God's faithfulness and provides an argument for realism. Arguably it is easier to believe in the reality of the world than in the incarnation! For Barth, however, the great mystery and miracle are the existence of the creation. Its status as reality and as creation can only be understood from a prior faith commitment to the center from which it all comes, namely Jesus Christ: "I believe in Jesus Christ, God's Son our Lord, in order to perceive and to understand that God the Almighty, the Father, is the Creator of heaven and earth. If I did not believe the former, I could not perceive and understand the latter" (*CD*, III/1.29).

John McDowell seems to think that I am mistaken here because Barth's argument is not about reality in the sense of the existence of the world but reality as creation.[24] I agree that for Barth the world can only be understood as creation on the basis of a prior commitment of faith in the triune God and the incarnation. One of Barth's more recent commentators, Kathryn Tanner, describes Barth's position in this way:

> One should turn to Jesus Christ for one's understanding of a world created and ruled by God rather than draw conclusions about such matters from more general observation of the world and its natural and historical processes. One should not, then, assume that the world exists and search for its cause; this way leads to the philosopher's God, the Creator as a world-cause.[25]

That Barth is questioning the reality of the world, not just its status as creation, prior to Christian commitment is borne out by quoting him more fully on the issue. In *Dogmatics in Outline*, Barth seems even more strongly to be making the case for realism from the incarnation:

> Has not each of us put to himself the question whether this entire world around us might not really be a seeming and a dream? . . . Whence can we be told authoritatively that that is a perversion and that life is not a dream but reality, that I myself am, and that the world around me is? From the standpoint of the Christian Confession there can only be one answer . . . that in Jesus Christ we have to do with God Himself, with God the Creator, who became a creature, who existed as a creature in time and space, here, there, at that time, just as we exist. (*DO*, 52–53)

Barth writes in similar vein in *Church Dogmatics*:

> The benefit of creation consists in the fact that the creature may be, and therefore is, through its Creator . . . that it really is, that it is not not, or not merely an appearance, or the subject of an illusion or dream. . . . God's creation is affirmed by Him because it is real, and it is real because it is affirmed by Him. Creation is actualisation. Hence the creature is reality. (*CD*, III/1.344–65)

So my point about Barth and realism stands. The phenomenal success of science in predicting and manipulating the behavior of the world would seem to be good reason for believing in the world's reality (see, for example, Arthur Peacocke[26]). The success of science might also lead one to believe that we inhabit a God-designed universe, for without God, chaos would be much more likely. These kinds of arguments (which of course need elaboration, but the point here is only an in-principle one), Barth of course denied himself, indeed repudiated. Perhaps it depends on the kind of person one is wanting to introduce to faith, but I would have thought that a rationally minded person could more easily be convinced of the reality of the world than of the incarnation. Ingolf Dalferth, to whom McDowell refers, would seem to support this point. Speaking of the eschatological presence of God in the power of the resurrection, whence Barth's realism stems, Dalferth writes, "Now it is far from self-evident that this is a reality at all."[27] Dalferth acknowledges that to adopt Barth's position is to stand our common notion of reality on its head.

While Barth seems to break radically with a strong line of common Christian tradition, he is in harmony with traditional Catholic and Protestant thinking when he asserts that God does not need the world or us but is wholly self-sufficient (*CD*, III/1.15). Barth writes that "God, who does not need us, created heaven and earth and myself, 'of sheer fatherly kindness and compassion, apart from any merit or worthiness of mine; for all of which I am bound to thank and praise Him, to serve Him and to be obedient, which is assuredly true'" (quoting Luther) (*DO*, 54; see also *CD* III/1.30. The Luther quotation is from the *Smaller Catechism*). In this sense we can agree that there is indeed mystery to the existence of the world—*a priori*, the world need not exist. However, surely *a posteriori* we know that the world does in fact exist and is real, and inferring that this is so because there is a Creator is not illegitimate.

God created freely and by grace, and he does not begrudge the creation its own reality, nature, and freedom. Here Barth would find more sympathizers in the camp of Christian scientists like Peacocke and Polkinghorne.

Barth is also traditional in asserting that it is wrong to think of the world as God (pantheism). It is also wrong to think of the world as an outflow, an emanation from God: "That would really not be creation, but a living movement of God, an expression of Himself. But creation means something different; it means a reality distinct from God. . . . Creaturely reality means reality on the basis of a *creatio ex nihilo*, a creation out of nothing" (*DO*, 55). Thus the Creator of the Christian confession is also not to be equated with Plato's demiurge (*CD*, III/1.17).

Barth asserts that God is eternal. He transcends the limitations of our (created) time and space—his time and space are different. However, that does not mean that "there is no time in Him" (*DO*, 56). In this way Barth might avoid some of the problems associated with the traditional doctrine of God's "timelessness."[28] However, he wants to retain from that doctrine the idea that God has "presence," which we do not. Moreover, his statements on the issue seem paradoxical, if not contradictory.[29] On the one hand, despite the above, he asserts that "eternity is the simultaneity of beginning, middle and end, and to that extent it is pure duration," and "time can have nothing to do with God" (*CD*, II/1.608). He also quotes with approval classic writers on timelessness such as Boethius. On the other hand, because God created time and especially because of the incarnation, "we cannot understand God's eternity as pure timelessness" (*CD*, II/1.617; see also *CD*, III/1.34ff.). God must be temporal to be a living God, and more importantly to become incarnate in Christ: "Without God's complete temporality the content of the Christian message has no shape" (*CD*, II/1.620). Richard Swinburne quotes the latter statement with approval.[30]

Barth agrees with Calvin that the object of creation is to be the theatre of God's glory—that is, of his manifestation or visibility. The goodness of the world consists in its being "the theatre of His glory, *theatrum gloriae Dei*," as Calvin says of it (*DO*, 58).

Why, according to Barth, is there no natural knowledge of God? William Nicholls[31] notes that for Barth God is not unknowable on the grounds of Kant's critique of pure reason—that is, because we experience only phenomena, and so can only have reliable knowledge of phenomena, and cannot have knowledge of "things in themselves." Rather, God is unknowable because of the ontological difference—the "infinite, qualitative distinction," as Kierkegaard put it—between God the Creator and man the creature, and because sin has corrupted man's nature. This goes further than Calvin's view that man *should* know God through nature (and Calvin urged the study of nature through the natural sciences), but can do so but imperfectly because of the fall and sin. Calvin says that the availability of this knowledge renders people "without excuse" in going their own way and not God's. For Calvin, revelation in Scripture both enhances the knowledge of God as Creator and is essential for *saving* knowledge of God as Redeemer.

To me, Calvin has it about right. Indeed it would seem that Calvin's view represents a limited form of natural theology, not dissimilar to that which I am advocating. A certain knowledge of God is available to all, whether members of the Christian community or not, through God's revelation of himself in nature. Indeed, God has implanted a religious sense (*sensus divinitatis*)[32] or seed of religion (*semen religionis*)[33] in all human beings whereby they can perceive God as Creator. Moreover, God has also been pleased "so to manifest his perfections in the whole structure of the universe, and daily place himself in our view, that we cannot open our eyes without being compelled to behold him."[34] This religious sense gives rise to what would later be called "points of contact" for the special revelation of God as Redeemer, in the Christ of Scripture. Barth denies the existence of such points of contact (see below) and asserts that even this general revelation cannot be authenticated by human reason, apart from faith. Indeed for Barth there is no distinction between "general" and "special" revelation, but only one complete revelation of God in Christ.

James Barr,[35] and more recently Alister McGrath, have disputed Barth's claim to represent natural theology in line with classical Reformed theology, notably that of Calvin. As we have seen, Calvin did have a place for a limited natural theology, which McGrath describes as "a theologically inoffensive and apologetically fruitful approach to natural theology, whether Barth cares to admit this or not"![36] Barr notes that Calvin used natural theology to prove that atheism is impossible, as must indeed be the case if the religious sense is planted in every human.[37] Even idolatry is evidence of natural knowledge of God for Calvin.[38]

This is a point of extreme importance for Calvin, and Barth is in error to represent his own view as that of the mainstream of the Reformation. As Barr says, "Actually, Calvin's debt to natural theology was, I believe, much greater than is suggested by Barth's very grudging admissions."[39] Indeed, for Calvin, "astronomy may justly be called the alphabet of theology."[40]

One is almost tempted to follow H. Richard Niebuhr, cited by Barr: "Something very nearly approaching a Barthian captivity of the history of modern Christian thought reigns in theology outside of ultramodern circles."[41] Niebuhr suspects there will be a move away from Barthian thought, just as in Barth's time there was a move away from Harnack. This is something I personally would regret since I agree with McDowell that there is a vast amount in the Barth corpus with which to engage.

Avery Dulles notes some of the problems with Barth's approach. How can there be revelation if men and women lack the capacity to receive it? And if the word can be received, it must be distinguishable from its contradictory: "The simultaneous yes and no cannot be final."[42] We return to some criticisms of Barth's approach later.

## *The Barth-Brunner Debate*

Barth and his erstwhile friend and colleague, and fellow dialectical theologian, Emil Brunner famously fell out following the publication in 1934 of the latter's "Nature and Grace."[43] Brunner was attempting to rehabilitate a natural theology and took as his basis the idea that man is created in the *imago Dei.* There is thus an analogy with the being of God—contra Barth, for whom there is no *analogia entis* that he perceives to be based on human insight, but only an *analogia fidei* created on the basis of God's self-revelation. Moreover, despite human sin there is, for Brunner, a "point of contact" (*Anknüpfungspunkt*) in human nature for God to reveal himself—that is, in man's recognition of God in nature and history. There is something implanted, as it were, in human nature that God utilizes in revealing himself. This might be awareness of God in nature, since for Brunner "the creation of the world is at the same time a revelation, a self-communication of God."[44] It might also be an awareness of what sin is so that the gospel imperative "repent and be saved" has meaning: "It will not do to kill the dialectic of this knowledge of sin by saying that knowledge of sin comes only by the grace of God. This statement is as true as the other, that the grace of God is comprehensible only to him who already knows about sin. . . . A man without conscience cannot be struck by the call 'Repent ye and believe the Gospel.'"[45]

Barth's peremptory reply to Brunner was *Nein!* (the ultrabrief title of his article).[46] He denied any such point of contact that might imply something a man contributes to his own salvation. The whole initiative of revelation is God's; there is no "natural theology." As Joan O'Donovan puts it, "Brunner argued for the indispensable role of the *imago* doctrine in articulating the universal being of sinful mankind apart from the redeeming and sanctifying grace of Christ, while Barth denied to the doctrine any nonchristological and pre-eschatological meaning."[47]

In the context of the Germany of 1934 Barth was keen to deny Luther's doctrine of divinely created "orders" such as the family, the church, and the state, particularly of course the last, which prevented creation's collapse into chaos. Brunner's position was, however, more subtle than would be one that lumped family, church, and state together. Thus he distinguishes marriage as an "ordinance of creation" from the state, which is an "ordinance of preservation," because the latter has to do with sin. Moreover, he was aware of the dangerous "false theology derived from nature" that was "threatening the Church to the point of death," and he acknowledged Barth's passionate leadership in resisting such a theology.[48]

Brunner argued that man's being possesses a formal and a material aspect.[49] The formal aspect is referred to at Genesis 1:26 and Psalm 8 and gives man superiority over the rest of creation because as a rational creature he is given a "capacity for words" and "responsibility." This formal structure is analogous to divine being and indestructible by sin. Moreover, "that is the 'point of contact': capacity for words and responsibility."[50]

In contrast, the material image, including original righteousness and free will, has been lost through sin. Brunner's view resembles that of Irenaeus, who split man's nature in a manner not too dissimilar from this. Irenaeus thought man retained the image—that is, rational nature and free will—at the fall, but lost the likeness—that is, moral virtue and righteousness. (Irenaeus, as pointed out by Luther and Calvin, failed to realize that Gen 1:26 exhibits typical Hebrew parallelism.) O'Donovan believes such a definition of human nature leads to rejection of those not obviously responsible or linguistically equipped (e.g., the unborn, the mentally handicapped), a point noted by Barth himself: "Are they not children of Adam? Has Christ not died for them?"[51] That is clearly a poignant question in the context of Nazi Germany, and it remains so today. It seems to pose a problem for Brunner's sharp distinction of the formal and material aspects of humanity. However, the simple point that God has revealed himself in nature, and that is something to which we have access simply by virtue of being human, is surely equally compatible with a relational view of human nature of the kind Barth adopts, even if for Brunner the formal/material distinction is so significant and informs the way he treats nature/grace. Similarly, by virtue of being human we have the capacity to be saved by Christ. Brunner would agree with Barth that we contribute nothing to our salvation, since our humanity is God-given and we do not make ourselves.[52] For Brunner, the denial of natural knowledge of God implies the denial of sin.[53]

Brunner ascribes to man "partial" knowledge of God's will and human sin. In his nature/grace dialectic, echoing St. Thomas Aquinas, grace is the completion, as well as the negation, of nature. In his response of repentance and faith, the formal image receives new material content, original righteousness restored. Whereas Brunner denies this, Barth nevertheless sees in Brunner's anthropology man contributing to his own salvation, in defiance of the Reformation doctrine of *sola gratia*. He denies the preexisting point of contact for divine grace. Rather this is renewed by Christ: "Man's capacity for God, however it may be with his humanity and personality, has really been lost. . . . The image of God in man . . . which constitutes the real point of contact for the Word of God, is the one awakened through Christ from real death to life and so 'restored,' the newly-created *rectitudo* now real as man's possibility for the Word of God. . . . This point of contact is, therefore, not real outside faith but only in faith."[54] Again, he writes, "The Holy Ghost, who proceeds from the Father and the Son and is therefore revealed and believed to be God, does not stand in need of any point of contact but that which he himself creates."[55]

Roman Catholic theologians also appealed to St. Thomas's dictum, "Grace does not destroy nature but perfects it," in order to justify a concordat between the Vatican and the Nazi regime. As with Brunner, this seemed to validate the claims of the German Christians who saw grace as not destroying *German* nature but perfecting it, and hence as seeing their own national folk-consciousness as a revelation of God.[56]

Clearly the context in which Barth was working is highly significant as we have begun to see, and we must now give it some more detailed attention.

## *Historical Background to Barth's Thought*

The dialectical theology of Barth and others has much to commend it. It came like a breath of fresh air as a necessary corrective to nineteenth-century liberalism, which had been, as Barth claimed, human-centered in its approach to theology. In analyzing Barth's theology, it helps greatly to see the context in which he worked. We have already seen something of this, but delving a little more into the historical background will be helpful.

When Barth arrived as pastor of Safenwil and found himself having to preach every week, he soon realized that his Reformed congregation expected to hear the Word of God spoken to them by the preacher. His university training had simply not equipped him for this task. He felt that it was essential to go back to the Bible and expound it, for there God had revealed himself in Christ. A further indictment of liberalism came when Barth found that almost all his former university teachers, whom he had hitherto greatly venerated, were among ninety-three German intellectuals who made a proclamation in support of the Kaiser's war aims in World War I. For Barth, theology must issue in a distinct ethics, and from this moment he knew he could no longer follow his teachers' ethics or dogmatics, or their understanding of the Bible and history.[57]

As noted above, Barth's dialectical theology dropped on the world of the theological establishment like a bombshell with the publication of the revised edition of his *Römerbrief* (commentary on Romans) in 1922. It shortly gave rise to a heated debate with his former teacher, the great church historian and grand old man of German theology, Adolf von Harnack. In 1923 Harnack published an article titled "Fifteen Questions to the Despisers of Scientific Theology among the Theologians" in the journal *Christian World*.[58] (Incidentally, the title echoes that of Friedrich Schleiermacher's classic *On Religion: Speeches to Its Cultured Despisers*, Schleiermacher being the pioneer of nineteenth-century liberal theology with whom Barth is chiefly at odds.) In his article Harnack wrote this:

> If it is certain that everything that is subconscious, non-rational, fascinating, numinous, etc., remains subhuman as long as it is not apprehended, understood, and purified by reason and protected in its proper character, how is it possible to wish to belittle, even reject, this reason? . . . Is there—admitting sloth, shortsightedness, and numerous other ills—really any other theology than that which has a firm connection and blood relationship to science? (*BDT*, 166)

Barth's reply contained this passage:

> If theology regained the courage to be objective, the courage to become a witness of the *word* of revelation, of judgment, and of the love of *God*, then it could also be that "science" in general would have to look out for its "firm connection and blood relationship" to theology, rather than the other way around. (*BDT*, 170)

This correspondence also exposes a marked divergence on the issue of history. Harnack asks how, if Jesus Christ be central to the gospel, one can ignore the findings of critical historical study in order to find a "reliable and common knowledge of this person" (*BDT*, 166). Barth's perfunctory reply is that "the reliability and common nature of the knowledge of the person of Jesus Christ as the midpoint of the gospel can be no other than that of a *faith* awakened by God" (*BDT*, 170).

We have seen how the rise of Nazism in the interwar period provided a further vital context for Barth's rejection of natural theology. The Barmen Declaration of the Confessing Church, made at the Synod of Barmen on May 31, 1934, was drawn up by Barth, so the story goes, while the other delegates were enjoying an afternoon nap. It is instructive to see the text of the first article of the theological declaration and Barth's interpretation of it:

> "I am the way, the truth and the life: no man cometh unto the Father, but by me" (Jn. 14:6).
>
> "Verily, verily, I say unto you, He that entereth not by the door into the sheepfold, but climbeth up some other way, the same is a thief and a robber. . . . I am the door: by me if any man enter in, he shall be saved" (Jn. 10:1,9).
>
> Jesus Christ, as He is attested to us in Holy Scripture, is the one Word of God, whom we have to hear and whom we have to trust and obey in life and in death.
>
> We condemn the false doctrine that the Church can and must recognise as God's revelation other events and powers, forms and truths, apart from and alongside this one Word of God. (*CD*, II/1.172)

In expounding the Barmen Declaration, Barth is adamant that a new form of natural theology confronted the Evangelical Church in 1933. This was seen in the demand to recognize "in the form of the God-sent Adolf Hitler, a source of specific new revelation of God, which, demanding obedience and trust, took its place beside the revelation attested in Holy Scripture, claiming that it should be acknowledged by Christian proclamation and theology as equally binding and obligatory." That demand for equality only obscured the even more outrageous demand that this new revelation was to be proclaimed the only revelation, leading to the "transformation of the Christian Church into the temple of the German nature- and history myth" (*CD*, II/1.173).

What is perhaps surprising is that Barth should equate this Nazi usurpation of God's revelation with developments in preceding centuries: "There can be no doubt that not merely a part but the whole had been intended and claimed when it had been demanded that side by side with its attestation in Jesus Christ and therefore in Holy Scripture the Church should also recognise and proclaim God's revelation in reason, in conscience, in the emotions, in history, in nature, and in culture and its achievements and developments" (*CD*, II/1.173). The "also" in these former demands also really meant to be an "only." Barth writes, "Even if we only lend our little finger to natural theology, there necessarily follows the denial of the revelation of God in Jesus Christ"

(*CD*, II/1.173). If these earlier proclamations of the knowability of God in Christ—alongside other proclamations of his knowability in nature, reason, and history—had been legitimate, then the same could be true of linking the proclamation of knowing God in Christ with racial purity.

John McDowell disputes the context of Nazi Germany as conditioning Barth's thought, particularly in the debate with Brunner, and he accuses James Barr of dismissing Barth's polemic against natural theology as a product of the times.[59] However, Barr's position is more subtle than that:

> I agree with C. Link, *Die Welt als Gleichnis* (Munich: Kaiser, 1976), 130, that it is wrong to suppose that Barth's polemic against natural theology was conditioned *purely* by the political controversies. I am sure this is not so. All I suggest is that these political circumstances acted as catalyst for the theological disagreement which soon broke out. In fact, as I indicate below, it seems more likely that it was precisely Barth's own theological requirements that led him to diagnose the German developments as constituting a case of natural theology.[60]

Barr vehemently asserts that to associate historical instances of natural theology with the German Christian movement is "a quite disgraceful smear on the careful, rational, and philosophical discussions which have generally been intended when the term is used."[61] Not only that, but the diagnosis of German Christian theology as "natural theology" at all seems misplaced.

Noting that many saw the advent of National Socialism as a new dawning and the opportunity for the renewal of national pride, Barr sees the theological import of the movement more in terms of "revelational" theology than "natural theology" in which "the new 'events' and the 'crisis' of modern experience formed an extension—or even in effect a replacement—of ancient revelation."[62] As Barr points out, two very distinctive features of natural theology are quite absent from National Socialism—namely, rationality and the tendency to universality. While the *völkisch* element might look like a "structure" or "order" of creation, and therefore resemble natural theology, it could equally if not preferably be understood as a revelational principle, for a particular people at a particular time (like the Israelites in the Old Testament).[63] Indeed, Barth himself used the category of revelation and saw the "German *Volkstum*" as a second source of revelation.[64] Barr goes further than I would want to in seeing Barth take on some of the characteristics of his opponents (that must count as a slur in its turn)—"an aggressiveness and totalitarianism," the "inability to use open-minded and reasoned forms of discussion," and "rhetorical and propagandist means of persuasion."[65] In the end, though, Barr sees, as I do, that the distinctions between natural and revealed theology are hard to maintain:

> If one believes that God has revealed himself in his creation and continues to do so, why is that "natural theology" and not "revealed"? If one believed that God was revealing himself in the German political experiences of a certain era, why was that "natural theology" and not "revealed"? If one believes that God was revealing himself in ancient Israel, why is this not "natural"? Perhaps all theology is both "natural" and "revealed."[66]

Owen Rees also portrays the German Christians as seeing the history of the German people in terms of *Heilsgeschichte*.[67] He speaks of the "exaltation of the idea of *Volk* and state into a divine ordinance possessing an absolute quality which gave to it the nature of revelation," and the recent revolution was "a manifestation of God's saving purpose" on a par with biblical history.

Dietrich Bonhoeffer, whom we shall consider in more detail in the next chapter, has an interesting passage in his *Ethics* in which he sees the values of "reason, culture, humanity, tolerance and self-determination," which had hitherto been used in opposition to Christianity, come back to find their home there, now united with the church in opposition to the "deification of the irrational, of blood and instinct, of the beast of prey in man" in National Socialism.[68] Yes, Christianity and reason belong together and should unite today as then against the forces of irrationality, examples of which abound.

An important question to raise concerning Barth's thinking is: "Did it change?" Did the radical challenge to the possibility of knowledge of God in nature moderate when the crisis of the Nazi era was over? It seems to me that the answer to this question is, in all essentials, "No!" Nevertheless this is not quite the angry "No!" of the Brunner correspondence. Perhaps the key text is Barth's 1956 lecture "The Humanity of God" (German, *Die Menschlichkeit Gottes*) (*HG*, 37–65). Here he is more generous to his opponents: "We are called upon today to accord that earlier theology, and the entire development culminating in it, greater historical justice than appeared to us possible and feasible in the violence of the first break-off and clash" (*HG*, 39). Nevertheless it was clear that that theology "could no longer continue as it was" (*HG*, 39), and although the challenge was made "somewhat brutally and severely" (*HG*, 41), that challenge was indeed essential.

While there is therefore no going back, Barth does acknowledge the need for a moving forward, indeed for a "revision" (*Retraktation*) (*HG*, 41). He further acknowledges that although the challenge to liberalism was right, "we were at that time only partially in the right" (*HG*, 42). The fundamental need in this revision is not now to see the deity of God, which was obscured by the liberal theology, but "the humanity of God." The "wholly other" or "infinite qualitative distinction," fundamental to that earlier theology, can ironically lead to a deity of God more resembling that of the God of the philosophers than the God of Abraham, Isaac, and Jacob (*HG*, 45). The counterbalance is that the deity of the living God must find its meaning in relationship to man. So the infinite qualitative distinction is bridged in Christ, who "comes forward to *man* on behalf of *God* calling for and awakening faith, love and hope, and to *God* on behalf of *man*, representing man, making satisfaction and interceding" (*HG*, 47).

This new emphasis on the "humanity of God"—seen, of course, christologically—means that there is still no natural theology. "We do not need to engage in a free-ranging investigation to seek out and construct who and what God truly is, and who and what man truly is, but only to read the truth about both where it resides, namely, in the fullness of their togetherness, their covenant which proclaims itself in Jesus Christ" (*HG*, 47). The initiative is all God's and the sequence of God's act inducing man's response irreversible: "Thus we have here no universal deity capable of being reached conceptually, but this concrete deity—real and recognizable in the *descent* grounded in that sequence and peculiar to the existence of Jesus Christ" (*HG*, 48).

## *Natural Theology and the Bible*

I have to agree with Barth that God's self-revelation in Christ as attested in Holy Scripture is primary. The absolute centrality of the person of Jesus Christ to Karl Barth is deeply impressive. In the crisis of the church struggle in Germany in the Nazi period, perhaps only a theology so utterly and unequivocally Christ-centered could have been effective. Jonathan Wright notes that even someone who developed theologically independently from Barth could say how indebted all were to Barth in the church struggle against National Socialism: "He forged weapons for us for our battle."[69] However, having said this, I must disagree with Barth that there is simply no such thing as natural theology. God as Creator has left evidence of himself in the natural world. Scripture itself attests as much. As Barr points out, Barth's insistence that "the church and human salvation [are] founded on the Word of God *alone*, on God's *revelation in Jesus Christ*, as it is attested in the Scripture"[70] is meant to imply the denial of all natural theology.[71] Barr writes, "But if the Bible accepted or implied natural theology this argument falls to pieces: the Word of God, as attested in the scriptures, must then *include* natural theology as part of revelation, or as the background to it, or as an implication of it or mode through which it is communicated."[72]

In Acts 17, Paul delivers a sermon on the Areopagus in Athens, which arguably constitutes the clearest example of natural theology in all of Scripture. He at first commends his hearers. He even identifies the "unknown god" that they worship with the God whom he, Paul, proclaims. Evidently the "God of the philosophers" *is* "the God of Abraham, Isaac and Jacob." He says, "And he made from one every nation of men to live on all the face of the earth, having determined allotted periods and the boundaries of their habitation, that they should seek God, in the hope that they might feel after him and find him" (Acts 17:26–27, RSV). Astonishingly, he quotes Greek poets, Epimenides of Crete and Aratus of Cilicia, in support. Paul seems to be building on what thinking Greeks knew about God from their philosophical reflection, contemplation, and experience. This all strongly suggests an *Anknüpfungspunkt*, a point of contact, for the gospel. Of course, Paul does go on to call his Greek listeners to repentance, because God has "winked at" former sins and idolatry stemming from an inadequate grasp of the nature of God. Natural knowledge of God (i.e., knowledge of God through his general revelation of himself in nature) is not adequate for salvation. Incidentally it does not matter from the point of view of the argument here whether the passage constitutes verbatim reporting of Paul or the words of Luke put into Paul's mouth, as some biblical critics would say. Either way, the argument is in Scripture and contradicts Barth's position.

Barr concludes from the Areopagus sermon that "Paul's approach as reported in Acts is entirely contrary to what any Barthian approach could have been."[73] Further, "there can be no doubt that it depends on, supports, and involves some sort of natural theology."[74]

Thus, for example, Paul doesn't compare or attack the two Greek philosophical schools (Stoic and Epicurean), as he does later the Jewish schools of the Sadducees and Pharisees (Acts 23:6ff.). Barr continues, "Nor, more important still, does he do anything to attack Greek philosophy as a whole or its modes of thinking."[75] In stark contrast Barth avers that the purport of Paul's speech is that "the stoic and epicurean philosophies and all other philosophies are at an end" ("*Die stoische und epikuräische Philosophie und alle andere Philosophie ist zu Ende*") (*CD*, II/1.123).[76] Barr pointedly asks, "If so, why did Paul say nothing to that effect?"[77] As Barr notes, the tendency in Barth's exposition is to emphasize the ignorance of the Athenians and to deny any continuity with what they knew before and what Paul now presents to them in his role as a Christian apostle: "If one of them now knows about the God proclaimed to them by Paul, it is definitely not in confirmation of what he knew before, perhaps as a member of the sect that worshipped the unknown God, or as a reader of Aratus. It is in a quite new knowledge of his previous complete ignorance. . . . Here absolutely everything that Paul has to say to the Athenians is plainly focused upon them and applied to them as the knowledge of a Christian apostle concerning them" (*CD*, II/1.123). However, it would seem to be a more straightforward reading of the passage to say that Paul does indeed build on the knowledge they had. Barr regards the arguments of Barth "as entirely invalid, because they do not constitute exegesis of the Areopagus speech at all: they pick out the few aspects that can appear to favour the Barthian dogmatic position, and they simply ignore the tenor of the total argument and its content."[78]

Barr makes the following serious charge: "What he [Barth] offers is not the slightest likeness to a serious exegesis of the text. On the contrary it is a travesty of exegesis, indeed a denial of exegesis: for it makes no attempt to follow out the content of the passage, and is a transparent endeavor to force his own modern dogmatic position upon the text."[79]

In Acts 14:17 (RSV), we read that God "did not leave himself without witness, for he did good and gave you from heaven rains and fruitful seasons . . ." A natural reading of this passage is that God has revealed himself to all, pagans and Jews alike, in the regularity of the natural order. As Barr notes, the passage displays a marked similarity to Paul's sermon on the Areopagus. There is no appeal to Moses or the specific revelation to Israel. Rather, "God made himself known through the created world; he will overlook past idolatry."[80]

In Romans 1:19–20 (RSV) St. Paul asserts that "what can be known about God is plain to them, because God has shown it to them. Ever since the creation of the world his invisible nature, namely, his eternal power and deity, has been clearly perceived in the things that have been made." In Romans 2:14 (RSV) he says, "When the Gentiles who have not the law do by nature what the law requires, they are a law to themselves, even though they do not have the law."

Barr supports the view that Romans 1 and 2 contain natural theology, although this is less clear than in the Areopagus case, particularly as there is some disagreement among New Testament scholars on the issue. Exegetes such as Cranfield and Barrett argue that there is no revelation of God apart from God's will (Rom 1:19 [RSV]: "God has shown it to them"). As Barr points out, no natural theology assumed that knowledge of God in creation was obtained apart from God's will, and in any case, if it is revealed to all, such knowledge amounts to the same thing as natural theology anyway. These exegetes also argue that the main (Cranfield says "only") point of Romans 1 is God's judgment, and people are without excuse. They *could* know God, but instead turn to idols and perversion. Barr says there is indeed no excuse "but there is no basis for insisting on the *only* at this point."[81] While it remains true that God's revelation in Christ is essential for salvation, that God reveals himself in the created world, and that therefore there is natural knowledge of God, seems inescapable and is a positive message from the passage.

Another kind of argument discussed by Barr sees Romans as containing natural theology but in the first part of the epistle it is an argument he is refuting. The example cited by Barr is W. Schmithals, for whom Paul is quoting a customary Jewish argument against the Gentiles in order to use it against the synagogue. Barr says of this argument that it is "to most of us a rather novel and paradoxical one."[82] A similar example, which postdates Barr, is Douglas Campbell, who suggests that Paul is arguing ironically here.[83]

Barr, however, notes similarities between Acts 17, where there is definitely natural theology, and Romans 1–2. In some ways Acts goes further, God guiding the nations so that they might "feel after him and find him," and Paul citing the Greek poets with approval. But in other ways Romans is more explicit: for example, in spelling out what is knowable about God—and indeed that "they knew God" (Rom 1:21)—and in the use of the highly significant word φύσις, "nature." Paul essentially uses a "natural law" argument to condemn homosexual relationships (they are παρὰ φύσιν, "against nature," Rom 1:26). Natural law and the law of Moses, which the Jews have, are in agreement, and both Jews and Gentiles are condemned by the lights they have but fail to honor.

Barr also sees Paul, not unnaturally, as dependent for his thought on Jewish tradition, even though he expressed his theology in Greek using Greek idioms. In particular, the Wisdom of Solomon definitely contains natural theology, which adds to the likelihood, given Paul's highly probable dependence on Wisdom, that Romans does also, there being a very similar type of argument in each. According to Barr, Paul has much in common with Wisdom that is not found in the Old Testament—for example, death coming into the world through Adam's fall and the fault with idolatry being that it substitutes worship of the creature for that of the Creator and leads to all sorts of moral depravity.[84] Regarding the fall, the Genesis story in fact says or implies the opposite—namely, that the humans were mortal but were expelled from the garden in case they ate of the tree of life and became immortal (Gen 3:22).

When it comes to natural theology, Wisdom 13:1–9 presents an argument from creation to knowledge of the Creator, appealing to the findings of Greek science: "For from the greatness and beauty of created things comes a corresponding perception of their Creator . . . for if they had the power to know so much that they could investigate the world, how did they fail to find sooner the Lord of these things?" (RSV). Arguably the findings of science, especially of the vastness of the universe, enhance rather than detract from our perception of the glory of God. But the main point here is that this argument is strikingly close to that of Paul in Romans 1. And the argument that instead of worshipping God they worshipped idols, and that led to moral degeneracy, is also present in both Wisdom and Paul.

The Old Testament also appeals to the natural world as revealing God's glory, and Psalms 19 and 104 deserve special mention. For example, in Psalm 19:1 (KJV) we read, "The heavens declare the glory of God; and the firmament sheweth his handywork." Moreover, there seems to be a universal communication of God's glory through the creation: "Day unto day uttereth speech, and night unto night sheweth knowledge. There is no speech nor language, where their voice is not heard. Their line is gone out through all the earth, and their words to the end of the world" (Ps 19:2–4a, KJV).

There is a nice complementarity in the psalm between God's revelation in creation and his revelation in the law, which the psalm goes on to extol: "The law of the Lord is perfect, converting the soul . . ." (Ps 19:7ff., KJV). As Barr points out, it is not, however, clear even here that it is specifically "the law of Moses" that is referred to. It could be more universally available divine instruction. To my mind nothing much hinges on that, once one concedes the universally available knowledge of God from the first part of the psalm, though if Barr is correct, the psalm is even more oriented toward natural theology.

Regarding Psalm 19, Barth says that there is a need to look at the psalm in the whole context of the Bible, and so, even conceding any natural theology there might be, this natural theology is completely overwhelmed (*CD*, II/1.101). In the same place Barth is insisting that in other places also, such as Romans 1:19ff. and 2:12ff., no matter what Paul says there, "he certainly did not intend the Gospel of his Romans Epistle to be gathered from what the heathen too can know about God. On the contrary, he grounded it exclusively on what the first chapter of this Epistle calls God's ἀποκάλυψις" (*CD*, II/1.102). However, as Barr says, nobody is saying that there is nothing but natural theology in the Bible, or, I would add, that natural theology is primary. However, Torah in Psalm 19 and other psalms is often closer to the meaning of wisdom in Proverbs, for example, where the law of Moses is not mentioned. Even the Mosaic law is supported by reason and could in principle be knowable that way, for example, from the way the food laws are conducive to health. There is also the commonality, if not dependence, of Mosaic law on earlier law codes such as that of Hammurabi. This would seem to contradict Barth's point that "when the witnesses in the Old Testament call upon God to bear witness, they do not appeal to a court which stands somewhere behind or above the God of Israel's history. They do not appeal to a God whom they expect to speak to men in some other way than in the history of Israel itself and as such" (*CD*, II/1.100). Of course it is the same God who speaks through the history of Israel *and* nature.

There is a very fascinating quotation of Psalm 19:4 in Romans 10:18 (RSV): "But I ask, have they not heard? Indeed they have; for 'Their voice has gone out to the all the earth, and their words to the ends of the world.'" Paul has just said that "faith comes from what is heard, and what is heard comes by the preaching of Christ" (Rom 10:17, RSV). Now he seems to say that the creation itself has in effect already preached Christ!

Psalm 104 is not obviously natural theology, more a theology of nature and so "revelational," starting as it does with God and moving from him to the marvels of the created world. However, as Barr points out, the information given about the creation is not specifically revelational or new, but comes from observation and so is open to all.[85] Barr notes an affinity with similar poems from Egyptian religion, and as he says, "Transreligiosity is always something that brings us closer to natural theology."[86] He also sees an affinity with Acts 14:17 referred to above, both passages extolling God's providence in nature.

We cited above the natural theology of the Wisdom of Solomon, and one could also mention Ben Sira in the Apocrypha. But there is also much natural theology in the canonical wisdom literature. Just to give one brief example, the instruction "Go to the ant, thou sluggard" (Prov 6:6, KJV) represents the gleaning of a moral lesson from observation of the animal kingdom. It is not an appeal to the law of Moses revealed on Mount Sinai, but wisdom open to all.

Here again, then, there is appeal to universal experience, and commonality with other religious traditions—for example, the parallels between the book of Proverbs and Egyptian wisdom noted by Barr. It is interesting to quote the verdict of John J. Collins, specifically commenting on the wisdom literature:

> There are certain fundamental aspects of the sages' approach to reality which are common to natural theology in all ages. Specifically the sages attempted to discern the religious dimension of common, universal human experience without appeal to special revelation or the unique experience of one people. This religious dimension was correlated with the distinctively Israelite tradition but it was not subordinated to it. The history and law of Israel did not replace universal wisdom, although the sages claimed that they did complement and illustrate it.[87]

It would seem that there is an inherent contradiction in Barth's position here. God's self-revelation in Scripture is all that matters, yet Scripture itself asserts that there is a knowledge of God to be obtained from observing nature.

Where I would agree with Barth is that natural theology is not adequate for salvation. It is also true that natural knowledge of God does not get one to the Trinity. Barth and his followers would argue that it is therefore *not* getting you to the same God as is revealed to us in Holy Scripture. Notwithstanding Acts 17, the "God of the philosophers" is *not* to be identified with the God of Abraham, Isaac, and Jacob, who goes on to reveal himself as Father, Son, and Holy Spirit. But since there can only be one Creator, and indeed the unity of the cosmos points to a single Creator, we must be speaking about the same God as is revealed in Scripture. What we learn from nature may only give us an incomplete and inadequate picture of God. Nevertheless, natural theology leads us not only to a Creator in the first place, but to a Creator with certain attributes—for example, majesty and power—that are associated with the biblical God. Arguably the universality of the laws of nature—that is, their applicability across all of space and time—in addition to an appeal to simplicity, would lead one to conclude, as Richard Swinburne does (contra Hume), that there is only one God.[88] This view, of course, needs to be supplemented and enriched by our biblical knowledge of God—for example, God is personal and is related to the world as the Triune God, and is not just some distant Prime Mover—but the view of natural theology is not wrong in itself.

Torrance puts Barth's position thus: "We are unable to achieve through our own natural powers and capacities the cognitive union with God which true knowledge of him requires."[89] But this is grossly to overstate the claims of natural theology. We are only claiming that the existence of the universe, and the order within it, enhance the prior probability that it was made and designed by some transcendent agency; and, following Richard Swinburne, one can equate this agency to God, on grounds of its being the simplest explanation, with a suitable definition of God in terms of a being possessing the attributes of omnipotence, omniscience, and so on.[90] Of course, this knowledge does not of itself give one a relationship with God.

We have seen also that in Scripture there is an appeal to evidence of a historical kind, which contradicts Barth's claim that such evidence is not to be sought. Especially important in this regard would be Paul's listing of eyewitnesses to the resurrection in 1 Corinthians 15. The Gospel accounts also give eyewitness reports of the resurrection, and rebut alternative explanations for the empty tomb—especially that the disciples removed the body.

I see natural knowledge of God, far from being a substitute for, as preparatory to the saving knowledge of Christ, and providing at least one point of contact for Christ to reveal himself (so, although not necessarily going along with Brunner's anthropology, I side with him on this point). In alternative phraseology, general revelation precedes and prepares for special revelation. The vast gulf between humans and God, due to human sin, emphasized by Barth, is also real. The revelation of Christ is necessary for salvation and must be received in faith. This revelation occurs when God is pleased to reveal himself in Christ through the proclamation of the gospel.

## *Barth and Rationality*

Dietrich Bonhoeffer accused Barth of introducing a positivist doctrine of revelation "which says, in effect, 'Like it or lump it!': virgin birth, Trinity, or anything else; each is an equally significant and necessary part of the whole, which must simply be swallowed as a whole or not at all. That isn't biblical."[91] We examine Bonhoeffer's statement in more detail in the next chapter, but here it is sufficient to note that Barth's approach isolates theology from rational scrutiny.

David Jenkins says that Barth "so isolates Theology as not so much to make it incredible as to make it impossible for us to know whether it is incredible or not."[92] He goes on:

> But it is by no means clear that there is the total discontinuity between belief and unbelief which Barth posits. If there is, then we can only wait for the miracle. But as we shall not believe in the possibility of such a miracle unless it has happened to us we shall not even wait. This seems an oddly hopeless position to be in in a world which God is both supposed to have created and to have been incarnate in.[93]

John Bowden makes a similar point in the context of sharing the faith:

> To take the most minor practical point: if knowledge of God is as Barth describes it, how can the Christian talk to his friend and persuade him to share his beliefs and concerns? He cannot point to any hints of God in experience, history, morality, for these are all ruled out of court. All that seems possible is to sit in silence and wait; and if nothing happens, atheism is a perfectly logical conclusion, on Barth's own premises.[94]

Roger Trigg is critical of Barth because he seems to be irrational, along the lines of the above quotations. Barth says that we must rely only on revelation, and not on human reason, yet of course his own arguments are a product of human reasoning.[95] Importantly Barth moves away from revelation as propositional truths about God to God himself as truth. What God reveals for Barth is God himself. There are indeed dangers in thinking we can confine God too tightly in propositions made in human words (can these ever be adequate?), yet Barth's theology itself is inevitably full of propositions. Torrance notes that for Barth, in orthodoxy, "objective descriptions of the truth were confounded with or mistaken for the truth itself, so that they were not subject to its critical questioning or judgment."[96] I think there is a lot of truth in this, but again, for Barth and his followers, the question is, "How can we *know* how God judges?"

To reiterate, the question is, "Why should we believe that which is purportedly God's revelation to us?" There are, after all, false prophets, and we need to "test the spirits." How do we know revelation is from God? The only way is surely by appeal to reason. Yet this is precisely the path that Barth denies to us.

In order to evaluate whether something is a revelation of God, we shall need the tools of reason. Indeed we shall need to have some prior concept of God in order to recognize the revelation. One source of such a prior concept is surely natural theology. Unless the critical tools of reason are brought to bear, our belief is arbitrary and impossible to commend to others. We end up in the sea of postmodern relativism, in which my beliefs and your beliefs, though incompatible, are equally tenable because we are not prepared to put them to the tests of rational justification.

Barth himself sees his theology as scientific and rational, not in Harnack's sense, but in the sense that it attunes its methods to its object—and it has nothing to learn from the methods of other "sciences." He makes this point in the very first section of *Church Dogmatics* (*CD*, I/1.10). In that section he engages in another dispute with a friend, Heinrich Scholz, who published an essay in 1931 titled "How Is an Evangelical Theology Possible as Science?" in the journal *Zwischen den Zeiten*.[97] Scholz put forward a number of criteria required to be fulfilled for any undertaking to count as science. These included freedom from contradiction, coherence, the capacity to be tested, congruity with what is possible physically and biologically, freedom from prejudice, and capacity of being expressed as a system of axioms and theorems. It seems to me that some of these are indeed essential, though I would quibble with the fourth, if it is meant to exclude the possibility of miracles by fiat. The last also sounds excessively rational; are all sciences to be set up just like mathematical systems?

Barth rejects Scholz's schema, just as he rejects any other attempt to straitjacket theology, along with other sciences, as unacceptable to theology (*CD*, I/1.7–9). He writes:

> The very minimum postulate of freedom from contradiction is acceptable by theology only upon the very limited interpretation, by the scientific theorist upon the scarcely tolerable one, that theology will not assert an irremovability in principle of the "contradictions" which it is bound to make good. But the propositions in which it asserts their removal will be propositions concerning the free action of God, and so not propositions that "remove" the contradictions "from the world." The remaining sections of Scholz's law can only remind the theologian that he should know what he is doing when he transgresses them, and that as a theologian he cannot escape the necessity of transgressing them. (*CD*, I/1.8)

As we shall see in subsequent chapters, I am not alone in seeing Barth's stance as irrational. Wolfhart Pannenberg and Alister McGrath both see freedom from contradiction and testability as essential to theology. A philosopher whom I consider when discussing Thomas Torrance is W. W. Bartley, who critiqued modern Protestant theology (and it was Barthian theology he had in mind) as irrational precisely because it makes itself immune from criticism. According to Bartley, this kind of theology starts from an unfalsifiable premise and argues in a circle, denying that it has to conform to standards of rationality adopted by other sciences.

John McDowell disputes my view that Barth is an "irrationalist" and sees the approach of Richard Swinburne, which I defend, as flawed, citing Alasdair MacIntyre and others in support.[98] MacIntyre is certainly a very significant philosopher, and his notion of tradition-based rationality recurs when we discuss McGrath's appropriation of it for theology later in this book. In the meantime it must be acknowledged that there are indeed differing approaches to rationality and much debate about them. Another approach that rejects natural theology, though for reasons quite different to Barth's, is the reformed epistemology of Alvin Plantinga. Plantinga, in reacting to foundationalist accounts of rationality, asserts that an individual's belief in or experience of God should be taken as properly basic. Barth's and Plantinga's approaches in particular might free the believer from any reliance on experts, whether they be theologians, historians, or philosophers, but they also share one big drawback: on these accounts, how is one to convince the outsider?

Swinburne's approach is "empiricist" in the sense that it seeks to evaluate the probability of God's existence given different pieces of evidence, though "evidence" is conceived much more broadly than in the natural sciences. The evidence considered in this context comprises such things as the very existence of a universe, the special overall character of the universe that does exist, the existence of consciousness and morality, and the fact of religious experience. I acknowledge that Swinburne's approach is itself not without problems (in particular that of assigning prior probabilities in Bayesian confirmation theory), but Swinburne does offer, at least in principle, an objective method for carrying out the task. That method is at home in the philosophy of science, and has antecedents in the work of Rudolf Carnap. There it is used to evaluate competing scientific explanations for observational or experimental data, but is equally applicable to the evaluation of competing metaphysical hypotheses.[99]

My intention in this book is not so much to expound the method of Bayesian confirmation theory, which has been done adequately elsewhere, but to address the concerns about natural theology stemming from Barth and other major theologians, and to identify what opportunities for natural theology may still be afforded.

Coming back to Barth, the question of his alleged "irrationalism" needs to be faced head-on. As McDowell admits, Barth certainly denies the appropriateness of empirical evidence. This is not just the evidence from the natural world deployed by natural theology, but historical evidence, such as that for the resurrection. I am far from wanting to deny that theological truth is different from scientific truth, and that revelation is the major source of truth for Christians. Nevertheless, if Christian claims are true, would we not expect evidence to that effect, and indeed is there not evidence in fact? In the case of the resurrection, one can point to eyewitness accounts of the empty tomb and the resurrection appearances.

Of course, there is a job of work to be done to make a full-blown case, and to counter objections, but this seems in principle an eminently sensible strategy to convince the skeptic. In the same way, if God is Creator, would we not expect, and do we not indeed see, evidence of his hand in the design of the universe? To put it another way, should nature qua nature give any pointer to its being created and so to its creator ("the heavens declare the glory of God"!)? Surely, if it is created we would expect it to do so. If it is not created we would expect a chaos. Again there is much work to do to make the case, and one may well have to say something about theodicy here, but that does not negate the usefulness of the exercise. Of course, as McGrath says, the danger is that one then relies on rational reflection rather than the Holy Spirit,[100] but perhaps there is a middle way. After all, we can be faced with incontrovertible evidence and still fail to believe, or we can believe the facts and fail to act appropriately (like the devils), so the aid of the Holy Spirit is still necessary to bring a person to a living faith.

As we shall see in chapter 5, even so fervent a Barthian as Thomas Torrance wants to move us on to an engagement of theology with the natural sciences, which ought to be possible by reason of "their common sharing of the rational structures of space and time conferred on the universe by God in his creating of it, and within their common sharing in the basic conceptions of the unitary rationality of the universe, its contingent intelligibility and contingent freedom."[101] My point is that if these rational structures are shared, why can there not be an argument from "publicly available evidence" in the natural world to God? Are not these rational structures public truth, as opposed to private truth revealed to individuals? If we only believe in the latter, are we not really in danger of sinking into postmodern relativism, or worse, a kind of Gnosticism—even, as McGrath says, "a ghetto mentality"?[102] These points would seem to be consonant with those of Richard Roberts on public truth and ghettoization, as cited by McDowell. Roberts writes: "The alienation of the natural order and its attempted recreation as a natural theology based upon revelation presents in a particular way the general isolation of Christian theology from the realm of commonplace secular reality. Such an alienation is nothing less than a comprehensive theological disaster."[103]

A question arises here as to why people reject the gospel. Is it purely because they are sinful, or are there genuine intellectual reasons why at least some people do so? Of course, people may have been mistaught; they may have imbibed false impressions from the surrounding culture, for example, about the weakness of the Christian position and the strength of the atheistic. If the latter is the case (and this would seem to be at least in part an empirical question!), then again the use of rational argument would seem to be indicated to assuage doubts. Yes, the pure and unadulterated proclamation of the gospel may work for some, but unless there is some intellectual undergirding, those who respond may find themselves wavering when they meet argument from the other side.

My view on natural theology and rationality is different from Barth's. I believe we can recognize the existence of the Creator from the creation. I agree with Barth that we need revelation to inform us of the other articles of the creed: the doctrines of the Trinity and of the person of Christ cannot be derived from pure reason, though even here I would argue that such beliefs are, or ought to be, rational. We believe them on good grounds, though now those grounds include the biblical revelation. Claims about the person of Christ are supported by the evidence of his life, death, and resurrection. Of course, faith is essential, and, moreover, faith is not simply believing the facts about Christ as stated for us in the creeds (which is more or less what St. Thomas Aquinas thought). Faith involves a response; as Luther said, it is putting one's trust in the living God. At the end of the day, though, the faith of Christians is not blind, irrational faith, but faith in a God of order and reason.

There seems to be a problem here for evangelism and apologetics: Christians are bidden by Scripture to "be ready always to give an answer to every man that asketh you a reason of the hope that is in you" (1 Pet 3:15, KJV), and to preach the gospel to all nations, but is conversion solely God's work of self-revelation? In one sense, the answer to this is, of course, "Yes," but at the same time God does use human beings as his instruments. It seems to me that arguments put forward using reason may at least prepare the ground for God's self-revelation in Christ—indeed, that God can and does work through such arguments—though of course God is free to reveal himself wherever, whenever, and to whomsoever.

It is worth repeating the limited nature of what natural theology, at least on the view of it I present here, is trying to do. It is *not* trying to erect an independent source of knowledge about God, "trying to know God apart from God's revelation," as Christoph Schwöbel glosses Barth.[104] It is *not* trying to replace the *sola gratia* of the Reformation with a *sola natura*, as Barth seems to think. Natural theology is *not* the be-all and end-all, merely the starting point, and its success is dependent on God's will. For me as a Christian, that pre-Christian knowledge of God from nature is not necessary because I am on the inside enjoying a relationship with God brought about through his grace, and received by faith, in Christ. Even so, for me it is confirming, and would be disturbing if it were otherwise, that persuasive, rational arguments can be produced for the tenets of my faith, and, at the very least, that the atheist has repeatedly failed to prove his case (cf. Calvin). No, all that natural theology is doing is pointing to creation and saying, for the benefit of outsiders, that it speaks of God as Creator. Of course, God could have made the world so that it did not point to him, or so that it didn't unless a person were among a select group enlightened by the Holy Spirit. But why would God want to disguise the fact that he made the world? Of course, the scriptural evidence is that he did design it so that it pointed to him (incidentally, that does not mean that there is no ambivalence about the world; there is the problem of evil to be considered).

Of course, as a Christian who believes that salvation is to be found in Christ alone, I do not want to leave those who hear the arguments from natural theology (or simply science) with just those arguments. There is much more to do. Yes, *fides quaerens intellectum* is vital. As a Christian, I want to say much more about God than natural theology can say. Indeed, one might well want to say more about nature—that is, develop a theology of nature from inside the fold. The question, though, is how to get our hearers over the first step, into the community in the first place, so that they can do their further seeking from inside. That is my concern. The internal development of theology by the church is essential, but how do we bring in those from outside to partake in the quest?

Thus, I agree with Barth that for Christians Christ must remain central. Natural theology will always be of secondary importance. We must also be aware of the dangers of natural theology. For Christians today, the main danger is not National Socialism. Instead we are faced with the more subtle and insidious dangers posed by religious pluralism on the one hand, and by militant secularism on the other. Natural theology gives us a point of contact with some of the world's major religions, as it did for Paul in Athens. It also gives us a point of contact with secular society, and especially with the scientific community. But we must insist that it is only a starting point, and that "Jesus Christ is goal of everything, and the center to which everything tends. He who knows him knows the meaning of all things" (Pascal).

Many of the points raised in this chapter are reconsidered as we see how the major theologians to be studied have reacted to Barth.

CHAPTER THREE

# Dietrich Bonhoeffer
## Disciple and Critic

THE GREAT GERMAN theologian and martyr Dietrich Bonhoeffer[1] is not widely known for engaging with scientific thought, having been heavily influenced by Karl Barth's celebrated stance against natural theology that we examined in chapter 2. Yet Bonhoeffer was brought up in a scientific household. His father was a professor of psychiatry at the University of Berlin and his brother Karl-Friedrich became an outstanding physical chemist. Moreover, Bonhoeffer began his theological studies at Tübingen under Karl Heim, who wanted to incorporate natural science into his theology.

There is not much sign of Bonhoeffer's engaging with scientific thought directly, however, in his earliest works, with the notable exception of his exposition of the early chapters of Genesis, *Creation and Fall*.[2] Here, while he effectively denied any relationship between the Christian doctrine of creation and scientific cosmology (as indeed did the Abbé Georges Lemaître, the father of the big bang theory), he fully embraced the Darwinian account of human origins. Indeed, it could be argued that Darwinism and Christian theology were thoroughly integrated in that work, in particular in the chapter expounding Genesis 2:7, where he asserts the thoroughgoing materiality of the human person in Genesis: "Even Darwin and Feuerbach could not use stronger language than is used here" (*CF*, 76). In this chapter I argue that Bonhoeffer's insights here link naturally with modern debates in the science-religion area—for example, that surrounding nonreductive physicalism, some form of which Bonhoeffer might well have embraced.

In *Creation and Fall* and in other, later works, Bonhoeffer interpreted Scripture theologically, specifically christologically, a much richer hermeneutic approach than engaging in a futile war with science. However, skepticism regarding natural theology is there, too—for example, in Bonhoeffer's concept of "orders of preservation" as opposed to the traditional "orders of creation" (*CF*, 140), although I argue that he provides opportunities for natural theology, even if unintentionally, both here and in the later *Ethics*.[3]

Bonhoeffer's maturing theology from the final period spent in captivity is presented, albeit in fragmentary and enigmatic form, in the famous *Letters and Papers from Prison*.[4] Here Bonhoeffer read a significant scientific work, Carl Friedrich von Weizsäcker's *The World View of Physics*,[5] which again led him to engage with science. From this reading he gained two major insights for his whole theological outlook. First, he realized that the notion of a "God-of-the-gaps" is futile, not just in science but in other areas of human inquiry. Second, he felt that an infinite universe, as considered by science, would be self-subsistent and could exist as if there were no God. Bonhoeffer replaced Barth's radical critique of religion with the even more extreme view that it is a mere passing phase in history with which grown-up humanity can dispense. At the same time Bonhoeffer began an important critique of Barth's reaction, namely, the latter's retreat to a "positivism of revelation." While Bonhoeffer did not go quite as far as one might like, his approach opened up hopeful avenues for an answer to "the liberal question" and even a revived place for some kind of natural theology.

## Creation and Fall

In the winter term of 1932 Bonhoeffer gave a lecture course at the University of Berlin on "Creation and Sin," published in 1933 as *Creation and Fall*. This is an exposition of Genesis 1–3, and if one wanted to know Bonhoeffer's early thoughts about the interrelationship between science and faith, and indeed natural theology, this would seem a good place to look. In what follows, I am much indebted to the introduction and footnotes provided by the editors to this volume.

Bonhoeffer accepted the science of his day and appreciated that the biblical cosmology was primitive, if it was to be interpreted literally. That did not mean, however, that there was no message for us today from the text: quite the contrary.

As John W. de Gruchy points out (in *CF*, 5–12), *Creation and Fall* is important for a number of reasons. It affirms the value of the Old Testament as Christian Scripture, in opposition to neo-Marcian tendencies in the church of the Third Reich. Rejection of the Old Testament was fed by anti-Semitism, which could even draw on the conclusions of Bonhoeffer's teacher, Adolf von Harnack, which the latter reached for other theological reasons.[6] Yet, second, Bonhoeffer is not engaged in a purely academic exercise of historical-critical exegesis, though the findings of these methods are also accepted. No, *Creation and Fall* is chiefly a theological exposition—indeed, more than that, a christological interpretation made in the light of the New Testament. As pointed out by scholars such as Green and Kuske, this is a method that Bonhoeffer utilizes frequently over the next few years.[7] It is perhaps best known in his manual for community life, *Life Together*,[8] in which he regards the psalms as the prayers of Jesus offered up by the church (the latter was written in 1938, shortly after the closure of Bonhoeffer's preachers' seminary by the Gestapo). Bethge notes that Bonhoeffer drew on Barth's christocentric treatment of the Old Testament and took it further; indeed, *Creation and Fall* marked Bonhoeffer as a member of the Barth school.[9]

*Creation and Fall* anticipates much that is to be found in the later Bonhoeffer, most especially the place of Christ "at the center of life." Bethge cites this as the first major appearance of this important theme and as one of the many examples of the continuity of thought between the early Bonhoeffer and his maturing theology in *Letters and Papers*.[10] Other Bonhoeffer scholars also comment on this theme.[11]

As we shall see, Bonhoeffer also introduces here the important notion of "orders of preservation" in nature as opposed to the traditional "orders of creation." As noted by many Bonhoeffer commentators, this is an anti–natural theological move and highly relevant to the context of the day when the concept of orders such as the "nation," deemed given in creation, were employed to support National Socialism.[12] Nevertheless there may be something positive, even here, for natural theology in the light of Bonhoeffer's talk later in the *Ethics* of "last and penultimate things."

It is suggested here that Bonhoeffer's high view of Scripture, and his exegesis stemming from this, ought to commend itself to modern evangelicals who are concerned that Darwinism undermines the authority of Scripture. Much less noticed are two insights that feed into modern discussions of science and religion. One is Bonhoeffer's assertion that number depends on God, and without him even mathematics cannot escape paradox. This observation might also be of positive import for natural theology. The second insight, drawn straight from the Genesis text, is a strong material aspect to human nature, stronger even than Darwinism. This ought also to impress evangelicals, but is important for another major area of contemporary science-religion discussion, namely, what it means to be human in the light of discoveries in neurophysiology. For example, what does it mean to talk of the "soul" in the modern context?

We shall cover these insights in more depth as we work our way through the text of *Creation and Fall.*

## *The First Creation Story*

Bonhoeffer begins by grappling with the notion of "creation in the beginning." All Christian theology begins from the end—that is, Christ. Our present situation in the middle makes it impossible for us to get behind the beginning. It defeats all notions of cause and effect. Bonhoeffer is thus not concerned with the big bang theory, which, even if not called that, was emerging at the time through the theoretical work of Belgian priest Georges Lemaître and the observation of the expanding universe by Edwin Hubble. Indeed he is not concerned at all with the beginning in temporal terms, because one can always go back behind such a beginning (*CF*, 32). The unique beginning spoken of in Genesis 1:1–2 is the creation in unconditioned freedom by God of what is distinct from God.

This is an important and classical assertion. Bonhoeffer does not, however, go down the route of arguing that the sheer contingency of the universe in some way points to its origin in God as necessary being, or any similar argument that might seem like natural theology or would "enthrone reason in the place of God" (*CF*, 27). On the contrary, Bonhoeffer asserts, quite radically, that we can believe in this creation out of nothing because of the resurrection of Jesus Christ. This is also a creation out of nothing (it is the "new creation"), since there is no continuum between the dead Jesus and the resurrected Christ, just as there is no continuity between nothingness and the created world.

Now, we might want to argue contrariwise that there is both continuity and discontinuity between the dead Jesus and the resurrected Christ. Jesus' disciples recognize him, albeit not initially. In the story of the Emmaus road, it is when Jesus carries out that most characteristic action of breaking bread that the two companions "eyes are opened" (Lk 24:31). That is no doubt true and important, since it must be the same person who dies and is raised again, as much for ourselves as for Jesus. Bonhoeffer's emphasis rather is on the sheer impossibility, and therefore discontinuity, of resurrection: "The fact that Christ was dead did not provide the possibility of his resurrection but its impossibility" (*CF*, 35). And certainly Christ would not be attested as Creator, as Bonhoeffer says, had he not risen from the dead. The resurrection was as powerful an act of God as the creation of the universe *ex nihilo*.

God's word in creation is also quite different from any human word of command, because for God to speak and for the thing to come about are one. Again there is no chain of cause and effect. This means that it is "not 'from' God's works, then, that we recognize the Creator" (*CF*, 41) as if there were some kind of continuum between cause and effect. We only know that God is Creator because his word says so "and we *believe* this word about his works!" (*CF*, 41). Here is a thoroughly anti–natural theological and quite Barthian statement. It is also similar to Emil Brunner's statement in his work of 1931, *God and Man*:

> The God who is known from the world is precisely not the creator. . . . As the creator he is only to be known by the fact that he is not to be known in continuity with the world, but

> from his Word alone. . . . The creator is known only by the Bible.[13]

There is thus no appeal to a cosmological argument, principle of sufficient reason, or the like, but a straight denial of such natural theological routes to God.

As we shall see, there are other, more positive lessons to learn from *Creation and Fall*. However, at this point I have to demur at the strength of Bonhoeffer's aversion to natural theology (and I do not disagree with scholars, such as Green, who affirm this aversion).[14] I agree that the classical arguments—ontological, cosmological, and teleological—cannot be construed as knockdown proofs of God's existence. Nor are they substitutes for God's self-revelation in Christ. Indeed I would concur with Wolfhart Pannenberg that God cannot be known anywhere, or by any means, unless he makes himself known.[15] I do, however, think that he provides us with some knowledge of himself in creation. I also concur with Richard Swinburne's approach of expressing the traditional arguments in probabilistic form. And I find the limited natural theology advanced by John Polkinghorne valid and helpful.[16] The very fact that physics is possible, and that the universe, from its tiniest particles studied in accelerators to all its vastness explored by cosmology, is open to human comprehension is best explained theistically. Moreover, the fine-tuning of the laws of physics and the initial conditions at the big bang are also suggestive of design by God, notwithstanding speculative alternatives such as multiverses.[17]

In expounding "and God saw the light that it was good," Bonhoeffer sees God's looking on his creation as his upholding it. Because the world is good and God sees this, he wills to uphold it. Thus, the importance of God sustaining the world he has made is there from the beginning.

In discussing the creation of day and night, he notes that, while the biblical writers were bound by the knowledge and limits of their time, this is irrelevant to theology. We are simply not concerned with the question as to whether "the creation occurred in rhythms of millions of years or single days" (*CF*, 52). Rather, the term "day" embraces all the rhythms of rest and movement in the universe given by God.

Again when speaking of the separation of the waters by the creation of the firmament, Bonhoeffer recognizes the primitive cosmology, which would be absurd if taken literally; he is presumably fully aware, unlike modern literalist readers of the text, that the Hebrew word *raqia* means "metal dome." However, while he knows this, he cautions against a "derisive attitude." The firmament, with its celestial inhabitants, "determines days, years and epochs of time" (*CF*, 52). It is the fixed background; as Bonhoeffer puts it, it is "number that rules with inflexible law" (*CF*, 52). While it is not easy to grasp this point, it leads to an interesting discussion of number (*Zahl*). Numbers too are upheld by God—they are also God's creatures "and so receive their truth wholly from the Creator" (*CF*, 53). This view, which sounds rather like Christian Platonism, is reinforced for Bonhoeffer by recent developments in the foundations of mathematics: "We have forgotten this connection; when we have numbers, we believe we have truth and eternity. What draws our attention to our loss of truth and eternity is the fact that in the end mathematics too does not rise above paradox. A knowledge of numbers that is godless ends in paradox and contradiction" (*CF*, 53).

It would appear that Bonhoeffer is aware of Bertrand Russell's finding (1902) of paradox in the transfinite arithmetic of Georg Cantor. Russell considered the set of all sets that have the property of not being members of themselves, and asked, "Is the set so defined a member of itself?" The answers "yes" and "no" both lead to contradiction. This is despite the construction being perfectly valid in Cantor's theory of infinite sets, indeed closely related to a procedure of Cantor himself.

It is possible that Bonhoeffer also knew about the publication in 1931 of the great paper by Kurt Gödel in which Gödel showed that any axiomatic mathematical system as or more complicated than arithmetic was either inconsistent or incomplete. If such a mathematical system is consistent, there will be statements within it that are true but nevertheless unprovable from the axioms by the logical deductive procedures allowed within the system.

From these developments Bonhoeffer draws the conclusion that truth and eternity are not to be found in numbers. My reading of the situation is that these developments were indeed quite devastating for mathematics, for mathematics had seemed the most secure and certain realm of human endeavor, since, being based on pure logic, it was not open to empirical correction, and it utilized deductive methods rather than the inductive methods of the natural sciences. And mathematics was now found to be paradoxical. Russell and Whitehead had produced a revised version of set theory so as to avoid paradox, and David Hilbert issued a challenge to mathematicians to show that this restricted set theory was consistent and complete. Gödel's theorem defeated the challenge by demonstrating that the opposite was the case.

It seems that a crack is opening up here for a kind of natural theology. This shattering of what humanly speaking had seemed most secure of all ought to lead us to what is truly secure and eternal: the Creator of all.

It is interesting that many modern mathematicians (such as Roger Penrose)[18] believe that mathematical truths inhabit a Platonic realm independent of conscious minds, whether human or divine. The incompleteness of mathematics does not drive Penrose to God. However, Penrose has utilized Gödel's theorem to argue that human beings are not simply computers, on the grounds that humans can perceive truths that computers, operating algorithmically, cannot prove. We shall see later how Bonhoeffer emphasizes the material aspect of human constitution, drawing on the Genesis text. This insight of Penrose balances that by saying that humans are at any rate more than "computers made of meat." There is a capacity of the organized complexity that is a human being that transcends the merely algorithmic. Some (such as J. R. Lucas[19]) see here an argument for mind-body dualism; Penrose himself seeks an answer in as yet unknown new physics.[20] Either way, the defeat of a purely mechanistic view of human nature, such as is advocated by the strong artificial intelligence school, might also lead one in the direction of a divine origin for humankind.

By extension Bonhoeffer could have concluded, ahead of modern physicists such as Paul Davies and Stephen Hawking, that physics, dependent as it is on mathematics, cannot provide ultimate truth. As a result, Hawking now recognizes that his earlier quest for a physical "Theory of Everything" is doomed to failure.[21] Thus, a natural theology based on the insight that mathematics does not possess "truth and eternity" leads on to a more traditional form of natural theology based on the laws of physics not possessing truth and eternity.

Of course, Bonhoeffer did not develop this argument, nor is it likely that he would necessarily find it congenial, given the rest of what he says. Indeed the argument about loss of eternity might be likened to the existential despair that Bonhoeffer repudiates as a way to God, both in his early review of Karl Heim's book *Glauben und Denken*[22] and later in *Letters and Papers from Prison* (*LPP*, 327). Nevertheless, it is intriguing how Bonhoeffer's remarks can be construed this way, and it seems legitimate for us to develop the idea in the most fruitful way we can.

Following from this, Bonhoeffer briefly alludes to "the old rationalistic question" about the creation of light on the first day and the sun on the fourth (a point that led Origen, c. AD 200, to decry a literalist interpretation of the text).[23] He makes the point that light makes the sun what it is and "because there is meant to be light, the sun shines" (*CF*, 55). Thus, light has a kind of metaphysical priority, even though we know that physically there has to be a source. In the sun, the unbound light of creation becomes bound (in the sense of "tied") to form [*Gestalt*], "to what is fixed, to numbers"; it remains, however, the creation of God. Although Bonhoeffer does not mention this, it is worth noting that the heavenly bodies are not given their names in the text, merely called "lights." Their names would connote deities in the Babylonian world in which Genesis 1 was written. It may also be that the author wishes to demote these lights from day one as the source of light, and of day and night, since otherwise that too might exaggerate their status.

So far all that is created is dead, but now God makes living creatures. The inanimate creation praises God by its existence, but living creatures praise him by carrying on the Creator's work in themselves creating life. The final stage is reached only when God as it were creates a being who reflects his very self. Man made in the image of God is utterly distinct from the rest of the creation, though Bonhoeffer again is not concerned with scientific accounts of human origins. "This has nothing whatsoever to do with Darwin" (*CF*, 62), he says of the creation of humans in the image of God. "We in no way wish to deny humankind's connection with the animal world—on the contrary" (*CF*, 62). His chief concern remains the theological one of the relationship between man and God, above all inaccessible questions of origins, and hence the uniqueness of human beings.

For man to be created in the image of God means that man is free. Nevertheless, he is not free in himself [*an sich*] but free *for* the other—free for worship of the Creator and free for other people. In the same way, God in Christ is free for humankind (the "man for others" in the phraseology of Bonhoeffer's doctoral thesis of 1927, *Sanctorum Communio*). As Green notes, this emphasis on sociality represents a far-reaching revision of the whole theological tradition.[24] The classical tradition regarded human reason as imaging God. The problems with the latter are that it does not do justice to the wholeness of man as *imago dei*, and it permits an individualistic theological anthropology. Marsh observes that Bonhoeffer's concept of us living "in the middle," through Christ, leads him away from speculative notions to the concreteness of Christ's sacrifice as the locus for human freedom (for others) and our affinity with God.[25] The likeness to God is then not *analogia entis* (human beings in themselves like God) but *analogia relationis* (a relationship in which they are set). In developing his doctrine of creation Barth followed up this point in the summer of 1942, *Creation and Fall* being the first of Bonhoeffer's books that Barth read.[26]

## *The Second Creation Story*

Bonhoeffer was well aware that the second creation story in Genesis 2–3 is completely different from the first, and accepts the results of biblical criticism (the scientific study of Scripture) that it comes from the much older J source as opposed to the P source. That means that what we have are only representations [*Darstellungen*] of the same thing from two different sides. Both are necessary for completion. The first account is from above—God's perspective—and portrays the world as distant. The second is about the nearness of the world and God. God is now given a personal name, Yahweh [*Jahweh* in German], and is anthropomorphically represented—walking in the garden. This represents his closeness, his fatherly care. So God is both majestic Creator and loving father.

The anthropomorphisms become "more insupportable," says Bonhoeffer, as God fashions man from the dust of the ground:

> Surely no one can gain any knowledge about the origin of humankind from this! To be sure, as an account of what happened this story is at first sight of just as little consequence, and just as full of meaning, as many another myth of creation. And yet in being distinguished as the word of God it is quite simply *the source* of knowledge about the origin of humankind. (*CF*, 75–76)

We note again Bonhoeffer's high view of Scripture.

This fashioning, theologically, signifies God's physical nearness to human beings. It is also important in signifying the connection of man with the earth. The Bible uses even stronger language than Darwin and Feuerbach (*CF*, 76n)![27] The message seems to be that if Christians found it demeaning that man was created from apelike creatures, then how much more demeaning to be created directly from earth! Genesis lays stronger emphasis on matter than these modern authors. And that signifies the importance of the body, which belongs to a person's essence.

In *God and Man*, Brunner had written: "Man is created as a bodily being, and his bodily nature is a part of his being. . . . The body is not merely an appurtenance of man, but—and here this psychology is in agreement with the naturalistic and romantic psychologies—man *is* body. . . ."[28] De Gruchy tells us that Bonhoeffer's copy of Brunner's book contains numerous markings in this chapter, on biblical psychology, and that Bonhoeffer recommended this reading for his seminar "Dogmatic Exercises: The Problems of a Theological Anthropology," also given in the winter semester of 1932–33 (*CF*, 76–77n).[29] Bonhoeffer writes: "The body is not the prison, the shell, the exterior of a human being: instead the human being is a human body. . . . People who reject their bodies reject their existence before God the Creator" (*CF*, 76–77).

Here Bonhoeffer links into contemporary debates in the science-religion area. He sees humans much more as body-soul unities than purely spiritual beings. Today he might well identify with nonreductive physicalism as opposed to substance dualism.[30] The former seems to be becoming the new orthodoxy, though there are some dissenters.[31] Human beings are a wonderful piece of earth "called by God to have human existence," and the earth is in this sense their mother. God's breath of life is what then distinguishes humans from the animals: "The human body differs from all non-human bodies in that it is the form in which the spirit of God exists on earth, just as it is altogether identical with all other life in being earth-like" (*CF*, 78–79).

Bonhoeffer's statement that "people who reject their bodies reject their existence before God the Creator" (*CF*, 77) also speaks to the modern age. The rejection of the body takes many forms nowadays. One example would be cosmetic surgery and, related to that, the use of the antiaging agent Botox. Certainly there are deformities, and it is legitimate to correct accidents of birth or injuries sustained in fire or war. In Britain, there has been concern that abortion has been used to prevent those with minor, surgically correctable deformities such as a cleft lip and palate from even being born. [Breast enlargement is not confined to Hollywood stars.]

The rise of eating disorders such as anorexia is also disturbing, and is not helped by the zero-size obsession of the fashion industry. This is also related to body image and a rejection of what we have been given in nature. A different problem, representing an even more major rejection of the body one has been endowed with, is transsexualism. In this condition, sufferers feel they have been given the body of the wrong sex. They are a "male trapped in a female body" or (more often) vice versa. Very often, only surgery can help such a person to "body-soul" harmony.

I am not for a moment saying that this and other body-image problems are not serious and should not be treated with the utmost seriousness by the medical profession, especially psychiatrists. On the contrary, those afflicted need all the help and compassion we can offer, and with some body-image problems, as indicated, surgery may be the only solution. Nevertheless they seem to be symptoms of something wrong with society or culture, especially in the affluent West, more generally. What I think Bonhoeffer would say is that we need to recover the theological perspective of the value of the material and of our basic constitution as material beings, since this is how God made us in the beginning. That would certainly accord with Bonhoeffer's recurring emphasis on God-given reality and concreteness, as noted by many of his commentators, in opposition to the abstract and metaphysics.

Bonhoeffer goes on to say that the only way one could possibly speak of the first earth is in the language of fantasy, in pictures, and so it is with the Garden of Eden. Regarding the taking of the fruit from the enchanted tree and being displaced from paradise, Bonhoeffer writes:

> This is a myth, a childlike, fanciful picture of the dim and distant past [*Vorzeit*]—so says the world. This is God's word; this is an event at the beginning of history, before history, beyond history, and yet in history; this is a decision that affects the world; *we ourselves* are the ones who are affected, are intended, are addressed, accused, condemned, expelled; *God, yes God*, is the one who blesses and curses; it is *our* primeval history [*Urgeschichte*], truly our own, every individual person's beginning, destiny, guilt, and end—so says the Church of Christ. (*CF*, 82)

In what follows, Bonhoeffer seeks to "translate from the picture language of the magical world into the new picture language of the technical world": "This must always be done, however, on the basis of the presupposition that, whether in the one language or the other, *we* are the ones intended to be addressed" (*CF*, 83). The difference between us and those who thought in those mythological terms is that Christ has appeared and "we can live only through Christ as people who have been lost and, whether in hope or in fulfillment, have been graciously pardoned" (*CF*, 83).

As Green notes, Bonhoeffer sounds rather like Bultmann here: he recognizes the naïveté of the text from a scientific point of view and says we must translate the "picture language."[32] However, he is different from Bultmann in not feeling the necessity to reject "myth" since he says that pictures are essential: "Why not see that all our speaking of God, of our beginning and end, and of our guilt *never* communicates these things themselves but always only pictures of them? Why not see that in both instances, with these ancient magical images as well as with our technical, abstract images, God must reach out to us, and that God must teach us if we are to become wise [*klug*]?" (*CF*, 82).

The result of the fall (or better, in Bonhoeffer's thought, "the destructuring of created reality," as Dumas puts it)[33] is that we suffer from an inner split [*Zwiespalt*]. This is manifested in our experience of pleasure and pain, of good and evil, and we are the ones who "have eaten from the tree of knowledge, not Adam." Paradoxically, the death that follows means the obligation to live, but to "live out of myself," that is, alone. Bonhoeffer continues:

> At this point, however, we need to remind ourselves again that this is not a tale about some primeval human being that hardly affects us. . . . Adam's history is our history, with the one decisive difference, to be sure, that for us history begins where for Adam it ends. Our history is history through Christ; Adam's history is history through the serpent. But precisely as those who live and have their history through Christ alone we are enabled to know about the beginning not by means of our own imagination but only from the new centre, from Christ. (*CF*, 92)

He notes, with a phrase that echoes Nietzsche, whose influence on Bonhoeffer is interesting in itself,[34] that we are unable to transport ourselves to "this paradise 'beyond good and evil.'" We are therefore not allowed to judge what the Bible calls good by our idea of what is good and on that basis "to criticize what the Bible says here about what is beyond good and evil."

Related to the story as it is presented literally, Bonhoeffer poses the question as to how Adam, who knows nothing of father and mother, can say, "That is why a man will leave his father and mother and cleave to his wife, and they will be one flesh" (*CF*, 100) (though it is not at all clear that that part of the text is in the mouth of Adam).[35] The answer lies in a basic fact that has been kept in the background hitherto: that "the Adam who speaks like this is we ourselves, we who have fathers and mothers" (*CF*, 100). We know what is the uniqueness of love between a man and a woman and how this is destroyed by our guilt. This statement is not a justification for running away from father and mother—that is, from the ties with them—but is the only way of expressing the depth and seriousness of belonging to one another.

When it comes to the fall, Bonhoeffer says, the intention of the Bible is not to explain the origin of evil "but to witness to its character as guilt" (*CF*, 105). Evil does not come from somewhere other than the creation (and it would exonerate Adam if there were some story as in Catholic theology or Luther about the fall of Lucifer). No, evil comes from within the creation and is utterly incomprehensible and inexcusable—its incomprehensibility being enhanced by its occurring in paradise.

The serpent's question is "Did God really say . . . ?" As Dumas notes, this is the "'religious' question, the pious question, which prefers the 'unreal' world of human temptation to the reality God himself has provided, and which thinks it can improve upon reality and penetrate more deeply than his commandment."[36] Bonhoeffer states:

> The decisive point is that through this question the idea is suggested to the human being of going behind the word of God and now providing it with a human basis—a human understanding of the essential nature of God. Should the word contradict this understanding, then the human being has clearly misheard. (*CF*, 106)

This question changes the attitude of the creature to the Creator: "It requires humankind to sit in judgment on God's word instead of simply listening to it and doing it. And this is achieved by proposing that, on the basis of an idea, a principle, or some prior knowledge about God, humankind should now pass judgment on the concrete word of God" (*CF*, 108). This is indeed a terrible temptation, and we see people succumbing to it all the time. "Did God really say, 'Thou shalt not commit adultery?' Isn't love the priority and doesn't that justify my new relationship?"

The temptation is to leave the creaturely freedom plus the boundedness given by God to become *sicut deus*, to be alone as Master, mankind acting out of its own resources, and unlimited. As Plant points out,[37] this links directly to the political situation of the time, and in particular the radio broadcast that Bonhoeffer made on February 1, 1933, and which, only two days after Hitler came to power, was cut off before the end (*NRS*, 190–204). There Bonhoeffer castigated the new *Führerprinzip*, in which authority is derived solely from the loyalty of the leader's followers. The dangerous tendency is then precisely toward the unlimited authority of *sicut deus*. This new Führer principle compares with the more traditional concept of the "office" (such as teacher, pastor, lawyer) where authority is genuine and limited, and exercised simply by virtue of holding the particular office in question.

But this becoming *sicut deus* amounts to death, says Bonhoeffer. In Christ we understand "the human being who is God incarnate, who was sacrificed for humankind *sicut deus*, in true divinity slaying its false divinity and restoring the *imago dei*" (*CF*, 113). At the end of *Creation and Fall*, Bonhoeffer brings his christological interpretation to its climax. The cross is the tree of life "in the midst of the world" and from it springs up the fountain of life:

> What a strange tree of life, this cross, this trunk on which the very God had to suffer and die. . . . The tree of life, the cross of Christ, the center of God's world that is fallen but upheld and preserved—that is what the end of the story about paradise is for us. (*CF*, 146)

In the opening chapter of the *Ethics*, written a decade later during the war, but in strong continuity with *Creation and Fall*,[38] Bonhoeffer returns to the subject of the fall. He notes that, whereas the subject of all ethical reflection is the knowledge of good and evil, specifically Christian ethics negates this (*Ethics*, 17ff.). This is because, in the Genesis narrative, acquisition of the knowledge of good and evil is a consequence of the fall, and so precisely not what Adam should have sought. This knowledge represents man turning away from his origin in God, and God's knowledge of good and evil, and seeking it *sicut deus* in his own knowledge. He thus comes to live out of himself rather than in dependence on God.

As in *Act and Being* (his *Habilitation* or university lectureship qualifying thesis, 1931) and *Sanctorum Communio*, in *Creation and Fall* Bonhoeffer sees Augustine's categories of *posse peccare, posse non peccare* (able to sin, able not to sin), and so on, as inadequate. Indeed, any attempt to make the deed comprehensible becomes an accusation against the Creator. Moreover, the biological propagation of original sin would not yield personal guilt. That comes about since the sin is committed by me and by humanity—and I am implicated in the latter. "I am infinitely burdened with the guilt of the other," he says (*CF*, 120). This is helpful in trying to preserve what is important from the doctrine of original sin without being tied to Augustine's misunderstandings of biology.[39] If Bonhoeffer is correct here, then this would have interesting consequences for such modern dilemmas as to whether the present generation should apologize for slavery or the Crusades.

Bonhoeffer's analysis of the primordial sin provides another instance of his approach that should commend itself to evangelicals. We should listen to and obey God's word rather than sit in judgment on it. In contrast, the "liberal" attitude is arguably to do the latter, such as through historical-critical analysis and the use of human reason. And while I have applauded Bonhoeffer's dictum above, there is also an ambivalence here, for the question arises, "How do we know what God's word is?" It is no good simply quoting Scripture, because (a) we need to establish that Scripture is indeed God's word and (b) Scripture needs to be interpreted (of course, Bonhoeffer himself is doing that—christologically). As Pannenberg notes, the Enlightenment and the historical-critical method challenge (decisively, Pannenberg thinks, though that may be too strong) the traditional doctrine of inspiration, and the doctrine of the perspicuity of Scripture is also problematic.[40] So in reality there is no escaping the use of critical methods, using our reason—doing some kind of natural theology—in order to discern God's will for us. Bonhoeffer's personal stand against the Nazis, which in his own terminology would be characterized as "responsible action in faith and in exclusive allegiance to God," is admirable, but what that expression means for us or anybody else cannot be read off in any simplistic way from what he tells us. Perhaps in the end some middle way is needed, since we also recognize the case characterized by Bonhoeffer when we know unequivocally what is right, what God has said, and we fail to do it.

Bonhoeffer's next point comes from Genesis 3:21, where we read, "And Yahweh God made cloaks of skin for Adam and his wife and clothed them with these." This Bonhoeffer sees as God the Creator now become the preserver. God acts to preserve the fallen world but also to restrain it.

This thought of God the preserver leads to a further important anti–natural theological turn, as mentioned earlier, which comes toward the end of *Creation and Fall*. Lutheran theology spoke of the "orders of creation"—state, family, marriage, and culture—which the German Christians appropriated in arguing that the German *Volk* was a God-given order. Barth had already opposed this form of natural theology christologically, and Bonhoeffer followed suit.[41] He denied the notion of "orders of creation" and coined the term "orders of preservation" (transmuted in the *Ethics* to "divine mandates") instead (*CF*, 140). He argued that these orders were not autonomous and independent of God's revelation but the means whereby God preserves the world from descending into chaos while it awaits its redemption in Christ. "They have no value in themselves; instead they find their end and meaning only through Christ," he says (*CF*, 140). In the *Ethics* he lists labor, marriage, government, and the church as mandates, God-given tasks rather than orders of being and directed toward Christ (*Ethics*, 207).

It seems to me that one can make an interesting connection between the provisionality of the "orders of preservation" and Bonhoeffer's later concept, also to be found in the *Ethics*, of "last and penultimate things." Importantly for this study, that connection gives yet another opening for natural theology. Although the main focus of this chapter hitherto has been on *Creation and Fall*, a slight digression to consider this passage from the *Ethics* might therefore be helpful at this point.

The distinction between ultimate and penultimate things seems to demarcate a place for the "natural" (*CF*, 120–87). The ultimate is the word of justification: it is grace, Jesus Christ himself, received in faith. The penultimate is everything that precedes grace; it is life before Christ comes to a person.

Bonhoeffer argues that there must be a place for the penultimate as a preparation for the ultimate. Feeding the hungry and freeing slaves, for example, are penultimate works. They are not grace itself, but the well-nourished person is better able to receive the word of justification than the starving. Christ can and does come to those suffering, but Christians should be preparing his way as Isaiah prophesies and John the Baptist preaches. In fact, Christians have to live in the penultimate until death, even though they are already risen with Christ.

What is good in the penultimate should be claimed for Christ. For example, while the order of marriage (later on called "mandate," as we have noted) is penultimate, it is nevertheless good that the marriage bond is observed and not violated.

This validation of the penultimate leaves room for the "natural." Indeed Feil sees the words as synonymous:

> One must not foreshorten the penultimate, or its synonym, the natural, for the sake of the ultimate. It is very significant that Bonhoeffer substituted the concrete and substantive term "the natural" for the rather formal and abstract terms "the preserved world" and "the penultimate."[42]

Having established the place of the natural, then, Bonhoeffer goes on to develop what looks very similar to a Catholic "natural law" ethic. He defines the natural as "the form of life preserved by God for the fallen world and directed towards justification, redemption and renewal through Christ" (*Ethics*, 145). There is now a place for human reason as the "organ of knowledge of the natural," albeit not a divine principle of knowledge—indeed, reason is fallen.

In discussing "natural life," Bonhoeffer affirms human rights as well as duties, with priority given to the former since God bestows life in the first place. Among human rights are the right to life, and more particularly the right to bodily life, including enjoyment and play. This is an individual right, not subservient to community rights. Bonhoeffer says that "it is incumbent upon reason to take account of the right of the individual, even though the divine origin of this right is not recognized"

(*Ethics*, 154). Bodily life is important theologically since, as in *Creation and Fall*, Bonhoeffer sees man as essentially an embodied being, in eternity as well as in time.

Arbitrary killing is wrong because it violates the right to life. Euthanasia is a particular example of arbitrary killing and is therefore condemned. All human beings, including doctors, have an obligation to preserve life. That includes those suffering from painful terminal diseases and wishing to be helped to die. It also includes those, such as the mentally disabled or sufferers from hereditary disease, whom society might regard as dangerous, but whom, Bonhoeffer asserts, in fact bring out the care and concern of others to the highest degree. "In the sight of God there is no life that is not worth living," he says (*Ethics*, 163). However, Bonhoeffer carefully draws distinctions between the deliberate ending of life and allowing a person to die.

Discussing marriage and procreation, Bonhoeffer regards the Roman Catholic restriction that both partners should be Catholic as "depriving marriage of its essential natural character" and transmuting "an institution of nature into an institution of grace." This restriction is on a par with the restriction of partners to members of the same racial group.

Abortion is "a violation of the right to live which God has bestowed upon this nascent life." The embryo's right to life is not at the disposal of the couple. It is also confusing to argue about whether this is a human being since "God certainly intended to create a human being." One can clearly see the attraction of Bonhoeffer's thought on many of these issues both for Roman Catholics and evangelicals engaged in contemporary ethical controversies. It is perhaps surprising to look back now on how Bonhoeffer was claimed for a radical liberal theology, and situation ethics, by John Robinson in the 1960s.[43] As noted by Bethge, Robinson's "fascinatingly one-sided" interpretation nevertheless had the positive effect of introducing "the most fruitful period for the study, translation and publication of all of Bonhoeffer's works in the Protestant, Roman Catholic, and secular spheres."[44]

Bonhoeffer suggested as a possible title for his book *The Preparing of the Way and the Entry into Possession*, and remarked that "this would correspond with the division of the book into the things before the last and the last things" (see Bethge's editor's preface in *Ethics*, 12–13).

Thus, he clearly intended this distinction to be central to the *Ethics*.

This idea of the penultimate as "preparing the way" for the ultimate strikes a chord with our interest in natural theology. Bonhoeffer did not venture into this territory, but it seems that he left an opening by developing his natural law ethic, even though, as Feil notes, Bonhoeffer would not have approved of an interpretation that rehabilitated "the kind of natural theology that Karl Barth had attacked with such vigour."[45] Might we not argue, however, that for some people natural theology could be a *praeparatio evangelica*, and to provide one would therefore be a service? There are those who find belief in God difficult, who have intellectual problems, or whose understanding of science is a deterrent to belief. It seems to me that engaging with those difficulties, which can inhibit faith as genuinely as physical deprivation, should rank as a penultimate task alongside those of bringing justice and material aid. If natural law is validated because God preserves the fallen world, surely natural theology has a place for the same reason. After all, God is Creator of the world that the natural sciences see their task as exploring.

## *What We Have Learned from* Creation and Fall

While one may not want to go with Bonhoeffer all the way, he provides a fascinating model for interpreting the early chapters of Genesis. He rightly sees the theological message as of overriding importance; indeed, his method of interpretation is thoroughly christological. The fact that the message is cloaked in mythological language in no way detracts from it being the word of God addressed directly to us. In fact, Bonhoeffer gives a far richer interpretation of the text than any naïve literalist approach could ever do. It seems to me that there is much here that should commend itself to evangelicals, most especially Bonhoeffer's high view of Scripture, his strong Christocentrism, his assertion that the text is addressed to us, and that we should not sit in judgment on God's word but obey it. I would hope that we could learn from his approach that challenging the findings of modern science is both futile and unnecessary, and that the findings of biblical criticism do not pose a threat either.

Where I would demur is with regard to the perhaps too stridently anti–natural theological stance. I believe we can get limited knowledge of the Creator from the creation, and it is important that we can do so because then the nonbeliever has access to some, albeit limited, knowledge of God. However, the much more important knowledge comes from revelation. It is also true that the ultimate sin is to put ourselves in the place of God, and to question his word rather than obey it. On the other hand, there must be a place for the use of our God-given reason in discerning how to interpret God's word, even though this were done in the context of prayer and worship as all theology should be. Bonhoeffer himself presents a beautifully reasoned theological interpretation of the early chapters of Genesis!

Having made the above caveats, there are, nevertheless, intriguing theological possibilities in what Bonhoeffer has to say. These relate both to a more positive outlook for natural theology and to other areas where theology interacts with the natural sciences in modern debate. Three we have examined are as follows.

### The Status of Mathematics

The status of mathematics as "eternal" and providing ultimate truth has been undermined by the discovery of paradoxes in its axiomatic formulations. We can be fairly confident that Bonhoeffer knew of Russell's paradox, and he may well have heard of Gödel's theorem, too: his remarks must relate to something like the shock waves caused by these discoveries for mathematics.

Loss of the eternal where we thought it most secure ought to drive us to where it truly can be found, the Creator. There is a knock-on effect on physics, too, since physics depends on mathematics. Any "theory of everything" will also not be complete, so physics also loses any claim to be the final word. The ultimate, the eternal must lie beyond physics, so this loss also points us to God.

The insight from thinkers such as Lucas and Penrose also impacts on our anthropological understanding. Although we are truly material beings, this is balanced by the knowledge that we are more than computers. The fact that a crude reductionism of the kind exemplified by strong artificial intelligence is defeated is again a pointer to our origin in God, rather than the accidental outcome of purely mechanical processes.

## The Materialism of Scripture

Bonhoeffer notes that Genesis is more strongly materialistic than Darwin or Feuerbach. That leads to an emphasis on human beings as bodies and to the insight that rejection of the body amounts to a rejection of the Creator.

I suggested that Bonhoeffer might today embrace some form of "nonreductive physicalism." Modern advocates of that position see it as more in keeping with the discoveries of neurophysiology than mind-body dualism would be. Bonhoeffer's point about rejecting the body is also of major relevance to instances of that in the modern world. Many people in rejecting their bodies are rejecting the reality of what God has given us in nature, in all its diversity and with its natural processes of aging, its God-given sexual differentiation, and so on. It amounts to a kind of detachment from reality. That is not to diminish the genuine suffering of those with body-image problems, but to suggest that modern obsessions in the wider culture, in the media, and so on are at the least a contributory factor to such problems.

## Orders of Preservation as "Penultimate Things"

In *Creation and Fall* Bonhoeffer substituted the term "orders of preservation" for the traditional "orders of creation." In the *Ethics* yet another term, "mandates," is used. Bonhoeffer's intention was to demote the orders from the kind of autonomous status they were given by the German Christians to a provisionality, upheld by God and receiving their meaning solely through Christ to whom they are directed.

I have suggested a link with Bonhoeffer's other concept from the *Ethics* of penultimate, contrasted with ultimate, things. The ultimate is the word of grace, of justification. The penultimate is what precedes grace, and it exists for the sake of the ultimate. In the penultimate we find a place for "natural" life. The link with "orders of preservation" or mandates can be made by direct examples. Thus, work is a mandate, and Bonhoeffer cites works such as freeing slaves as "penultimate." Marriage is a mandate and is penultimate. Its status as "natural" is violated by the insistence of the Roman Catholic Church that the partner of a Catholic must also be Catholic.

It seems to me that the above, together with Bonhoeffer's development of a natural law ethic and his discussion of human rights, certainly leaves room for the "natural," as he himself says. What he does not do is extend this to the realm of natural theology. However, to me such an extension would seem a logical step. Providing evidence for the existence of God from nature could be regarded as a penultimate work. It is not a substitute for the proclamation of God's self-revelation in Jesus Christ, but a preparation for it. Those who are persuaded by evidence and reasoned argument that the idea of God as Creator best explains the universe in all its vastness and majesty might be led on to explore the more specific claim that the same Creator also wills to redeem the world and does so through the life, death, and resurrection of his Son, the incarnate Word of God, Jesus Christ.

We move now to a consideration of important strands in Bonhoeffer's maturing theology as evinced in *Letters and Papers from Prison*.

## *Bonhoeffer's Reading of Weizsäcker*

The highly cultured Bonhoeffer read widely, and this continued in prison. During the critical period leading up to the July 20, 1944, plot and the discovery of Bonhoeffer's links with the conspirators, he was thinking most creatively, and this was when he read physicist Carl Friedrich von Weizsäcker's book *The World View of Physics*.[16] He first refers to it in a letter of May 24, 1944 (*LPP*, 308), where he says he hopes to "learn a great deal from it" for his own work and longs to read and discuss things with his friend Eberhard Bethge as of old. He returns to the topic in a letter of May 29, 1944 (*LPP*, 310–12). Comments in the seminal letter of July 16, 1944, also reflect this reading matter (*LPP*, 357–61).

### Letter of May 29, 1944

Early on in this letter Bonhoeffer describes the one-dimensional life of his fellow inmates: all fear when there is an air raid, all greed when food is around. In contrast, "Christianity puts us into many dimensions of life at the same time." He tells people trembling under an air raid that it is much worse for a small town. "We have to get people out of their one-track minds," he says. But there is a circularity here. Getting people out of their one-track minds is a "kind of 'preparation' for faith," yet it is faith that makes possible a multidimensional life!

Maybe there is a parallel in Bonhoeffer's thought here with the ambiguity of natural theology: as a *praeparatio evangelica* (preparation for the gospel) on the one hand but, conversely, as the idea that nature is only appreciated properly in all its richness as creation from within a theological perspective.

Reading Weizsäcker gave Bonhoeffer the important insight that God is not to be used as a stopgap [*Lückenbüßer*] for the incompleteness of our knowledge:

> If in fact the frontiers of knowledge are being pushed further and further back (and that is bound to be the case), then God is being pushed back with them, and is therefore continually in retreat. We are to find God in what we know, not in what we don't know; God wants us to realize his presence, not in unsolved problems but in those that are solved. That is true of the relationship between God and scientific knowledge, but it is also true of the wider human problems of death, suffering, and guilt. . . . God is no stop-gap; he must be recognized at the centre of life, not when we are at the end of our resources. (*LPP*, 311–12)

This is a crucially important passage, and it is a pity Bonhoeffer was disturbed at this point, although he does return in later letters to the vital topic of the centrality of Christ, which is probably the key to the whole of his thought. He is of course right to inveigh against a "God of the gaps." Weizsäcker later described how he was moved to learn that Bonhoeffer got this insight from him in prison.[47] Weizsäcker also remarks in the same work how the importance of science in Bonhoeffer's upbringing would have impressed on him the unshakeability of scientific progress.[48]

Bonhoeffer preempts here by a decade the better-known discussion of the God of the gaps by Charles Coulson.[49] Coulson wrote about how the gaps have a habit of shrinking as science advances, and he popularized the "God of the gaps" terminology to describe this strategy as adopted by some Christians. Coulson too argued that God must be found in what is known, not in what is not known.[50] In his 1958 Eddington Memorial Lecture, Coulson goes even further and says, "When we come to the scientifically unknown, our correct policy is not to rejoice because we have found God: it is to become better scientists, and to think a bit more deeply and imaginatively until we can devise some model, or some concept, that will bring the previous unknown into the pattern of the known."[51]

Long before Coulson made the term well-known, the idea was in Weizsäcker and Bonhoeffer. The term itself can be traced back to the nineteenth century when the evangelical Henry Drummond contrasted the God of the gaps with the immanent God of evolution, who is far grander:

> There are reverent minds who ceaselessly scan the fields of Nature and the books of Science in search of gaps—gaps which they will fill up with God. As if God lived in gaps? What view of Nature or of Truth is theirs whose interest in Science is not in what it can explain but in what it cannot, whose quest is ignorance not knowledge, whose daily dread is that the cloud may lift, and who, as darkness melts from this field or from that, begin to tremble for the place of His abode?[52]

Some Christians still make the mistake identified by Bonhoeffer and these other writers. Bonhoeffer specifically mentioned theology's "taking up arms" against Darwinism, although in reality Darwinism was readily accommodated by mainstream theology. There are biblical literalists today who still reject Darwinism despite the overwhelming evidence for it. The modern Intelligent Design movement, while more subtle, does precisely what Bonhoeffer describes—seeks to explain particular features in the natural world by invoking design when there may well be scientific explanations. Indeed, the idea that the bacterial flagellum (the almost invariably quoted paradigm) is "irreducibly complex" in ID terminology and therefore requires a particular act of God, whereas the vast majority of other features that on the face of it would seem to be equally complex can be explained by natural causes, seems a disastrous strategy from an apologetic point of view, because the gaps may well be filled. On the other hand, to view God as responsible for the whole of nature, and to see that there is an ordered structure to nature and argue that this points to God, is logically entirely different. God is in the big bang, and God is in the whole process of evolution—in what we can explain scientifically, not just what we cannot.

However, some developments in natural theology today may still be open to the God-of-the-gaps charge. Let us examine briefly two of them, both advocated by John Polkinghorne, for example. These are (1) seeking to explain divine action in the supposedly open processes of an unpredictable and indeterminate universe and (2) explaining the fine-tuning of the universe as the product of divine design. Interestingly, there are scientific alternatives in each case—or, more accurately, there are alternative ways of interpreting the scientific data. In the first, there is the alternative interpretation of quantum theory in terms of hidden variables, which makes the theory deterministic (interestingly, Weizsäcker in the book Bonhoeffer read was of the view that quantum theory is ontologically indeterminate); in any case, classical chaos theory, Polkinghorne's more favored locus of divine action, is deterministic even if unpredictable. Polkinghorne has to make a metaphysical leap in his claim that "epistemology models ontology."[53] This bold claim requires some justification. Nevertheless the claim *is* different in kind from that of ID because it relates to the nature of scientific laws (as ontologically indeterminate or unpredictable), not supposedly inexplicable lacunae in the processes of nature.

In the second case, one needs to be open to the possibility that the anthropic coincidences might conceivably be explained scientifically, either by a better theory or by a multiverse. It is then a question of arguing why design is a more satisfactory explanation, and the explanation relates even more strongly to the nature of scientific laws: why are they conducive to the appearance of intelligent life?

In both these cases the explanations are metaphysical rather than scientific (in the case of a multiverse, because of its lack of contact with observation in principle). A key criterion in both instances is also that of simplicity: Which is the simpler of competing explanations? And that brings us right back to another line of argument found in Weizsäcker.

Although not using this terminology, Weizsäcker would seem to be open to a form of natural theology that appeals to the simplicity of mathematical laws that are found to obtain in physics. Why should the laws of nature take such a form? Even if Bonhoeffer did not pick up this particular line of argument, he was nevertheless right to highlight the God-of-the-gaps problem from Weizsäcker.

In a crucial passage Weizsäcker notes a remarkable development in the interpretation of astronomical data from Kepler to Newton.[54] Kepler devised his laws of planetary motion to fit the careful observations of Tycho Brahe. He set two conditions for this derivation: agreement with observation and mathematical simplicity. This latter condition, found time and again to be successful in physics, Weizsäcker likens to a miracle. Kepler, in discovering the mathematical laws of nature, was "thinking again God's thoughts at creation."[55] He thought of nature as a "symbol" pointing to God.

Newton's great achievement was to derive Kepler's laws from his own, more fundamental laws of motion and law of gravity. The problem was that this still left a lot to be explained—for example, why the solar system is so stable. This was where Newton saw the need for God to be at work—that is, precisely as a God of the gaps. Then as now, the gaps were filled, in this case by Pierre-Simon, Marquis de Laplace, whose nebular hypothesis removed the need for such interference by God. "I have no need of that hypothesis," Laplace famously remarked. Interestingly, Gottfried Wilhelm Leibniz had already criticized Newton for demanding that, in effect, God needed to correct his faulty workmanship.

All this took place within a theistic framework shared by all the scientists involved, not least the Roman Catholic Laplace. Nevertheless, the turn from Kepler's approach to that of Newton was fundamentally flawed, and Bonhoeffer was correct to see this. Kepler saw God indicated positively from what he knew from science; Newton saw the gaps in what he knew as pointing to God. Weizsäcker points out the mistake; Bonhoeffer recognizes it and takes it further, arguing that God must be at the center, not the periphery, of life.

## Letter of July 16, 1944

In this highly theologically significant letter, Bonhoeffer picks up on another important point from Weizsäcker. Just before he comes on to the sequence of thought of Kepler, Newton, and Laplace, Weizsäcker discusses how Nicolas of Cusa was the first to teach that the world is infinite; the second proponent of this view was Giordano Bruno a century and a half later. This represents a remarkable departure from the classical view of the finiteness of the world, which spoke to the Greeks of order and intelligibility. The medieval view maintained the finiteness of the world, contrasted with the infinitude of God.

Cusanus gets his view that the world is also infinite from the idea that God infuses the world with as much of his own perfection as is possible while still making the world different from himself. The geometric symbol of God as the infinite sphere is transferred to the world as concretely imaging God. This gives rise to the twin dangers of identification of the world with God and total separation. Bruno still admits the distinction between God and world but speaks only of the world. The glory of the infinite God has been transferred to the infinite world.

This line of thought leads in three possible directions, says Weizsäcker: pantheism, the unlimited technological exploitation of the world, and, connected with this second, disenchantment.

In modern times the critique of the inference from the finite to the infinite has led to a crisis in science, says Weizsäcker. All the conclusions of modern physics and cosmology depend on the laws of physics being valid throughout space and time, and many strands of evidence point to them being so. However, physics is showing limits to the infinitely small (through quantum theory with its minimum quantum of action) and the infinitely large (through the second law of thermodynamics, which leads to a finite period between maximal order at the beginning and heat death at the end).

We have better estimates of the finite age of the universe than Weizsäcker did. The current estimate from the big bang theory is 13.7

billion years. Moreover, general relativity, coupled with non-Euclidean geometry, leads to the possibility of either a spatially finite universe or an infinite universe. Indeed, at present (again long after Weizsäcker's book) there is tentative, if controversial, evidence that such a finite model might be right—controversial because the universe actually sits on a knife edge between spatial infinity and finitude making an empirical determination very difficult if not impossible.[56]

The striving for the infinite—now this is not God, but the world—leads to disillusion, says Weizsäcker. There are limits to human knowledge; we cannot get behind the appearances of things to the things in themselves. Does this mean that the world, which as infinite and open to human exploration had been invested with ultimate meaning, is meaningless after all? For Weizsäcker the question demands a decision: whether we wish to hear God at all. Where does God speak to us? Do we have to move away from science to find God?

Weizsäcker calls us back to Kepler, who, he says, achieved the "last great union of natural science with objective symbolism."[57] The criterion of mathematical simplicity in the search for the laws of physics remains as valid now as for Kepler, if not more so. The success of this criterion cannot be explained from within science but is presupposed in order to do science. Immanuel Kant tells us that lawful order is the precondition for meaningful experience, but not why such order should exist in the first place. The explanation of this order as God-given is in fact a powerful argument of modern "natural theology," advanced convincingly by such thinkers as Polkinghorne and Roger Trigg.

Bonhoeffer picks up this theme of the infinity of the world in the July 16 letter in the following important (even though bracketed in the original) statement:

> It seems to me that in the natural sciences the process begins with Nicolas of Cusa and Giordano Bruno and the "heretical" doctrine of the infinity of the universe. The classical *cosmos* was finite, like the created world of the Middle Ages. An infinite universe, however it may be conceived, is self-subsisting, *etsi deus non daretur*. It is true that modern physics is not as sure as it was about the infinity of the universe, but it has

> not gone back to the earlier conceptions of its finitude. (*LPP*, 359–60)

The "process" to which Bonhoeffer refers is the movement of the world and humanity toward their own autonomy. This is also at work in other disciplines. In theology, reason is sufficient for religious knowledge; in ethics, "rules of life" replace the commandments and Hugo Grotius's "natural law" is set up as international law that is also valid *etsi deus non daretur*, "even if there were no God"; in philosophy, the deistic view is of the world as a mechanism running by itself.

Is Bonhoeffer correct, at least with regard to science? It is certainly interesting that in modern cosmology the idea of an infinite universe (usually because allowing a multiverse in some form) is conceived by many proponents in an antireligious sense,[58] as eternally self-subsisting and thus removing the need for God as creator. An infinite cosmos is, as Peter Bussey argues,[59] put forward as an alternative causal explanation to God. Moreover, through its throwing up all possibilities, an infinite cosmos is also said to explain the particularity (the fine-tuning referred to earlier) of our "neck of the woods," as our world is just something that is likely to arise sometime somewhere in an infinite universe.

That these arguments are put forward, however, does not make them valid. Leibniz's question "Why is there something rather than nothing?" has no explanation on the basis of an infinite cosmos, just as it had no explanation on the basis of a finite one. The cosmological argument remains. Leibniz formulated the principle of sufficient reason, according to which nothing exists without a reason for its existence and for being the way it is. And even if one does not accept the necessity of the principle, it is surely metaphysically more satisfactory to have an explanation than not, and God conceived as necessary being in the manner of St. Thomas Aquinas does provide an explanation for the existence of a contingent universe, whereas even an infinite universe cannot explain its own existence. Moreover, there are cogent arguments that God provides a much more satisfactory answer for the fine-tuning than does an infinite cosmos.[60]

These are not knockdown arguments, however—only arguments on the basis of balance of probabilities. It is certainly open to atheists to accept an infinite cosmos, and, to the extent that atheistic scientists utilize the concept in an attempt to shake off any reliance at all on God, Bonhoeffer is correct.

## *Christ the Center*

For Bonhoeffer, as is clear from the quotations we have noted, rejection of the God of the gaps goes much further than natural science, although it includes it. In the letter of May 29, 1944, we saw how in the "wider human problems of death, suffering, and guilt" God is also not to be used as a "stop-gap" solution. In the letter of June 8, 1944, Bonhoeffer writes:

> Man has learnt to deal with himself in all questions of importance without recourse to the "working hypothesis" called "God." In questions of science, art, and ethics this has become an understood thing at which one now hardly dares to tilt. . . . As in the scientific field, so in human affairs generally, "God" is being pushed more and more out of life, losing more and more ground. (*LPP*, 325–26)

He traces the development of this human autonomy from the thirteenth century on. He thinks that Christian apologetics has been wrong to try to persuade a "world come of age" that it still needs the tutelage of God. The ultimate questions—death and guilt—remain, but what if they too can be answered without God? The "secularized offshoots" of Christian theology—existentialist philosophy and psychotherapy—try to persuade the perfectly contented and happy that they are really in despair. This tactic Bonhoeffer labels "secularized methodism." He says a few might succumb to this, but the ordinary man "has neither the time nor the inclination to concern himself with his existential despair, or to regard his perhaps modest share of happiness as a trial, a trouble, or a calamity" (*LPP*, 327).

Richard Bube, who has also noted Bonhoeffer's use of "God-of-the-gaps,"[61] argues that although Bonhoeffer may be exaggerating in this passage, it is nevertheless true that the Christian should see God at work in modern psychiatry and reject the God of the gaps in this context also as the only hope for curing mental illness.

Bonhoeffer charges that the attack on the adulthood of the world is pointless, ignoble, and un-Christian—pointless because it attempts to take man back a stage in his development, ignoble because it is exploiting a weakness for ulterior purposes, and un-Christian because it confuses Christ with a human law. Bonhoeffer here repeats the charge of "despair or Jesus" that he made against Karl Heim, as we noted above, in a review (*NRS*, appendix 1) of the latter's book of 1931, *Glaube und Denken*: "Heim sought, on pietist and methodist lines, to convince the individual man that he was faced with the alternative 'despair or Jesus.'" However, there seems to be an even more radical shift in Bonhoeffer's thought here since the Heim review, because Bonhoeffer had then allowed despair at one's sin, if not at meaninglessness, to be the problem to which Christ is the answer.

Bonhoeffer was equally critical of Paul Tillich's religious socialism, which attempted the interpretation of culture (though Bonhoeffer simply uses the word *Entwicklung*, development or evolution), religion giving culture its *Gestalt*. However, "the world unseated him and went on by itself" (*LPP*, 327).

Bonhoeffer praises Karl Barth as being the first to realize the error in all this in "leaving a clear space for religion in the world or against the world." Barth "brought in against religion the God of Jesus Christ, '*pneuma* against *sarx*.'" However, Barth's failing was to give no guidance in the "non-religious interpretation of theological concepts." This brings Bonhoeffer to repeat the charge of "positivism of revelation" against Barth, raised in earlier letters of April 30 and May 5 (*LPP*, 278–87), a topic to which we return in a later section.

At the end of the letter of June 8, 1944, Bonhoeffer picks up a question of Bethge's, namely, "whether Jesus didn't use men's 'distress' as a point of contact with them" ("*an der 'Not' der Menschen* angeknüpft *hat*" [emphasis added]), and therefore whether the "methodism" that Bonhoeffer had criticized earlier was not right (*LPP*, 329). He breaks off at that point and says he will come back to this. This happens in the letter of June 30, 1944 (*LPP*, 341–42). Here he again sees God "being increasingly pushed out of a world that has come of age . . . since Kant he has been relegated to a realm beyond the world of experience." On the one hand, while theology has "taken up arms—in vain—against Darwinism," on the other hand "it has accommodated itself to the development by restricting God to the so-called ultimate questions as a *deus ex machina*." Bonhoeffer repeats the point that existential philosophy and psychotherapy are rather good at showing those who do not feel despair that they really do suffer. He goes on to say that Jesus, in contrast, while blessing sinners, calls them away from their sin, not into it. St. Paul realized he was a sinner after conversion, not before it (Bonhoeffer may have had Phil 3 and Rom 7 in mind). And although Jesus cared about those on the fringes of society, he never questioned "a man's health, vigour, or happiness, regarded in themselves as evil fruits; else why should he heal the sick and restore strength to the weak?" Bonhoeffer's point is that Christ claims the whole of human life in all its manifestations for himself and his kingdom.

Again in the letter of July 8, 1944, Bonhoeffer writes that we should recognize that the world has "come of age" and confront humanity with God "at his strongest point" (*LPP*, 346). He seems to be saying that it is wrong tactically and indeed morally to go for a person's weakness—sin, despair, ill health—and say Jesus is the answer. God meets us at our strongest point, which is presumably in what we know, not what we do not know, in science and so forth, and in our health and psychological self-satisfaction and reliance rather than existential despair or, now, even our sin. And Bonhoeffer seems to see worldliness or the "world come of age" as a good thing, a positive development.

The attack on "religion" goes back to the letter of April 30, 1944, that is, before the reading of Weizsäcker. Bonhoeffer states that the whole history of Christian preaching rests on the "religious *a priori*" of humankind, which he had in fact already criticized years before in *Act and Being*,[62] but which no longer exists because it belonged to a historically conditioned period of human self-expression. Bonhoeffer apparently does not regard this development as a bad thing, but his question is, How can Christ become the Lord of the religionless as well?

Barth began this line of thought, Bonhoeffer says, but did not complete it, ending with a "positivism of revelation" (an expression we explore in the next section). Nothing was gained, because this was in reality a restoration. The questions needing to be answered have to do with how we speak of God without religion—that is, "without the temporally conditioned presuppositions of metaphysics, inwardness, and so on" (*LPP*, 280).

Bonhoeffer's thoughts are tantalizing here because they are incomplete and raise many questions. However, it is clear that he is concerned fundamentally with the centrality of Christ. If Christians regard themselves from a religious point of view not as especially favored but as belonging wholly to the world, Christ becomes not an object of religion but "really the Lord of the world" (*LPP*, 281).

That is the key to which all this is pointing, and in his resumption of this letter after a break Bonhoeffer makes the point more explicitly: "Religious people speak of God when human knowledge (perhaps simply because they are too lazy to think) has come to an end," and then God is "the *deus ex machina* that they bring on to the scene." But Bonhoeffer wants to speak of God "not on the boundaries but at the centre. . . . God is beyond in the midst of our life. The church stands, not at the boundaries where human powers give out, but in the middle of the village" (*LPP*, 282).

In the letter of June 27, 1944, Bonhoeffer repeats the point: "Christ takes hold of a man at the centre of his life" (*LPP*, 337). The unanswered question is how God does this, because, as for Barth, there is no *Anknüpfungspunkt* (point of contact in human nature). One can see in Bonhoeffer how a Christian might live but not perhaps how one becomes a Christian.

The frustration from our point of view is that Bonhoeffer was unable to spell out for us what his religionless Christianity really would look like, although in the letter of July 16 he sees the starting point for his "secular interpretation" in the suffering God who "lets himself be pushed out of the world on to the cross":

> Christ helps us, not by virtue of his omnipotence, but by virtue of his weakness and suffering. Here is the difference between Christianity and all other religions. Man's religiosity makes him look in his distress to the power of God in the world: God is the *deus ex machina*. The Bible directs man to God's

> powerlessness and suffering; only the suffering God can help. To that extent we may say that the development towards the world's coming of age outlined above, which has done away with a false conception of God, opens up a way of seeing the God of the Bible, who wins power and space in the world by his weakness. (*LPP*, 360–61)

This notion of the suffering God has been vital in postwar, post-Auschwitz theology, notably in the writing of Jürgen Moltmann. For Bonhoeffer the key to what it means to be a Christian is to be found in sharing the sufferings of God in the world. This goes back to his cry in *Cost of Discipleship* that "when God calls a man he bids him come and die."[63] It is also central to the nonreligious interpretation being expounded in the prison letters, and expressed clearly, for example, in the poem "Christians and Pagans" (noted helpfully by Selby[64]).

## *Positivism of Revelation*

What did Bonhoeffer mean by the expression "positivism of revelation" in the charge leveled against Barth? It puzzled Barth himself, who after the war expressed the hope that "in heaven at least he has not reported about me to *all* the angels (including the church fathers), with just this expression" (quoted in Selby[65]).

The charge first appears in the letter of April 30, 1944. Bonhoeffer argues that the religious *a priori* has gone and asks what a religionless Christianity might look like. He says that Barth began this line of thought, and did not bring it to completion, but arrived at a positivism of revelation, which is essentially a restoration. This does not help the nonreligious person (*LPP*, 280).

The most serious formulation of the charge comes in the letter of May 5, 1944, where Bonhoeffer says that Barth replaces religion with "a positivist doctrine of revelation which says, in effect, 'Like it or lump it!': virgin birth, Trinity, or anything else; each is an equally significant and necessary part of the whole, which must simply be swallowed as a whole or not at all. That isn't biblical." Bonhoeffer goes on: "There are degrees of knowledge and degrees of significance; that means that a secret discipline must be restored whereby the *mysteries* of the Christian faith are protected against profanation. The positivism of revelation makes it too easy for itself, by setting up, as it does in the last analysis, a law of faith, and so mutilates what is—by Christ's incarnation!—a gift for us" (*LPP*, 286).

At first sight this is a strange accusation. Positivism (due originally to Auguste Comte) says that only direct sense experience can be the object of human knowledge and the criterion of knowledge. Positivism denies the existence of a personal God. In the twentieth century it transmuted into the even stronger logical positivism, whose verifiability criterion stipulated that statements which could not be verified by sense experience (synthetic truths) or directly from the meaning of the words (analytic truths) were meaningless. Bonhoeffer now seemed to be applying the term "positivism" to theological statements that one is expected to accept as meaningful and true on the basis of revelation rather than either empirical evidence or logical reasoning.

Andreas Pangritz tells us that Bonhoeffer may have adopted the phrase "positivism of revelation" from his teacher Erich Seeberg, who uses the expression twice in his *Luthers Theologie*. By it, Seeberg seems to mean that "the word of God revealed in Jesus Christ is accepted as something positively given, that is to say, as a truth of faith natural reason cannot analyze or question."[66] Even more pointedly it is "the 'irrational' assertion of divine revelation as the 'positively given' reality against all reason, in opposition to the possibility of natural knowledge of God."[67] Pangritz argues that Bonhoeffer had accepted a revelation positivism like this in his *Habilitationsschrift* (university lectureship qualifying thesis), *Act and Being*. He invokes the emphasis on the contingency of revelation from the medieval nominalists Duns Scotus and William of Ockham. In its contingency, revelation transcends reason and "can only be welcomed or rejected in its positivity—that is to say, received as a reality—but not elicited from speculations about human existence as such" (*AB*, 80).

There is, nevertheless, a counterargument to this. As noted by Bethge,[68] *Act and Being* also contains Bonhoeffer's most critical questioning of Barth, even if Bonhoeffer means to criticize from a position of enthusiasm for the Barthian message. After that point it became much more important to unite in the church struggle.

Perhaps the main criticism is that, as a Lutheran, Bonhoeffer was convinced of the *finitum capax infiniti* (the finite can hold the infinite), whereas for the Reformed Barth, humans are *incapax infiniti* (incapable of holding the infinite) (*AB*, 84). At the time of the Reformation these terms applied to the Eucharistic elements and distinguished the respective Lutheran and Reformed doctrines. By extension, for Bonhoeffer, God is accessible despite everything— "haveable" or "graspable" as he puts it (*AB*, 91)—whereas Barth's Kantian transcendentalism makes God remote. This point reinforces what we have already noted from the much later *Letters and Papers from Prison*, namely, the importance for Bonhoeffer of finding God in what we know and not in what we do not know.

According to Pangritz, in *Letters and Papers* Bonhoeffer is more critical of positivism of revelation in conservatives, because they have moved from positivism to "conservative restoration" (*LPP*, 328). Pangritz believes, quite plausibly, that Bonhoeffer has Hans Asmussen in mind.[69] Asmussen rejected the demythologizing paper of Rudolf Bultmann outright as incompatible with the theology of the Confessing Church. Bonhoeffer welcomed it, although he did not agree with it. He admired Bultmann's intellectual honesty, which he had also seen in his teacher Adolf von Harnack.

Let us examine the matter in a little more detail. The conclusion may be somewhat different from that of Pangritz.

Barth is accused of "positivism of revelation" because the virgin birth, resurrection, and so on have to be taken as a whole package (letter of May 5, 1944). This sets up a "law of faith" that negates Christ's incarnation, which is a gift for us. The conservatives are accused of taking this even further (letter of June 8, 1944). They reject Bultmann's demythologizing approach. Bonhoeffer believes that Bultmann's approach should be on the table. In one sense he believes Bultmann has not gone far enough; indeed Bultmann (and Barth) is still responding to liberal theology, although Bultmann's approach leads in the opposite direction from Barth to a total reductionism.

Bultmann is right that miracle, eschatology, and the rest are essential to the New Testament but wrong to say that we have to reject them since they are unbelievable to anyone who switches on the radio: "It is impossible to use electric light and the wireless and to avail ourselves of modern medical and surgical discoveries, and at the same time to believe in the New Testament world of daemons and spirits."[70] No, says Bonhoeffer, they are indeed essential (they are not "mythological clothing of a universal truth" but "the thing itself") but must be interpreted in a "non-religious" fashion. Just what does this mean? One thing he says in the letters of April 30 and June 8, 1944, is that religion must not be made a precondition of faith in the same way that circumcision could not be made a precondition for Paul: "Only in that way, I think, will liberal theology be overcome . . . and at the same time its question be genuinely taken up and answered" (letter of June 8).

The letter of May 5 also pointed to a way of holding to the truths of the New Testament, namely through the *disciplina arcana* (secret discipline), whereby the "mysteries of the faith are preserved from profanation." It would seem that what Bonhoeffer is saying is that the *Church Dogmatics* (Barth,[71] beginning with volume I.1 in 1932)—indeed, the Barthian theology from the *Epistle to the Romans*[72] on—can be accepted by the church, but it is of no use for the "religionless."

This is the crux of the whole argument with Barth. As Pangritz explains,[73] Barth was aware of this problem in Luther. In an address of 1922, "The Word of God and the Task of the Ministtry,"[74] Barth says that Luther bids us to give up thinking, to slay the harlot reason, and to accept the doctrine of the Trinity, for example. Even for Barth that will not do, because humankind's question about God is thereby quashed![75] There is an ambivalence in Barth. While in *The Epistle to the Romans* he quotes Luther approvingly,[76] in his book on Anselm he brings reason back in by saying that "the *quaerere intellectum* [seeking understanding] is really immanent in *fides* [faith]."[77]

I think there is a lot in this latter position. We learn and grow in our faith by exploring from within the fold. I do believe in the virgin birth and the Trinity as well as the resurrection, although I think the last is the best grounded empirically and will stand up to rational scrutiny and can count as public knowledge. The first two doctrines are more likely to arise as convictions from within by seeing their coherence with other tenets of belief, including the resurrection. The question is how to get someone across the threshold so as to begin these deeper explorations. For this step it is no good, as with Luther, to deny the place of reason. That is like a red rag to a bull for atheist Richard Dawkins, who vilifies belief in God precisely because he sees it as irrational (see, for example, *The God Delusion*[78]). If one is to engage with the thought of Dawkins and other atheists, one needs to start from a position that the Christian faith is rational, Luther notwithstanding. For Bonhoeffer the way will be through the "non-religious interpretation," which precludes at the least "the temporally conditioned presuppositions of metaphysics, inwardness, and so on" (*LPP*, 280). In this way Christ will become center stage.

What does the nonreligious interpretation mean? This comes out in the poem "Christians and Pagans" referred to earlier and in the letter of July 18, 1944. It is the reversal of seeing God at humanity's beck and call. It is human beings sharing the sufferings of God in a godless world. "Could you not watch with me one hour?" Jesus asked the disciples (Matt 26:40, RSV). In the poem, both Christians and pagans go to God "when they are sore bestead," but the difference is that "Christians stand by God in his hour of grieving" (*LPP*, 348–49, 361).

Bethge[79] thought that the difference between Barth and Bonhoeffer was that the former believed that religion was a natural condition of man and the latter saw it as merely a temporary phase in human history. Notwithstanding Pangritz's wanting to play this down, it does seem to be an obvious point of difference. A question mark over Bonhoeffer's view might arise in more recent times, because religion seems resurgent, so much so that Alister McGrath could write *The Twilight of Atheism*.[80] It is perhaps critical for Bonhoeffer's view that Europe's passing through the Enlightenment led ultimately to its loss of religion, and other cultures have not as yet had that experience.

Bonhoeffer considers Christian life at the time he is writing to consist of "prayer and righteous action" within the silence of the arcane discipline (baptismal letter, May 1944 [*LPP*, 300]). This is because the church has only fought for its own self-preservation during these years and effectively abdicated its right to speak. When it does speak again, it will be in a new, "perhaps quite non-religious" (*LPP*, 300) language, and will once again proclaim God's peace and righteousness and the coming of God's kingdom.

As we have seen, Bonhoeffer says that Barth demands we take the whole package, "virgin birth, Trinity, or anything else," and that is to set up a law of faith. Instead, "a secret discipline must be restored whereby the *mysteries* of the faith are protected against profanation" (*LPP*, 286).

In responding to the 1933 Altona Confession of Asmussen, which he welcomed, Bonhoeffer remarked that doctrine (*Lehre*), proclamation (*Verkündigung*), and confession (*Bekenntnis*) are to be distinguished. The first two are for the world, but the last is only for the Christian community (*Arkandisziplin*).[81] This statement puzzles me somewhat, because in the creed (*Glaubensbekenntnis*) we confess doctrinal truths, making it difficult to distinguish doctrine from confession. However, what it is right for the church to say, and when, was clearly a topic exercising Bonhoeffer's mind at that early date. It also features in the *Ethics*, in his discussion of the ultimate and the penultimate, as well as the baptismal letter of May 1944. As we saw above, this section of the *Ethics* is another place in Bonhoeffer's later writings where one may get a glimmer of hope for natural theology, as Bonhoeffer develops there what looks like a natural law ethic. The ultimate is the word of grace, of justification, but it is necessarily preceded by the penultimate, and penultimate works of justice and compassion receive validation for the sake of the ultimate.

Barth and Bonhoeffer recognize that we are indeed dealing with mysteries, and there always will be an irreducible sense of mystery in Christian dogmas. Their understanding of the Trinity is similar, and orthodox, but, as Pangritz notes[82] their understanding of the virgin birth differs significantly, even though they both accept the Chalcedonian definition, with all its paradox, and therefore the truth of the incarnation. Barth sees the virgin birth as part of the historic faith and to be believed as historical, even despite the critical questions of the liberals.[83] Bonhoeffer finds the virgin birth more problematical. In a brief reference in *Christology* he writes, "It is both historically and dogmatically questionable. The biblical evidence for it is uncertain."[84] In arguing that it is less well attested, he is more accepting of the liberal agenda; indeed, he claims that the liberal question has still not been answered by Barth or the Confessing Church—and it needs to be (*LPP*, 329).

My position includes elements of both Barth and Bonhoeffer here. Yes, the virgin birth is a clause of the creed and to be accepted as part of the historic faith, but, as Bonhoeffer says, the liberal question remains. Surely the liberal question is best answered by better scholarship in the area of historical Jesus research, and that research should be without the kinds of antisupernatural presuppositions of nineteenth-century liberals. In my view, one should accept the miracle on the basis of reliable testimony (although not as a precondition of faith), following critical analysis, including analysis of its coherence within the Christian belief system as a whole.

Interestingly, in the letter of August 3, 1944, Bonhoeffer seems to suggest precisely that the liberal question is valid and must be answered on its own terms: "We must move out again into the open air of intellectual discussion with the world, and risk saying controversial things, if we are to get down to the serious problems of life. I feel obliged to tackle these questions as one who, although a 'modern' theologian, is still aware of the debt that he owes to liberal theology" (*LPP*, 378). In the outline for a book he encloses with this letter, he writes, "Karl Barth and the Confessing Church have encouraged us to entrench ourselves persistently behind the 'faith of the church,' and evade the honest question as to what we ourselves really believe." For Bonhoeffer the answer will involve characteristic features of his theology—relationship to God through participation in Christ, the "man for others," and so on—but the way he expresses this indicates that there must be a place for reasoned argument and debate with the church and the world. And that represents a distinct departure from the assertive theology—or "revelation positivism"—of Barth.

## *Conclusion*

Perhaps contrary to expectations, Bonhoeffer did indeed engage with scientific thought in several places in his writings. Notable examples are his acceptance and integration of Darwinian thought in *Creation and Fall* and his reading of and commentary on von Weizsäcker's *The World View of Physics* in the prison letters. From early in his career he was heavily influenced by Barth's stance against natural theology and critique of religion. Nevertheless, while firmly in the Barthian camp, in prison he sees signs of its weakness and begins a criticism from within. There are also indications in the *Ethics* that there is a place for natural law, and this line of argument might be extended to yield a place for natural theology, even if Bonhoeffer himself never did that.

Weizsäcker's book led Bonhoeffer to two main thoughts. The first was that a God-of-the-gaps strategy is completely wrongheaded. God is not to be used to fill in gaps in the scientific account of natural processes both because God gets squeezed out as science advances and, more important, because God is to be found in what we know, not in what we don't know. Second, Bonhoeffer considered the notion of an infinite universe. In modern physics this arises as a possible solution to Albert Einstein's equations of general relativity applied to the cosmos as a whole (although a finite universe is also a possibility). An infinite universe would be self-subsistent and could exist as if there were no God (*etsi deus non daretur*). One may disagree with Bonhoeffer about this, but some modern cosmologists are treating an infinite universe in precisely this way.

Bonhoeffer extended these insights to other areas of human inquiry and experience—for example, ethics, existentialist philosophy, and psychotherapy. Thus he attacked as ignoble the Christian's trying to persuade his neighbor of a despair he does not feel, and indeed this is futile because it is putting God into yet another gap. Most important is that he sees religion as a passing phase in human history and Christian preaching on the basis of the religious *a priori* as mistaken. His critique of religion is thus more radical than that of Barth. Bonhoeffer's whole thrust is that Christ should be at the center of life, not confined to small niches not yet filled by either the natural or human sciences.

How to help a person make Christ the center is not spelled out, but Bonhoeffer comes back to the "liberal question," which has not been answered by Barth or the Confessing Church. Barth is charged with "positivism of revelation" in expecting a person to accept various dogmas of Christianity lock, stock, and barrel. Bonhoeffer recommends protecting the dogmas within the worshipping life of the community of believers, because their public presentation is of no use for the "religionless" whom Bonhoeffer wishes to reach. His "non-religious interpretation" involves the Christian sharing in Christ's sufferings in the world, unlike the religious person who seeks God only when in trouble. The Christian is to be involved in prayer and righteous action, and all Christian thinking will stem from that. In his own day the Christian cause was to be a hidden affair, and the church's prime concern for self-preservation made it incapable of speaking the word of redemption and reconciliation to the world.

In the West today, Christians are engaged in both self-preservation and righteous action. There is the concern to guard the church against laws passed by a secular state that might compromise the church's moral stance. This is understandable but would be dangerous were it the only public face of the church. Thankfully, Christians are also engaged in matters of justice, such as debt relief for third-world countries, fairness in trade, and the eradication of poverty. Global warming is another very important issue as this will affect the poor far more than the affluent. It is vital that Christians stand with the poor and those who suffer, for they are then, as Bonhoeffer would say, sharing in Christ's sufferings in the world. As for Bonhoeffer, that may well mean cooperating with others who are similarly concerned but do not confess Christ. It would mean, in his terminology in the *Ethics*, being engaged with the penultimate for the sake of the ultimate.

Bonhoeffer's thought is immensely impressive. His own life and martyrdom testify powerfully to the Christian faith involved in "righteous action." Perhaps one way of helping the nonreligious to faith is by living an exemplary life—identifying with the outcast, sharing Christ's sufferings, doing penultimate works of justice, and so on. I am sure that is true. Nevertheless, the intellectual battle goes on. The place for reason and evidence in grounding Christian belief is not thereby removed, and engaging with scientific thought could also be regarded as a penultimate task. In the end, there must be a place for the "liberal question" to be answered on its own terms, and in that endeavor natural theology still has a significant part to play. It seems to me that Bonhoeffer was pointing in that direction as he began to distance himself from his master, Barth.

# Wolfhart Pannenberg
## Theology, Truth, and Science

As we saw in chapter 2, Karl Barth, acknowledged as possibly the greatest theologian since the Reformation, famously repudiated natural theology as the denial of God's revelation in Jesus Christ. Moreover, he felt no need to engage in any kind of dialogue with the natural sciences, writing his volume on the doctrine of creation without any such reference. For Barth, the object of theology must be studied in the way appropriate to it, namely through God's self-revelation to us in Jesus Christ.

If one wishes to commend the Christian faith to nonbelievers, it seems to me that Barth's approach will not do. It opens up the charge of obscurantism and leaves the, albeit hopelessly one-sided and unscientific, arguments of Richard Dawkins[1] and his friends commanding the field. Christians are after all bidden to give a reason for the hope that is in them (1 Pet 3:15). A theologian who brings a necessary corrective to the debate within theology is Wolfhart Pannenberg. In contrast to Barth, Pannenberg regards dialogue with the sciences as essential, and all truth claims of Christianity dependent on linking the doctrine of creation to the findings of modern science. For example, he writes:

> Only if we can understand the world as the creation of the biblical God and God himself as its Creator can we raise a truth claim for belief in the sole deity of God. Furthermore, only on this same assumption can we set forth the history of Jesus Christ as the reconciliation of the world by the one

> true God, only then do the proclamation and mission of the Christian church take place in obedience to this one true God, and only then can the Christian hope of the future have a sure basis in him. . . . Theology must make this claim in dialogue with the sciences. . . . A failure to claim that the world that the sciences describe is God's world is a conceptual failure to confess the deity of the God of the Bible.[2]

And again:

> If the God of the Bible is the creator of the universe, then it is not possible to understand fully or even appropriately the processes of nature without any reference to that God.[3]

Moreover, for Pannenberg, Christianity makes truth claims based on publicly checkable evidence, even if there is a provisionality in those truth claims until the eschaton.[4] Supremely it is the resurrection of Jesus that brings that eschatological reality into the present, thereby making sense of the whole of cosmic history.

In this chapter I present some of Pannenberg's key arguments. I begin with a brief biographical sketch before considering his early groundbreaking work on history, his critique of Barth, his engagement with the philosophy of science, and his aims to establish theology in the public arena as a science in its own right. This is followed by an exploration of his attitude to natural theology, his work on the doctrine of creation, and his more direct engagement with the sciences. I consider key aspects of his thought, such as contingency, where he sees consonance between the biblical and scientific views, and, more controversially, the concept of "field." I also briefly consider some suggestions for furthering his program of providing rational support for theological claims.

## *Biographical Sketch and Outline of Pannenberg's Work*[5]

Wolfhart Pannenberg was born in Stettin, now part of Poland, in 1928. His family moved several times during his childhood, settling in Pomerania after their house in Berlin was destroyed. Here the young Wolfhart had a life-changing numinous experience in January 1945. Although called up at age sixteen, he was saved from fighting and dying with others of his unit on the Eastern front through his having contracted scabies. Instead he was taken prisoner by the British and released in the summer of 1945.[6]

After the war Pannenberg studied theology in Berlin, Göttingen, and, following a term under Barth in Basel, from autumn 1950 in Heidelberg. He received his doctorate from the University of Heidelberg in 1954; his *Habilitationsschrift* in the following year procured him a teaching post there as *Privatdozent*. Subsequent posts included a professorship at the Kirchliche Hochschule in Wuppertal, where Jürgen Moltmann was a colleague, the chair in systematic theology at Mainz, and finally the similar chair at Munich (1967–1993).

Pannenberg broke on to the theological scene in a major way with *Revelation as History*,[7] which he edited and to which he contributed. This small volume from the so-called Heidelberg Circle came as a theological bombshell, perhaps not with the same impact as Barth's *Epistle to the Romans* nearly half a century before, but nevertheless presenting a serious challenge to the Protestant theology of the time. Pannenberg's view marked a significant departure from Barth's "positivism of revelation," as Bonhoeffer had characterized it. Faith is rooted in a history that has to be interpreted as exhibiting revelation. Many of the themes for Pannenberg's later work are set out in this early volume. In *Jesus—God and Man*,[8] he defends the historicity of the resurrection. The resurrection is central for christology, validating the pre-Easter claims, and it means that the end of the world has broken into the present.

Pannenberg's concern with historical rationality is developed further in *Theology and the Philosophy of Science*[9] and *Anthropology in Theological Perspective*.[10] In contrast to Troeltsch, whose "principle of analogy" led him to rule out the resurrection as historical, on the grounds that it would be unique, Pannenberg denies that historical events have to be like other historical events. The "principle of analogy" can function as no more than a working tool.

For Pannenberg, Christian theology must argue with atheism on the grounds of a shared rationality. Theological truth claims are made on the basis of universal and publicly accessible evidence. History, which resembles the natural sciences in some, though not all, respects, can only be understood through Jesus Christ. He has revealed the end of history proleptically through his resurrection. The apocalyptic world-view of the New Testament is thus essential to understanding it (cf. Bonhoeffer's criticism of Bultmann on this point[11]).

The resurrection of Jesus tells us who he is, confirming his divine nature. This is an objective "Christology from below," in contrast to that of Schleiermacher, which, it can be argued, merely reflected subjective human experience or feelings of redemption back onto Christ.

In *Systematic Theology*, Pannenberg again argues for the truth of the Christian faith. Only the pursuit of truth in theology can justify the place of the subject in the university. Indeed, only if it is true can Christianity occupy any place in the public sphere, and can it be worthwhile adhering to it. A privatized belief that is "true for me" but not for others is ultimately not even true for me. These are important statements, not only with regard to the relationship between science and theology but in the postmodern context of the late twentieth and early twenty-first centuries.

A useful collection of Pannenberg's essays, particularly relevant to creation and the relationship of theology to the natural sciences, is *Toward a Theology of Nature*.

## Revelation as History

As noted above, *Revelation as History* broke new ground, and its themes remained important for Pannenberg's whole approach to theology, as seen both in *Jesus—God and Man* and *Systematic Theology*; and indeed in his engagement with the natural sciences in *Theology and the Philosophy of Science*. Given that our main theme in this chapter is creation, and connected with that natural theology and the importance for theology of the natural sciences, we cannot do justice to Pannenberg's treatment of history. However, since it is important for everything else—and not least because Pannenberg sees God's creative activity as not confined to the beginning but continuing in history—we do give a summary.

Instead of Barth's authoritarian approach, and in a different way from Bultmann, Pannenberg prefers the "open rationality of the Enlightenment," but "combined with a concern for the substance of the Christian tradition" (*RaH*, ix). That is reflected in this book and throughout his oeuvre. The book was a direct challenge to dialectical theology, although Pannenberg later acknowledges (*ST*, 1:227–28) that the book did not do justice to the full variety of the biblical data on revelation.

In common with Barth, Pannenberg starts with revelation as meaning God's self-disclosure in Christ. However, evaluating the scriptural material, both Old and New Testaments, Pannenberg concludes that, while God does indeed reveal himself in history, he does so in an indirect way. That is to say, the content of God's revelation is not his essence. God's acts in history may be interpreted as originating in him, which is quite different from saying they *are* him.

The problem with indirect revelation, Pannenberg argues, is that there are then as many revelations as divine acts in nature and history. How can we then speak of revelation as self-revelation of God? Two possibilities present themselves: either total reality as cosmos is God's indirect communication, which leads back to natural theology; or the totality of reality in history is God's self-communication, which then leads to the questions, "How can a specific event within it, such as the fate of Jesus, have absolute meaning as revelation?" and "Could there not be progress beyond Jesus Christ?" (*RaH*, 17–18). Elsewhere he argues that revelation is confirmed by experience—dreams coming true, prophecies fulfilled, and so on (*ST*, 1:191).

It seems to me that there is a tension in Pannenberg's thought here. History is undoubtedly primary, and God's revelation in history remains central for him. And yet God is also the "all-determining reality" so that it is essential to engage with the natural sciences. This is most obviously done by exploring how the doctrine of creation relates to what science has to say. We shall see shortly how Pannenberg goes about that latter task.

With his biblical scholar colleagues, Pannenberg considers the importance of the move from Old Testament prophetic thought to apocalyptic. In apocalyptic, God's vindication comes in the eschatological future. This is when the decisive revelation of God occurs, namely at the end of history. Interestingly in *Systematic Theology* (*ST*, 1:208–9) Pannenberg notes that the one major exception to the apocalyptic schema of a present disclosure and then a future universal disclosure is the revelation of the power and deity of God in creation that Paul refers to in Romans 1:19. We return to that important passage later.

Most significantly for Pannenberg, the fate of Jesus anticipates the end of all events, and only at the end will revelation be fully understood and be given its full meaning, retrospectively as it were. Nevertheless the historical revelation is open to anyone with eyes to see: it has a "universal character." He writes (*RaH*, 136), "Nothing must mute the fact that all truth lies right before the eyes, and that its appropriation is a natural consequence of the facts." Indeed the truth of God "can prove itself to us *only* in the course of a history" (*ST*, 1:171, emphasis added). This last statement is a sign of the tension I referred to earlier between history and the natural sciences for Pannenberg.

All this does not mean that unaided reason can give the knowledge of this truth: the *events* provide the data, and a reasonable person ought normatively to believe as a consequence. Otherwise, Pannenberg says, "The Christian truth is made into a truth for the in group, and the church becomes a gnostic community" (*RaH*, 137). Contra Richard Dawkins, who defines faith as "belief without evidence or in the teeth of the evidence," for the Christian theologian Wolfhart Pannenberg, "a person does not come to faith blindly, but by means of an event that can be appropriated as something that can be considered reliable. True faith is not a state of blissful gullibility" (*RaH*, 138). This reliability and reasonableness of the facts given in Christian proclamation leads quite reasonably to the Christian being able to "risk his trust, life, and future on them."

Pannenberg notes that the Greeks also saw God reflected in the totality of events, but in the unchangeable structures of order in the cosmos; history gives a superior and more complete view of the same God, he says, because it also includes the contingency of real events.

Since the end of history has been proleptically revealed in Christ, that means there can be no fundamentally new self-revelation in history, though, of course, God continues to act in history.

This again is a very important point that relates to what Pannenberg says elsewhere. As we shall see, there is in his thought a place for metaphysics and philosophical theology, with the traditional arguments for the existence of God, and so on, playing a role. However, this is relatively minor and certainly secondary to the place of history. From the point of view of natural theology, however, it seems to me that the public availability of evidence for events in history, which Pannenberg affirms, even if our understanding is provisional, is itself a kind of natural theology. Indeed Pannenberg might well agree that the boundaries between natural and revealed theology are broken down in his thought. Historical evidence might also be regarded as contributing to a kind of "ramified" natural theology that seeks to provide grounds for belief in the particulars of the Christian faith, rather than simply belief in a more abstract "Absolute." One argument against Richard Swinburne's approach to the justification of Christian belief, which I myself favor, has been that probabilities diminish as they are multiplied together to evaluate the credibility of the finer details of the faith.[12] This would be redressed by the adducing of more evidence of a historical kind. This would also apply to the alternative developments of Pannenberg's "scientific theology," which we shall see have been offered by Philip Hefner and Nancey Murphy.

## *Pannenberg's Critique of Barth*

In *Theology and the Philosophy of Science*, Pannenberg takes up Bonhoeffer's accusation against Barth of positivism of revelation (*TPS*, 265–76).[13]

For Barth the starting point of theology is God's self-revelation, and what makes theology a science in its own right is treating its object in the manner appropriate to it. This self-revelation of God cannot be "justified," and the appropriate response to God's word is to obey it and preach it.

Barth first gave this definition of scientific theology in his *Christliche*

*Dogmatik* of 1927. Martin Kähler had already made the point that a particular subject requires its own scientific procedure in 1883, but Kähler insisted that this must be "within the general method of universal epistemological laws" (*TPS*, 268). Barth denied this last point.

As we saw in chapter 2, Heinrich Scholz in 1931 (*TPS*, 269) asked how an evangelical theology can be a science, given that he could not find any criterion to judge whether an idea is appropriate to its subject. Pannenberg agrees that no judgment can be made independent of formal criteria of scientific validity. He criticizes Torrance (in *Theological Science*[14]) who takes Barth's line without recognizing Scholz's disagreement. Torrance in fact sees different natural sciences having different methodologies with some aspects common to all, though he does seem to agree with Barth about the givenness (positivity) of God in his word.

Scholz laid down formal postulates, which included the requirement of lack of contradiction of propositions and that the claim to truth should be subject to testing, though he wants a wider sense of this than the verification principle of the logical positivists. Barth asserts that even the principle of lack of contradiction can only be asserted with reservation in theology and rejects the notion of testing for theology. As Scholz says, theology cannot then be a science but only "a personal confession of faith exempt from all earthly questioning" (*TPS*, 271).

Here it seems Barth is on weak ground. He asserts contra Scholz that theology is investigating a "definite object" by a "self-consistent path." Yet it is clear that if the principle of noncontradiction is denied, then all statements are allowed and the search for truth becomes meaningless. And if there is no means of testing God's call to obedience as actually being from God, then how can the theologian justify himself or anybody else following the path? As Pannenberg asserts, Barth's rejection of reducing the subject matter of theology to human religious consciousness leads in the end, however unintentionally, to its being just that! His "venture of faith" rests on "no more than irrational subjectivity." We do need the methods of rational inquiry to judge whether what we are receiving is genuinely God's revelation and command. Wentzel van Huyssteen, also commenting on the Scholz-Barth dispute, comes to a similar conclusion to Pannenberg: "Methodologically, then,

Barth ultimately fell prey to precisely that psychological subjectivism from which he had sought to escape."[15]

Later, in his contributions to Barth's *Festschrift* of 1936, Scholz insists again that theological statements cannot breach the laws of logic and still say anything meaningful. "It is always dangerous for a thinking being to renounce logical argument," he says (*TPS*, 275). That certainly goes for the law of noncontradiction, and it is also the case that there must be some way of determining at least in principle the conditions under which a statement is true for it to have meaning, though again not being restricted to sense experience as in logical positivism.

Concluding this section of *Theology and the Philosophy of Science*, Pannenberg remarks, "If we consider Scholz's arguments carefully, we must agree that even theological statements cannot be exempt from logic. But if we admit this, we admit a great deal including that a view of theology based on the positive nature of revelation is untenable" (*TPS*, 275–76). In *Systematic Theology* (1:44) he likens Barth's approach to that of Schleiermacher. Schleiermacher based dogmatics on faith as self-evident; Barth based it on the Word of God as self-evident. Barth acknowledged that this meant taking a risk, implying that he is still basing dogmatics on faith—even if that is faith as risk rather than faith as experience.

## *Is Theology a Science?*

This is the major theme of Pannenberg's *Theology and the Philosophy of Science*.[16] Pannenberg is concerned that theology is only eligible for a place in the university if it is a science. This approach contrasts with Schleiermacher, who thought it enough for theology to be essential for the education of clergy. This is inadequate; theology must be there for what it is, for its pursuit of truth, and it cannot be immune to criticism (*TPS*, 255; also *ST*, 1:5).

Today in Britain, Richard Dawkins does not believe that theology warrants a place in university education precisely for the reason that it is not a science, so Pannenberg's theme is directly relevant. Dawkins and other atheistic scientists such as Lewis Wolpert might concede its study as a historical phenomenon, though presumably alchemy and astrology would also warrant a place for the same reasons. Interestingly this was essentially the approach of Ernst Troeltsch, which again Pannenberg rightly deems inadequate (*TPS*, 256ff.).

Thus the question of the truth of theological claims and of their scientific rationality is essential for anyone who believes that theology is worthy of university study. Otherwise it should be relegated to the seminary.[17] As we have seen, some theologians (notably Barth) play into the hands of the opponents of theology because the former make theology immune from rational criticism.

Before the great philosopher of science Karl Popper came on the scene, positivism had asserted that arguments should proceed from the basis of what is known via sense perception. Logical positivism added the criterion that propositions be testable and formulated the principle of verification, which made statements about God meaningless. Barth played into the hands of the logical positivists by saying that one cannot verify religious experience to a third party. Bonhoeffer's charge against Barth was that taking God's revelation in Christ as the basis for all subsequent theological argument itself constituted a form of positivism—"positivism of revelation"—and would presumably suffer from the same weaknesses as other forms of positivism.

Popper argued that scientific laws are meaningless on the basis of logical positivism because you cannot verify a generalization of infinitely many instances by only observing a finite number. Instead he proposed that hypotheses should be open to falsification, which means that no hypothesis can ever attain certainty since there is always the possibility of falsification. Popper was mistaken, though, in arguing that a theory should be abandoned rather than modified if a falsifying observation is made. Science sometimes works that way, but not always. Indeed, Thomas Kuhn argues that, contra Popper, the normal way is precisely by accommodating anomalies—for example, the perturbation of Uranus's orbit could be accommodated by invoking a new planet (Neptune) rather than a new law.

While metaphysical propositions cannot be falsified, they remain important for Popper as "helping to organize the world." However, Popper's pupil W. W. Bartley took the view that Protestantism represented a "retreat to commitment," as exemplified by Barth. Faith becomes irrational fanaticism and plays into the hands of an atheistic psychology of religion, which traces the irrational need to believe back to its secular roots (*ST*, 1:47–48). This latter is the kind of exercise secularists such as Dawkins and Dennett[18] have been engaged in more recently, however unsuccessful or open to criticism their approaches may be.

In superseding positivism, Popper's falsificationism does not suffer from taking irrational starting points but presupposes no ultimate certainties. However, Popper is not the last word because falsificationism (critical rationalism) has its problems. We have seen the problem that falsified theories *can* be modified. There is also the problem of Popper's basic propositions, which are observation reports (singular "there is" statements). However, these basic propositions are only accepted on the basis of other basic propositions and ultimately by a group's decision or agreement, and are thus to be regarded as "conventions." Carnap, I think rightly, replaced falsification with the notion of confirmation. It is still true that confidence in a law of nature can never be final, though it does grow as the number of observations mounts. I would argue that the modern form of confirmation theory, as pioneered by Richard Swinburne, is a valid way not only of evaluating scientific hypotheses, but metaphysical ones, too.[19] Here the ability of different theories to explain the evidence at hand is important, and that is something Pannenberg affirms as a criterion for their scientific status (a point we return to shortly).[20] Van Huyssteen's basic criticism of his position is that, even so, the subjective commitment of the religious believer is never eliminated by Pannenberg, although van Huyssteen seems to think that that is in any case not a barrier to finding an ultimate basis for scientific rationality since scientists themselves exercise their own commitments.[21]

For Pannenberg it is important to know whether history and metaphysics can be conceived as sciences. Clearly history does not conform to the falsification criterion since an exception to a regularity would not break a law. History concerns unique and unrepeatable events. However, so do the sciences of cosmology and biology; hence, this factor clearly does not make history unscientific. However, the ability to explain evidence is common to historical, metaphysical, and scientific hypotheses. A hypothesis that unifies and interprets the data is to be sought in history just as in science. Moreover, metaphysics is also included here, too, for philosophical assertions can be tested for their "coherence (freedom from contradiction), the efficiency of their interpretative components (the avoidance of unnecessary postulates), and the degree of simplicity and subtlety they achieve in their interpretations of reality" (*TPS*, 69). The uniqueness of philosophical assertions lies in their being concerned with the whole of reality; they are, however, scientific in the ways suggested.

Later in *Theology and the Philosophy of Science* (326–45), Pannenberg returns to the question of whether theology is a science in the sense in which Scholz maintained in criticizing Barth. He says that it is coherent in being able to give an account of how the all-determining reality of God gives meaning and unity to the whole of reality other than it. Again, a philosopher who would agree is Richard Swinburne, who has argued for the coherence of theism and for its explanatory power.[22] Philip Hefner sees Pannenberg as providing a "scientific research programme," in the terminology of Imre Lakatos.[23] The "hard core" of this research program would be God as the all-determining reality bestowing meaning to the as yet incomplete totality of reality, completion coming eschatologically. "Auxiliary hypotheses" relate both to the biblical/theological tradition (these would be open to various forms of falsification), and to scientific descriptions of reality which at least "leave open" (Hefner's phrase) the conjecture that they manifest the effects of God's all-determining reality. I would broadly agree with Hefner, although, again, my preference would be for "confirm" in the sense of confirmation theory rather than the weaker "leave open"; indeed, although I cannot develop the arguments here, it will now be very apparent that my overall preference is for confirmation theory, as expressed through Bayesian probability theory.[24]

As we have seen, history is of central importance for Pannenberg. Only God can give meaning to the whole of history, and that meaning is anticipated in the resurrection of Christ. Nancey Murphy sees Pannenberg here as failing to counter Hume's alternative view of history as without transcendent reference and so without the consequent unity of meaning.[25] Moreover, Hume does not, of course, accept the resurrection. He utilizes the logic of the Port-Royalists whereby the probability of an event is weighted in accord with the frequency of its past occurrence (the effect being not dissimilar to that of Troeltsch's principle of analogy). Murphy thinks Pannenberg does not defeat Hume because their two systems are incommensurable. However, like Hefner, Murphy sees Pannenberg as providing the starting point for a Lakatosian research program (see later).[26] Murphy argues that this is a sound move since Lakatos represents the modern form of probable reasoning in the line of Hume, though I would argue, as noted above, that it is Bayesian confirmation theory. One point to note is that the latter utilizes "epistemic probabilities" rather than the frequency interpretation.

Pannenberg further argues, correctly in my view, that religious statements are to be understood as making assertions about states of affairs. They are therefore open to testing, though this must be understood, as for Scholz, as going beyond the strictures of logical positivism. This testing must, again rightly in my view, be other than by reliance on authoritative dogmatic statements. Indeed, traditional assertions such as Scripture being the word of God are themselves not sources of proof of theological statements but candidates for verification (or, again preferably in my view, confirmation in the sense of Carnap and his successors today such as Swinburne). The factual status of the state of affairs is indeed more important than coherence (*TPS*, 331).

Now it is clear that statements about God—and for Pannenberg theology is "the science of God"—cannot be verified directly. God is not under our control; he is not an object like others to be examined in the same way. Thus statements about God must be tested on the basis of their implications. This applies in the sciences and in history.

We have seen that the verification criterion does not work for hypothetical scientific laws (which are generalizations). Nor is falsification necessarily applicable since, as Kuhn showed, there arises the option of accommodating an anomaly to the present paradigm as an alternative to paradigm shift.

As Pannenberg writes, "The fundamental contribution of general statements within general theories is their ability to 'explain the evidence at hand'" (*TPS*, 335). This is as true equally of theological as scientific theories. Pannenberg concludes that "we may speak of a theory as 'proved' when it is able to explain the facts at hand" (*TPS*, 336). The term "proved" here, like "verified," is too strong for my liking. Rather, he should use the term "confirmed," in the sense of "increasing the probability," as do Carnap, Swinburne, and others. Van Huyssteen reads this aspect of Pannenberg's thought as shaped by Kuhn's paradigm theory. As I have said, I prefer to see it as tending toward the more objective approach of confirmation theory, though Pannenberg does not actually pursue this (or a Lakatosian approach) in any detailed way. Surprisingly, for example, he does not make the connection at this point between all he says about the resurrection elsewhere and the evidence for it "confirming" a theological hypothesis. Of course that is essentially what Pannenberg is indeed doing in other places, most notably in *Jesus—God and Man*.[27]

Predictability is important in the natural sciences but clearly less so in historical and theological science, although there can be discoveries that contradict hypotheses. And in the natural sciences it must be remembered that predictability is not all, since laws are abstractions and concrete instances are contingent and unique (we return to the vital issue of contingency in Pannenberg's thought later). Even so, Pannenberg has said that he is prepared to venture into this territory, as noted by Murphy (see below).

In history there is documentary evidence and archaeological evidence, for example, which may permit conclusions to be drawn about events being investigated. Theology goes beyond the establishing of historical facts to the appearance of the all determining reality, which reveals itself in them and in present experience. Theological statements resemble those of philosophy in dealing with the whole of reality and must be evaluated in a similar way. While verification (confirmation) is possible, it is questionable, as in science but perhaps more so, as to whether a final conclusion can ever be reached. Given that the process is still open and continuing, that must only happen in the eschatological future; again we meet this characteristic emphasis of Pannenberg, though here he cites John Hick and I. M. Crombie in support (*TPS*, 343). He also cites Ebeling to the effect that God verifies himself by verifying us—that is, by bringing our lives into his truth, taking this to mean that theological explanations give a more convincing interpretation than alternatives of the reality that includes all human experience, not least religious experience. In *Systematic Theology* (1:23) he notes that, while verification is important, affective and practical verification must complement the theoretical.

I would argue that theological explanations are worldviews. Science is not a worldview unless scientism—the idea that science can answer all questions (Dawkins, Atkins)—be adopted. With Alister McGrath I would agree that worldviews cannot be proved (e.g., predictability is a greater problem than for science), though I would argue that they can be confirmed in the sense of Bayesian probability theory.

Pannenberg gives helpful criteria whereby theological hypotheses may be deemed nonsubstantiated (*TPS*, 344–45): (1) they do not express implications of biblical traditions; (2) they do not connect to reality as a whole as understood by present philosophical inquiry; (3) they are not integrated with the appropriate area of experience; and (4) their explanatory force is not greater than that of alternative hypotheses. Hefner sees these criteria as conforming to the Lakatosian structure of scientific research programs.[28] Hefner suggests some helpful directions for this program, though I was somewhat surprised that he thought Pannenberg protects the biblical traditions from falsification. As we have already seen, Pannenberg does think that the place of Scripture should be a problem for dogmatics rather than a "given."

As noted above, Nancey Murphy also sees Pannenberg's approach as expressible in terms of a Lakatosian research program. Both Hefner and Murphy see this as a hybrid theological-scientific research program whose "hard core" (in Lakatosian terminology) is God as the all-determining reality and whose auxiliary hypotheses draw from physics and anthropology as well as theology. The success of such a program, according to Murphy, will be measured by its ability to "predict and corroborate novel facts." She notes that, at a symposium in Chicago in 1988, Pannenberg accepted her reconstruction of his program and suggested several predictions for corroboration.[29] These included anthropology finding a more constructive place for religion, and physics developing a new form of field theory that includes the irreversibility of time. We return to field theory below but note here the boldness of theology making essentially scientific predictions. Is

Pannenberg offering a hostage to fortune, or is he right that theology really ought to make a difference to science? This controversial question deserves a good deal more analysis than we have space for here.

## *The Knowledge of God and the Truth of Christian Claims*

For Pannenberg, history is primary. Christian doctrine "rests on the historical revelation of God in the historical figure of Jesus Christ and on the precise evaluation, by historical interpretation alone, of the testimony that early Christian proclamation gives to this figure" (*ST*, 1:x). Nevertheless, all knowledge of God is provided only by God (*ST*, 1:72, 189) and comes through the working of the Spirit, and the questions of how that knowledge is obtained and who has it to what degree are not decided merely by stating this.

Pannenberg is insistent that truth cannot be relative (*ST*, 1:51): "*My* truth cannot be mine alone. If I cannot in principle declare it to be truth for all—though perhaps hardly anyone else sees this—then it pitilessly ceases to be truth for me also." This is an important statement for those seduced by the current form of relativism in the shape of postmodernism.

For Pannenberg, doctrinal statements are "hypotheses" (*ST*, 1:56; *TPS*, 332–45). They are "propositions which are not self-evident and which do not follow with logical necessity from self-evident propositions." Thus, the crucifixion and resurrection are hypotheses, to be evaluated on normal historical criteria, though clearly the latter is more complex because resurrections are not common; it must be presupposed that such a thing can happen, not ruled out *a priori* as Troeltsch did through his "principle of analogy."

A critic of Pannenberg here is Tom Wright, who argues that Pannenberg gives too much away by conceding that the ultimate verification of the resurrection will come at the eschaton.[30] That means, of course, there will ultimately be an analogy. The rise of the early church is sufficient counterexample, says Wright, since it too is a unique phenomenon and on Troeltsch's principle one could say nothing about it. While Wright has a point, it seems to me that Pannenberg is essentially correct because he denies absoluteness to Troeltsch's principle anyway, and the resurrection must remain only probable rather than certain until the eschaton.

History concerns the whole breadth of doctrine, however, not simply that recorded in Scripture (*ST*, 1:59), even though that concerning God's self-revelation in Christ is fundamental: "In the sequence of creation, sin, reconciliation, and consummation, Christian teaching is viewed and structured in terms of a history which aims at the salvation of humanity and the renewal of creation." The deity of God is manifested in this history.

Pannenberg argues (contra Barth) that dogmatics cannot begin with the reality of God (*ST*, 1:61). The reality of God has to be presented initially "only as a human notion, word, or concept."

Pannenberg notes (*ST*, 1:70) that philosophical theology speaks of the one God as the origin of the unity of the cosmos. Today, Swinburne has argued against Hume's positing the possibility of many gods precisely on the grounds of the uniformity of natural law across space and time. Pannenberg says that Christians can speak into what philosophical theology says by identifying the Creator with the God manifested in Jesus Christ. In doing so they are in continuity with what the Israelites did in the Old Testament (e.g., Isa 40:12–13 and Isa 45:18–21). The concept "God," as Ian Ramsey said, makes possible an ultimate explanation of the world as a whole. I have argued elsewhere that alternative hypotheses, such as multiverses, do not provide an ultimate explanation for the existence and special nature of our universe; only God does so.[31]

## Natural Knowledge of God and Natural Theology

The idea of a natural knowledge of God has been there from the beginning and is enshrined in Romans 1:19–20. Up to the twentieth century, nobody disputed that there existed a provisional knowledge of God that needed to be filled out with historical knowledge of Christ. Even Barth recognized that we are guilty before God because we know him by his revelation in creation (*Church Dogmatics* [hereafter cited as *CD*] I/2.306–7).[32] However, for Barth that knowledge comes in and with the revelation in Christ and is ascribed and imputed to us from without (see especially *CD*, II/1.121).[33] It is not preceded by knowledge of the same God into which is proclaimed the wrath of God, because that is incompatible with Barth's understanding of the revelation in Christ as the one revelation of God.

Pannenberg thinks that Barth's view is defective: "Might it not be a feature of this revelation that it presupposes the fact that the world and humanity belong to, and know, the God who is proclaimed by the gospel, even though a wholly new light is shed on this fact by the revelation in Christ?" (*ST*, 1:75). Jesus came to *his own* and his own received him not—they were his own people, however. And Romans 1:20 talks about knowledge of God's deity from the creation of the world—that is, long before the historical revelation in Christ.

This natural knowledge of God is not at all the same thing as natural theology, however. Natural theology is to do with a "special human possibility" of developing a philosophical doctrine of God by argument (*ST*, 1:76).

## The Proofs of God and Philosophical Criticism of Natural Theology

Pannenberg claims that the ontological proof, rejected by Aquinas, has been to the fore in modern philosophical theology rather than proofs from the world, though the modern example of Richard Swinburne would be a counter to this. Descartes used the identity of God's essence and existence to reframe the ontological proof. Discussion of the tenability of his proof was found to need a cosmological argument.

The cosmological argument from the contingency of the world to a cause of its existence that needs no other but is of itself, its essence identical to its existence, led to the idea of a necessary being and was the key to the proof. This was satisfactory until Kant claimed that it was illegitimate to extend the boundaries of causation beyond the sensory world. In a footnote (*ST*, 1:86) Pannenberg notes that in a significant work of 1763, Kant accepted the inference of an independent origin from the contingency of things, but not inferences of absolute perfection and unity.

Pannenberg notes some problems with the argument from causes. One is the problem of infinite regress. A second is that a cause of something does not need to continue in existence, as seen from human generation. That is countered by the need for a sustaining principle for the process. However, Newton showed that not even a sustaining principle is needed because things have a tendency to stay as they are. The mechanistic universe defeats both first-cause and first-mover arguments.

Pannenberg (*ST*, 1:90) says that Kant destroyed the arguments of speculative reason for a necessary being but still required an ideal of necessity to give unity of knowledge (*Critique of Pure Reason*[34]). In *Critique of Practical Reason* Kant argued that the absolute necessity of moral laws rightly requires the postulate of a supreme being, and thereby Kant completes the move begun by Descartes from a cosmological to an anthropological basis for thought of God.

This might seem to leave the traditional arguments in a somewhat ambivalent position, as far as Pannenberg is concerned. However, he says that the philosophical proofs make talk of God intelligible and can establish criteria for it, and they witness to the need for humans to rise above their finite existence to the thought of the infinite (*ST*, 1:94–95, 106–7), even if the debate is not decisively closed. Indeed, I would argue the debate is very much alive. As I have said, Richard Swinburne is a proponent of the cosmological and teleological arguments (Pannenberg himself notes the move to consider purpose and contingency in the universe, and we return to that topic below), and other arguments as well; William Lane Craig is another philosopher who defends the traditional arguments. As Pannenberg rightly says, philosophical theology still has a critical function regarding Christian theology's talk about God (*ST*, 1:95).

## Theological Criticism of Natural Theology

Natural theology has been strongly attacked from within theology itself, most notably by Barth but by others as well. Even Schleiermacher (in *Speeches on Religion*[35]) regarded natural religion as an anemic common denominator abstracted from the positive religions and therefore incapable of forming the basis of a religious fellowship. However, asks Pannenberg, was not Schleiermacher's appeal to the feeling of absolute dependence a form of "natural theology"? And similarly Ritschl, while rejecting metaphysical bases for the concept of God, was he not doing natural theology in concentrating on morality?

"Against the synergistic idea of a natural and a revealed knowledge of God that harmoniously complement one another," writes Pannenberg (*ST*, 1:102), Barth charged that "the distinction between a theology of the Word of God and a theology based on anthropology" was being erased: "Natural theology was an expression of human self-justification." Pannenberg goes on: "Barth never made any material revision, although in his doctrines of creation and reconciliation he abandoned the tone of sharp encounter and claimed the 'lights' of creation for a christologically based universalism" (*ST*, 1:102–3). In contrast, for Pannenberg himself, the natural theology of the Baroque Age and Enlightenment did at least support the Christian claim that the world and humans are dependent on God for their existence: "Barth has little to offer in this regard but rhetoric" (*ST*, 1:106).

Pannenberg writes (*ST*, 1:127) that Barth is correct that "the deity of God stands or falls with the primacy of his reality and his revelation over religion" (note that Barth's target until 1929 was "religion" rather than "natural theology"). The problem is that we cannot approach this directly because, if we do, we are then merely asserting. We need the mediation of reason. The reasons for the domination of the concept of religion must be taken into account, which Pannenberg sees as (1) the decay of the doctrine of biblical inspiration through Enlightenment critiques; and (2) the reduction of natural theology to anthropology. So how do we get back to the primacy of revelation over religion without just asserting it? That is the crux of the matter, as Pannenberg sees it. The older theologians (he mentions Buddeus and Dorner, but includes even Schleiermacher) were seeking to validate the truth claims of Christianity given the conditions of their own times. That is the task in today's very different climate, too.

Regarding religious experience, Pannenberg says (*ST*, 1:157) that its being a constitutive feature of human nature is a necessary but not sufficient condition for the truth of religious claims, if God is taken to be the creator of the world. More than that (*ST*, 1:158), God is not an illusion associated with narcissistic wishful thinking if the world is created and controlled by God. Hence, the question of truth is answered in our experience of the world (*ST*, 1:159), "as the world shows itself to be determined by God." This is not the cosmological proof, however. The concept of God is the starting point for the appeal to experience of the world, and that experience either confirms the truth claim involved in the concept of God or disconfirms it (note the language of confirmation here, though not, I am sure, in the technical sense of confirmation theory). In the latter case God would be merely a human concept (see also *TPS*, 300, 301ff.). Interestingly there are also modern studies of the evidential value of religious experience,[36] and it is also one of the factors in Swinburne's building up of a cumulative case for the existence of God.

Ultimately the truth of the Christian religion is not proved from metaphysics or the philosophy of religion. These can give only a general limited concept of the "Absolute," which Christianity in its debate with other religions must endow with concrete meaning as the Christian God by giving the best account. Metaphysics and philosophy of religion can have a regulative function in this debate but of themselves can come to no final judgment "because of the openness of worldly experience" (*ST*, 1:176). The Absolute per se is insufficient, since it is impersonal, compared with the God of religion (*ST*, 1:176–77).

Following a long section reiterating his views on revelation as history, which we have covered earlier, in the end (*ST*, 1:257) Pannenberg says that "verification of the truth claims of Christian revelation will take place in the form of a systematic reconstruction of Christian doctrine, beginning with the understanding of God which is contained in the event of his revelation to which the scriptures bear witness and which was the express theme in the theological discussions that led to the formation of the doctrine of the Trinity." In volume 1 of *Systematic Theology*, Pannenberg goes on to a discussion of the Trinitarian God, which again features in his doctrine of creation to which we now turn.

## *The Doctrine of Creation in Pannenberg*

In beginning his presentation of the doctrine of creation in volume 2 of *Systematic Theology*, Pannenberg reiterates the point that Christian doctrine makes claims to truth that are open to possible confirmation at the bars of human experience and reason. The champions of secularism today (perhaps Richard Dawkins most notably at the present time) would have us believe that such matters have long since been decided by clever people in the negative, so we need to provide good reasons for belief (*ST*, 2:xiii).

Pannenberg begins (*ST*, 2:1) with the classical Christian affirmation that the world owes its existence to a free act of God. The world is distinct from God. It is essential to the Christian understanding that creation does not "emanate by necessity from the divine essence or belong by necessity to the deity of God." The divine act of creation concerns "the free origin of a reality distinct from God" (*ST*, 2:9, 20).

Very importantly, and we devote a section to this topic below, the world is contingent. It might not have existed. It did not need to exist for, if it did not, "nothing would have been lacking in the deity of God" (*ST*, 2:9). It is also contingent in the sense that, given its existence, it could have been different from what it is.

## The Nature of Creation

Pannenberg notes that in Deutero-Isaiah the prophet appeals to the idea of God as Creator to motivate the expectation that God will do something new in history. The question this raises for Pannenberg is whether creation is thus to be seen as something occurring at the beginning only or whether it epitomizes God's creative action in world history: "Tension between these two aspects marks the biblical testimonies to God as Creator" (*ST*, 2:12). Perhaps this delineates the tension in Pannenberg's own thought, too, which I noted earlier, between the primacy of history and the need for theology to engage with the natural sciences. I would hope this also justifies this chapter on creation and the sciences also devoting so much space to history! As Wentzel van Huyssteen remarks, for Pannenberg theology is "fully and most profoundly concerned with God's revelation in Jesus Christ." Nevertheless, because the concept of creation implies the universality of the concept of God, *all* knowledge and every aspect of reality can only be understood in relation to God's revelation.[37] We have seen how, for Pannenberg, history and theology must be shown to be sciences in their own right, and the natural sciences then inevitably end up as secondary to the main thrust of his thought, even though he engages seriously with them.

The P account in Genesis 1 testified to God's unrestricted power in creation by "focusing on the divine Word of command as the only basis of the existence of creatures." Furthermore the "effortless nature of the simple command" illustrates the unrestricted nature of God's power compared with Babylonian or Ugaritic-Canaanite myths of battles with chaos or the sea, respectively (*ST*, 2:13).

Even so, creation by word is not unique to the biblical account, occurring as it does for example in the third millennium BC Egyptian Memphis theology. In the latter the royal God Ptah thought in his heart and commanded by his tongue the existence of all the elements of the universe, including all other gods.[38] No, the decisively distinct feature of creation by the Word in the Hebrew account is "the unlimited freedom of the act of creation, like that of the historical action of the God of Israel." Again we have the important linkage between history and creation in Pannenberg's thought.

This idea of unrestrictedly free creation by God later found expression in the formula "creation out of nothing" (first found in 2 Macc 7:28; cf. Rom 4:17; Heb 11:3). Pannenberg notes that the doctrine of *creatio ex nihilo* was established decisively by Theophilus of Antioch and Irenaeus.

Pannenberg criticizes Barth again, this time for ascribing a reality to "nothing" under the name "nothingness" and seeing it as resistant to God (*CD*, III/3.289–368).[39] "Genesis 1 makes no reference to any resistance to God's creative activity," he responds. Pannenberg is surely right that this is what the later doctrine of *creatio ex nihilo* was meaning to affirm.

Also erroneous is the dualistic thinking of the process thought of Whitehead.[40] Whitehead's God works by "persuasion" and not by mighty creative action (*ST*, 2:15). This is a seductive view because the biblical God is also patient and kind, seeking out his creatures in love. But they always owe everything to his "almighty creative action." For the biblical God his patience is not a sign of his weakness but "an expression of the love of the Creator, who willed that his creatures should be free and independent" (*ST*, 2:16).

Process theologians argue that the God of classical theism cannot be the God of love because he would have the power to prevent evils. Their more restricted God can be loving because he lacks the power to prevent evils. But then, Pannenberg argues, it would not make sense, as for the Israelites, who traced evil back to God, and for whom Satan was a servant of God, to put their trust in God to provide a way out of suffering. To Pannenberg, the creation is an expression of divine love through its freedom of origin.

## The Trinitarian Origin of the Act of Creation

For Pannenberg, it is important that creation is an act of the triune God and relates distinctively to each of the persons of the Trinity.

Creation relates first to the Father as origin. Second, it relates to the Son whose self-distinction from the Father is the ontic basis of the distinction between creature and Creator and the independent existence of all creaturely reality (*ST*, 2:23).

Pannenberg balks at the notion of the Son's mediation of creation being through the ideas held in the Son's mind, which the divine will effects. There are problems with that, such as the seeming necessity of the creation that is not the classical, nor Pannenberg's, view as we have seen.[41] Pannenberg prefers Hegel's thesis that "in the Trinity the Son is the principle of otherness, the starting point for the emergence of the finite as that which is absolutely other than the deity" (*ST*, 2:28).

Hegel linked this notion to a "logically necessary self-development of the Absolute in producing a world of the finite." For Hegel this meant absolute subject moving out of unity with itself. However, Pannenberg argues that if one takes seriously the mutuality of the relations of the Trinitarian persons, then no such necessity arises. Self-distinction is a condition of the fellowship of the persons in unity, and the unity needs nothing outside itself: "Nevertheless, in the event of the incarnation, in the relation of Jesus of Nazareth to his heavenly Father, the Son moved out of the unity of the Godhead" (*ST*, 2:29).

This was part of the Son's humility in accepting creatureliness. However, he remains united to the Father through the Spirit. The Spirit is also involved in creation as a whole (Gen 1:2), and then also as the life-giving principle of creatures—animals, plants, and humans (Gen

2:7; Ps 104:29ff.; *ST*, 2:76ff.). The Spirit is responsible for the fellowship of the creatures with God and their participation in his life. Equally the new life of the resurrection is the work of the Spirit (Rom 8:11; 1 Cor 15:44ff.). The Spirit is also the principle of movement, and Pannenberg notes the biblical models of wind and breath. Later we consider his appropriation of the scientific term "field," which he sees as relating the idea of the Spirit to modern understanding.

## God's Creation, Preservation, and Rule of the World

Preservation is correlative with creation and is not unchanging conservation but "continued creation, a constantly new creative fashioning that goes beyond what was given existence originally" (*ST*, 2:34). We have already seen how the discovery of inertia has affected the credibility of the notion of preservation and will return to this again shortly.

Pannenberg notes that in Scripture God is very active; for example, he feeds the animals (*ST*, 2:35). He cites Augustine (*ST*, 2:36) (*The Literal Meaning of Genesis* 4.12.22ff.) that God is preserving on the seventh day—that is, he is ruling and governing by his power, and if he were not, then what is created would sink back into nothingness.[42]

Clement of Alexandria (*Stromata*, 6.16) argued that time came into being with creatures: "And how could creation take place in time, seeing time was born along with things which exist."[43]

Augustine (*City of God* 11.6) is better noted for saying the same thing: "Assuredly the world was made, not in time, but simultaneously with time."[44] Pannenberg (*ST*, 2:39) sees the merit of Augustine's view as twofold: (1) it avoids the appearance that the world's origin rests on an arbitrary resolve of God—it is a free act, not capricious or based on a whim; (2) it opposes any restriction of divine action to the beginning of the world—the eternity of the act of creation is a presupposition for God's "preserving activity as continued or in continuous creation."

Pannenberg further agrees with Augustine that miracles are not violations of the natural order, since we have limited knowledge of this. He writes (*ST*, 2:46), "Since it is not self-evident that anything should take place, not merely the emergence but above all the continuation of creaturely forms and states is at every moment miraculous." Later

(*ST*, 2:73) he writes, "The idea that God can bring forth what is new and unusual only by breaking the laws of nature has been overruled by the insight that for all their regularity the laws of nature do not have the character of closed (or, better, isolated) systems." He recognizes (*ST*, 2:45) that his view is in contrast to David Hume's definition of a miracle as a violation of the laws of nature.

Pannenberg (*ST*, 2:49–50) compares Descartes, who thought that God didn't intervene after the initial creation, with Newton, who thought that absolute space, and gravitation that acted without touch, demonstrated the ongoing activity of God. However, as we have seen, the principle of inertia represents a problem for the idea of God's activity, and there is consequently a need to take account of more modern developments in physics, such as fields and quantum physics. We return to this important topic in Pannenberg's thought in a separate section below.

Pannenberg (*ST*, 2:50n125) believes that the engagement of science and religion in philosophical reflection on theory construction affects the process of scientific theory appraisal. This is somewhat stronger than Ernan McMullin's view that theology should not interfere but help in constructing a broader view.[45] We have seen the boldness of Pannenberg in making certain predictions of a scientific nature in discussion with Murphy, which seem to go further even than his remark here.

Persisting implies more than inertia, writes Pannenberg, because it involves change (*ST*, 2:51). Thus it is identity in change that is important (of course, the argument to a prime mover can be reexpressed in terms of a first changer). Self-awareness also brings awareness of contingency and thence the need for preservation from outside of oneself.

## World Government and the Kingdom of God: The Goal of Creation

The preservation of creatures rests on God's faithfulness. That is the basis for the identity and continuation of creatures. Contingency, the creatively new at each moment, is posited in the concept of preservation (*ST*, 2:53).

The notions of world government by God and of God's having the good of all creatures in mind can seem problematic in the light of suffering (*ST*, 2:54). Faith can affirm God's sovereignty in these respects only in expectation of a renewed creation; this is "the goal of all creaturely reality (Rom 8:19ff.)" (*ST*, 2:55). This seems to be Pannenberg's answer to the theodicy question, which arises also in the context of his critique of process theology, as we have seen.

Pannenberg states (*ST*, 2:58): "World government [providence] relates to integrating into God's purposes for the world the actual results of the independent conduct of creatures, namely their failures and the evil that these failures cause. The central theme of the divine world government is God's supremacy over the misuse of creaturely independence" (*ST*, 2:59). God's skill is shown in his ability to bring good out of evil and the final vindication is eschatological. This reminds me of a helpful analogy from J. R. Lucas concerning Persian rugmaking.[46] In a family the father weaves from one end of the rug and the children from the other. The children make many mistakes but the father is so skillful that he can weave the whole into a beautiful pattern.

At this point (*ST*, 2:59) Pannenberg asserts what we saw at the beginning, namely that theology must make sense of the world as God's creation prior to making known his reconciling work in Christ and consummating work in the new creation. Only if we begin this way with creation can we make the truth claims of Christian faith have a secure basis, and this must be done in dialogue with the sciences. Again we see this seeming tension in Pannenberg's thought between the primacy of the historical, including above all his affirmations about the resurrection, and the importance of creation and the sciences—though we have now also seen that his doctrine of creation embraces preservation and continuing dynamic activity rather than simply being confined to "creation at the beginning."

Referring to the big bang, Pannenberg also now sees the role of the *Logos*, in conformity with what he has said earlier, working as the generative principle of diversity. As the expansion of the universe progresses, new forms and structures develop according to physical laws. The order of the world, seen in its laws, is an expression of the wisdom of God, which is identified with the *Logos*. The *Logos* is, however, also the principle of the concrete particularity and unity of the way in which this universe has contingently unfolded, and that is seen especially in the incarnation and will be perfected in the eschatological future. Again we return to the issue of contingency below.

Pannenberg addresses a question raised much earlier in this chapter: "Are humans really the goal of creation?" (*ST*, 2:74). He affirms that they are in view of the incarnation. And he sees this as in conflict with earlier science—for example, Copernicus—but in conformity with modern science. Modern cosmology has shown what the conditions must be for life to evolve through the "anthropic principle." The constants of physics need to be what they are, the age of the universe needs to be what it is—a host of parameters need to be "just right"—for humans to evolve in the cosmos. As I note a number of times in this book, I myself believe that these contingencies provide powerful evidence for the universe's being designed by God and have so argued in *God, the Multiverse, and Everything*.[47] It seems that Pannenberg is also impressed by these anthropic fine-tunings and sees them as confirming that humans are the goal of creation. They are, of course, the conditions for anything interesting at all to happen, and in particular for "intelligent life" to evolve. Thus, Paul Davies, notes how the term "biophilic principle" is more accurate than "anthropic principle."[48] Pannenberg is not worried about the existence of extraterrestrial intelligent life forms, who might need redemption, since there are already precedents for such in Christian tradition, namely the angels. Their existence would not challenge the credibility of the incarnation of the *Logos* in traditional Christian teaching. But Pannenberg agrees that the discovery of the remarkable fine-tunings signals a reversal of the trend since Copernicus to remove humans from the center of the universe.

## *Contingency*

In modern times "God has been expelled from physics step by step," writes Pannenberg (*TTN*, 73). The role of God has thus been reduced to the deistic one of creating the world in the beginning, but then leaving it to its own devices. There is some truth in this, and even anthropic arguments, which seem positive for theology, could leave one with a deistic view of God.

Pannenberg notes again (*TTN*, 74, 113n3) Barth's making theological discourse about creation immune from criticism by the natural sciences. This makes theology irrelevant not only for the sciences but for the present worldview of humanity, which is rightly informed by the sciences. Theology has to think of God as the creator of the world described by science and to connect to the scientific view. But then the problem arises that science itself seems to be able to do away with God, certainly an all-determinative God who interferes in natural processes.

Pannenberg commends Karl Heim as a pioneer theologian who saw the need for theology to relate to science. However, a problem with Heim is that he did not really find the common ground on which to seek a consonance. Instead he used scientific terms, most notably that of "dimension," in a metaphorical way to represent different orders of reality, so that theological claims come to supplement scientific ones. The trouble is, as Pannenberg notes, that the scientist is not compelled to accept these extra claims (*TPS*, 75–76). Rather, the common ground must be the key to the relationship, and that is where contingency comes in.

Contingency is central to the biblical understanding of God, since "new and unforeseen events take place constantly that are experienced as the work of almighty God" (*TTN*, 76). This understanding is essential for prayer to be meaningful. This is, of course, a historical understanding of contingency, and it implies the lack of determination of the present by the past (*TTN*, 116n11). This is not the same as quantum indeterminacy, Pannenberg asserts, though it bears similarities to it. For example, there might be statistical patterns in historical events, rather than strict determinacy.

The biblical view also recognizes regularity but as dependent on the contingent will of God, and thus not in the sense in which natural laws have come to be regarded as immutable and admitting of no exceptions. The only contingency in classical physics is that at the beginning. In quantum physics there is in contrast ontological indeterminacy, and outcomes of measurements can only be described in probability terms. Another feature of physics is its revisability—our current laws are only approximations and need to be revised when new observations are made. Both these points are taken up by John Polkinghorne, though given the latter point he finds it more profitable to build his metaphysical position on the unpredictability of chaotic systems (even though these would be classically deterministic) rather than quantum indeterminacies (see later).[49]

Pannenberg repudiates the "God of the gaps," the idea of finding gaps in the scientific account of natural processes. He would thus identify with theologians such as Bonhoeffer[50] and Christian scientists such as Coulson[51] in this respect. In the modern debate Pannenberg would separate himself from the Intelligent Design movement. This is welcome both theologically and scientifically. Science has a habit of filling gaps as new discoveries are made, forcing God ever more out of the picture, as Pannenberg recognizes and as we saw in chapter 3. Scientific answers should be sought for scientific questions, and there is no reason to think science is incapable of finding answers to present unknowns. Theologically Pannenberg recognizes that God must be the Creator of the whole world process.

But contingency is manifest in many natural processes—quantum physics, macroscopic turbulent motion, mutations driving evolution: "The total process of natural events presents itself again as a mesh of contingency and regularities" (*TTN*, 78).

Interestingly Pannenberg draws on Carl Friedrich von Weizsäcker as did Bonhoeffer in his prison letters. From the 1954 edition of *Zum Weltbild der Physik*, he gleans the insight of "the inexhaustibility of reality" to individual inquiry (*TTN*, 79). A final "theory of everything" in modern parlance is probably unattainable, and science will continue to be characterized by the interplay between contingency and regularity.

The contingency of occurrences is in accord with the biblical view, but what about the regularities? Pannenberg argues that only if the laws of nature too are contingent will the biblical view be confirmed. He does not, however, want to pursue that question scientifically, but from the point of view of reflection on the whole of reality, for which the God hypothesis might make most sense—though in the scientific discussion the anthropic fine-tunings are predicated on the contingency of the laws.

Pannenberg notes that there is contingency at the beginning even of the sequence of regularities, but wants to go further. The key to the biblical understanding is that all reality is history—that is, historical actions of God. History is experienced as "a series of ever-new occurrences, which despite many similarities are unforeseen." God's faithfulness gives meaning and connection between contingent events, as God is faithful to his promises—even though these get transformed over time, are fulfilled in unexpected ways, or, ultimately, in the future. Pannenberg speculates as to whether it is even possible for there to be any unity in history apart from theology. And in science it is God's faithfulness that is expressed in the uniformity of natural laws (*ST*, 2:72).

Here Pannenberg brings in his characteristic insights from eschatology. New events throw light on earlier ones, and the whole will be given meaning in the ultimate future. Creation must then be seen from its end. However, that future is not determined; creation is not directed entelechially toward it. That would contradict the idea of contingency. The theory of evolution fits this perspective nicely, involving chance as it does.

Pannenberg goes on to ask whether nature can be included in the total reality as history. Again drawing on Weizsäcker, he notes the importance of irreversibility and unrepeatability in nature. The apparent repeatability—the recurring seasons, revolving stars, and so on—vanishes over larger timescales. And here we have a tension with the notion of laws of nature, which are predicated upon repeatability, though an exception is the second law of thermodynamics.

Again drawing on Weizsäcker (*TTN*, 90)—and this is actually quite old material now in this context (Pannenberg's original article came out in 1970; the book of collected essays dates from 1993), considering the advances made by cosmologists—Pannenberg discusses the big bang theory. This seemingly required an "absolute miracle" at the beginning, even though there is a regular naturalness about its subsequent evolution and further contingency in the way density variations here and there give rise to galaxies as the universe expands. He also makes the point, which seems to recur much more recently in Paul Davies, that the laws of physics do not exist in an ideal Platonic realm, but only exist once the universe itself exists and has embarked on its expansion.[52] Pannenberg notes (*TTN*, 106–8) that laws are of the form "If A then B." There will be a first A, on the big bang model at any rate, and he speculates that subsequent "A to B" causal links occur following the first B's "latching" onto the first A. This is similar to gestalt psychology's account of perception. Natural law is thus not eternal but dependent on time. Moreover, our existence is dependent on a host of seemingly fortuitous events, not least from the origin of life through the evolutionary process via innumerable mutations, which were exceptions to the general rule of being unhelpful in making creatures fit to survive and flourish. In *Systematic Theology* (2:71) Pannenberg argues that we would be talking about a "God of the gaps" if we confined contingency to particular branches of physics—quantum theory—since history teaches that gaps tend to get filled. While Polkinghorne, for example, sees the indeterminacy of quantum theory as ontological and not epistemological, Pannenberg makes the point that the *whole* of nature is contingent and therefore we are not simply dealing with gaps.

Against Bondi and the steady-state theory, Pannenberg takes issue with the assumption of uniformity (in fact Bondi calls this the "perfect cosmological principle" in his book *Cosmology*[53]) by extrapolation from present experience, because present experience includes the second law of thermodynamics and does *not* give constancy in time. Also, postulating the new origination of matter goes against the law of conservation of mass, which is experimentally confirmed, and which we have no other reason to doubt—even if the hypothesis puts mass creation below the measurable threshold.

Pannenberg also considers oscillating models of expansion and contraction, which, he says, are propounded, even though they have no empirical evidence, in order to retain an unlimited past and future for the universe. Indeed it would appear that there is quite a bit of ideological motivation at work in some of these theories. Oscillating theories are entirely speculative but do not need the creation of new matter. Pannenberg asks, "Should a theological interest in the finiteness and irreversible historicity of the world also become involved?" (*TTN*, 95). Pannenberg argues that the present-day prejudice is against theological motivations, so the big bang really only does survive because of the empirical evidence. A similar debate today surrounds the more recent "God or multiverse" debate.[54] As we have already seen, Pannenberg would be the bold theologian putting his head above the parapet in siding with certain scientific theories on theological grounds, just as atheistic grounds have motivated other theories in the recent past.

Pannenberg states, "When natural science, in seeking laws and especially the origin of the present world with its forms and laws, comes upon contingent conditions and events, it opens up nature in such a way that the Christian can discover the expression of the creative act of God" (*TTN*, 98). In contrast, other possible models of the universe are not in accord with the biblical view of creation by God, for example, "a world order that has not come into existence but is eternally without change, perhaps in the sense of the ancient cosmos conceived in accordance with the model of the revolution of the stars, is opposed to the idea of creation." Similarly, "the deistic conception, according to which God indeed has brought forth the world but then withdrawn from it, produces a similar negative result, because the perfection of the divine action has effected the existence of a perfect world machine that runs completely by itself" (*TTN*, 99).

As we saw in chapter 3, Bonhoeffer thought that an infinite world, as conceived by Nicholas of Cusa, is self-subsisting and therefore God is no longer necessary. Interestingly, some modern cosmologists and physicists, including Martin Rees[55] and Leonard Susskind,[56] see a multiverse (the way an infinite universe is now conceived) as a substitute for God. Peter Bussey argues that it is being used causally as a God substitute.[57]

Pannenberg, who like Bonhoeffer has read Weizsäcker on the subject, regards an infinite world as "a marginal possibility for the Christian theology of creation" (*TTN*, 100), for such a world could still be subject to change, and theological eschatology could apply. When he was writing, Pannenberg thought the evidence firmly in favor of a finite age for the universe, and that is still very likely on the scientific evidence, though the very tiniest fraction of a second from the origin takes us into territory where we do not know what laws of physics to apply, and there must therefore remain some uncertainty as to whether an actual singularity is attained. While Polkinghorne is skeptical about multiverses, he does not see an infinitely old universe as presenting problems: what is important for Christian doctrine is the ontological origin, not the temporal beginning, of the universe.[58] We have seen that Pannenberg agrees that God's creative activity is not confined to the beginning. Perhaps another bold step, if one were to pursue Pannenberg's program in the Lakatosian fashion advocated by Hefner and Murphy, would be to make a prediction that multiverse theories would in the end prove a fruitless diversion in physics.

Pannenberg considers inertia in *Toward a Theology of Nature* (109) as well as in *Systematic Theology* (vol. 2), where we have already encountered it. The problem posed by the discovery that bodies continue in their own condition unless acted on from outside was that this removed the need for God's sustaining the process. Interestingly, Murphy notes that some historians have seen the concept of inertia in Newton's "hard core" as reflecting his Calvinist theology.[59] Nevertheless, I am inclined to agree with Pannenberg that inertia poses a problem and that the newer realization of the contingency of all natural occurrences essentially solves it. The uniformity given by inertia can then be seen as an expression of the faithfulness of God (unlike for Descartes, where it was a sign of his unchangeability). This faithfulness, as seen by the Israelites in his maintenance of their election in history, is in fact the ground for the development of any uniformity in laws of nature at all. It explains why contingent events have the tendency to "latch" (see above) into regularly repeated forms of process.

Pannenberg notes (*TTN*, 111–12) that it is only with humans that history becomes meaningful, as theologically events are connected and unified, and only with humans that extrahuman nature takes on meaning and the unity of its contingent processes through natural law is understood.

Finally, he concludes that the incompatibility of knowledge of nature with the idea of God is groundless, although clearly "faith in God has to be gained in other areas of life than that of scientific knowledge." However, "the significance of the idea of God for a connected understanding of nature is just as clear" as this (*TTN*, 112–13). He writes, "The connection between the contingency of occurrences and of persevering form, whether of material figures or of regular forms of process, can be interpreted on the basis of the contingency of divine action in the sense of the Israelite-Christian experience of God because God alone remains one and the same in the contingent sequence of all occurrences" (*TTN*, 113). This production of a connection "has the stamp of a personal power, not of a mere structure of laws. In this way—and perhaps only in this way—does the unity of occurrences with the preservation of their contingency become understandable" (*TTN*, 113).

In commenting on Pannenberg's engagement with the natural sciences, and in particular his analysis of contingency, Philip Hefner remarks that Pannenberg intends that theology add something to the story that science tells. This is in accord with Pannenberg's view that theology is itself a science, as we have discussed earlier. In the case of contingency, this something extra is the knowledge that "the contingency of events is rooted in a source of that contingency, namely, the action of God."[60] Hefner argues that Pannenberg's discussion of field theory, to which we now turn, has a similar intention. As we have seen, Murphy also thinks Pannenberg's theology open to such "additions," though of a more particular kind, and we have seen other possibilities for Pannenberg along the way, such as the rejection of multiverses.

## *Field Theory*

One of the concepts that Pannenberg borrows very boldly from the natural sciences for his theology is that of "field." It is probably the most controversial aspect of his theology from the point of view of scientists, or indeed theologians trained in science.

Forces were originally conceived as acting through material bodies, essentially having contact with each other. Newton's gravitational force acted at a distance, and Newton saw this as a form of God's activity analogous to the action of the soul on the body. This brought criticism from physicists of later generations, who wanted forces to be associated with bodies, an antitheological turn for Pannenberg since God is not a body (*ST*, 2:80). However, the field concept (as developed from Faraday onward) allows for the nonmaterial to act at a distance since fields permeate the whole of space; indeed, for Faraday the field became primary and bodies were particular concentrations of field lines. This is better for theology both from the nonmaterial aspect and because it was antireductionist, the whole now acting on the parts. Pannenberg links the dynamic work of the Holy Spirit to this concept of field, and theologically God grounds the whole of creation. Here, Hefner remarks, Pannenberg's addition to scientific knowledge is the insight that the "largest field of all, which embraces all of reality, is God."[61]

A problem with the older view of Aristotle, which was taken into medieval theology, was that movement required a cause—hence, the argument to a prime mover. With Newton's laws it was seen that movement required no cause. Modern field theories give a different take, however.

Sidestepping potential criticism, Pannenberg writes, "The principle differences between the ways of describing reality in physics and in theology prohibit us from offering a direct theological interpretation of the field theories of physics" (*ST*, 2:83). Differences in use of the concept in the two disciplines are to be expected (*ST*, 2:84). Pannenberg is thus well aware of possible equivocal uses of language (*TTN*, 39). He also makes another point here *against* making too close an identity between the Spirit's activity and fields, namely that scientific models are only approximations (*TTN*, 40; *ST*, 2:83), conceived from the point of view of the regularities of natural law. These caveats should be borne in mind when we consider the criticism of Pannenberg's position by Polkinghorne, who, as we have seen, would agree that the laws are approximations.

The role of the Spirit in creation is different from that of the Son. The Son's self-distinction from the Father gives rise to the distinction between creatures. The Spirit "relates to the link and movement which connects the creatures to one another and to God." In the Trinity the Spirit mediates the fellowship of the Father and the Son, and similarly in creation the Spirit is the dynamic in creaturely relations, though in the latter having to overcome the rifts and collisions between creatures.

I am not sure that Pannenberg's positing the metaphysical use by the Stoics of the divine *pneuma* as direct predecessor of the modern field concept helps his case, however. That is a bit like the ancient element "quintessence" equating in some sense to the modern concept of a generalized "dark energy," when in reality the name has simply been appropriated for something that has a very specialized meaning, even while remaining mysterious.

A significant critic of Pannenberg's position here is John Polkinghorne,[62] who finds Pannenberg's discussion of fields "baffling."[63] If the language were simply metaphorical, denoting "extended relationality," that would be acceptable, but it would still be regrettable to use a term with a precise meaning in physics. This strikes me as rather like Pannenberg's criticism of Heim (see above) being applied to himself. However, Polkinghorne's criticisms would of course be blunted if we took account of Pannenberg's own qualifications of his use of the field concept as cited earlier. Charles Gutenson suggests that Pannenberg would help if he made it clear that he uses fields as a model or conceptual tool,[64] though it seems to me that he comes quite close to that.

The important thing about fields in physics is that they are not "spiritual," says Polkinghorne. Physical fields such as Maxwell's electromagnetic field carry energy and momentum, which are "inertial properties that function in the same way for the field as they do for particles of matter." So Pannenberg's claim that the Stoic concept of *pneuma* as "subtle matter" has been theologically improved by the modern, more spiritual concept, since no ether is required, does not make sense in terms of physics (*TTN*, 39–40).

For Polkinghorne, rightly I think, the activity of the Spirit is better discerned in chaotic systems, where unpredictability is inherent, and complexity theory, wherein one sees the spontaneous generation of order out of disorder. Polkinghorne postulates (boldly in his turn) a kind of pattern-forming causality, which he terms "active information," supplementing the usual energetic causality of physics.[65] Complex systems also exhibit irreversibility, an important theme for Pannenberg, for whom another major theme, as we have just seen, is the contingency of the world and its history.

Pannenberg is also right to see whole-part interaction, which is again a feature of complex systems, and also of quantum systems, as important. The notion of emergence, and the associated concept of downward causation, is an important theme in the modern science-religion dialogue.[66] This relates well to what Pannenberg says elsewhere about the inadequacy of reductionism (see above and *TPS*, 129ff.). It also relates to his discussion of biological evolution, in which he sees organisms (supremely humans) as transcending their bodily constitution through interaction with their environment (*TTN*, 133ff.). As Hefner notes, Pannenberg also associates these latter empirical phenomena with the creative activity of the Spirit.[67]

However, when discussing fields Pannenberg seems tied to classical concepts. As Polkinghorne points out, classical fields are local in the sense that values at different points of space can be varied independently. It is quantum fields that are truly integrated into a whole, and these unite particle and wave pictures of reality and display contingent behavior.

Regarding contingency, Polkinghorne points out that even on the mechanical picture of nature, where Pannenberg finds the persistence of a state not in need of God and therefore problematic, the laws themselves are contingent (I think Pannenberg would agree with that, from what I have said above). Contingency in the sense of openness to the future, however, is more characteristic of modern physics, both quantum theory and classical chaos theory (as discussed above).

## *Conclusion*

Pannenberg is one of very few theologians of major stature to have engaged rigorously with the natural sciences. This is reflected in his doctrine of creation, even though God's revelation in history remains his first and most important concern. There is thus a tension in his thought between these concerns to see God as the all-determining reality and therefore the God of creation and the natural sciences, and the God who has revealed himself in Jesus Christ in history.

It is possible to see this tension being resolved through Pannenberg's arguments that history and theology are themselves sciences, and thus open to the same criteria for evaluation as other sciences, and that God's creative activity is continuing in history. Pannenberg is thus critical of Barth, who makes theology immune from criticism. He believes that natural theology and the traditional arguments for God's existence still have a role to play, and that theological claims should be evaluated on the basis of their ability to unify and explain the evidence at hand.

Regarding history, the resurrection of Jesus Christ is the key. This event is open to rational scrutiny that confirms its occurrence. It will, however, remain probable rather than certain until the end of history, which the resurrection anticipates. Then the unity and meaning of all of reality will be fully realized.

Pannenberg presents an orthodox doctrine of creation as owing to the totally free decision of God to make a reality distinct from himself. This creation is, moreover, an act of the Triune God. The self-distinction of the Son from the Father is the basis of the distinction between creature and Creator, and the Spirit gives life to the creatures and is responsible for their participation in the life of God.

God's preservation of the world is important, as is his ongoing creative activity; creation does not occur just at the beginning. Preserving or sustaining has been problematic since Newton's work on inertia, but is more easily accommodated by modern physics with its emphasis on contingency. Indeed Pannenberg sees contingency, now very much a part of the scientific picture, as totally consonant with the biblical picture of God's activity. The correlative of contingency is regularity, in which Pannenberg sees God's faithfulness reflected. Pannenberg sees the big bang theory and the contingency of anthropic fine-tuning as more favoring the theological interpretation of creation being God's activity than alternatives such as the steady state or an infinite universe (and therefore the presently popular multiverse).

Pannenberg proposes a model of the activity of the Holy Spirit based on the physics of field theory. This enables him to think of God acting throughout space. Polkinghorne agrees with Pannenberg's aim—to utilize physical concepts to speak of divine action—though Polkinghorne sees chaotic systems with their inherent unpredictability as more suitable loci for this.

I believe Pannenberg has very much to offer the modern science-religion debate. In arguing for the scientific nature of theology and for theological claims to be evaluated by similar criteria to those for the natural sciences, he implies that we can utilize appropriate tools from the philosophy of science. As we have seen, Hefner and Murphy have proposed a Lakatosian methodology; I would prefer Bayesian confirmation theory. Either way we can use the evidence at hand, such as that for the resurrection from history and the anthropic fine-tuning data from science, in applying such methodologies. Particularly interesting to see will be whether Pannenberg's approach to theology as a science really does provide "additions" to the other sciences. That is his boldest and, I believe, most controversial move.

# Thomas Torrance
## Natural Theology Redefined

THE LATE Thomas Forsyth Torrance is widely regarded, according to his biographer Alister McGrath,[1] as the most significant British theologian of the twentieth century. He was born on August 13, 1913, at Chengdu in Sichuan Province, China, of Scottish missionary parents. He studied philosophy, classics, and theology at Edinburgh, and in Basel under Karl Barth, who deeply impressed him from the first.

After lecturing at Auburn Theological Seminary during 1938–1939, Torrance was approached by Princeton University regarding a new post to establish the teaching of religion on an "objective basis" and "in a dispassionate way" in the arts faculty. Torrance explained that he would be interested in teaching theology *as a science*, which meant that "we think not as we choose to think, but as we are compelled to think in accordance with the nature of the object," a view that is often repeated in his mature writings, as we shall see. He found to his surprise that they still offered him the job, despite his distaste for "dispassionate" approaches to theology and his statement that he could not guarantee that no one would be converted through the lectures![2]

However, it was June 1939 and war was looming. On a walk through the grounds of the Institute for Advanced Study with Emil Brunner when future plans were discussed, Torrance decided at once to return to Scotland, where he felt he belonged. He became an army chaplain and was a parish minister until 1950, when he was called to become professor of church history at the University of Edinburgh. A couple of years later he became professor of Christian dogmatics at Edinburgh, a position he held from 1952 until his retirement in 1979. A very difficult personal decision was to turn down an invitation that came in 1961 to succeed Barth at Basel.

Torrance has written a significant book about Barth,[3] which he begins by stating, "Karl Barth was unquestionably the greatest theologian that has appeared for several hundred years. His stature rivalled that of the real giants of the Church." He names Luther, Calvin, Athanasius, and Augustine, and furthermore he quotes Pope Paul as saying that Barth was the greatest theologian since St. Thomas Aquinas, which means he is ranked above Duns Scotus—a truly amazing tribute to a Protestant from a Roman Catholic pontiff. All this is high praise indeed, and consequently it comes as no surprise that Torrance's own theology is so deeply indebted to Barth.

Torrance was in large measure responsible for the reception of Barth in Britain. One key element of this was his supervising the English translation of *Church Dogmatics*. Torrance chose Geoffrey Bromiley (both for his mastery of the German language and of theology) as his coeditor for this project, and the two would supervise the larger team of translators. This project was begun in 1952 and completed in 1977 following the retranslation of volume I/1, originally translated by G. T. Thomson in 1936.

Torrance also founded, with J. K. S. Reid, the *Scottish Journal of Theology*, which was used to promote Barthian ideas to the English-speaking theological world—though without adopting an uncritical stance.

Torrance once challenged a student who had written an essay propounding the "moral influence" theory of the atonement with a reproduction of Grünewald's famous Isenheim altarpiece. He explained that it was "FOR our sakes, to save us from sin and judgment" that Christ endured the amount of suffering so graphically portrayed.[4] It can surely be no accident that this is the painting that also meant a great deal to Barth—indeed, Barth retained a picture of John the Baptist, from a panel of this painting, with his elongated finger pointing to Christ and with the Latin words "He must increase, I must decrease" on his desk.

Torrance's attitude to natural theology—namely his outright rejection of it outside main theological discourse—is clearly a Barthian theme. However, he differs significantly from Barth in two ways: (1) by reappropriating natural theology from within dogmatic theology proper, and (2) by his willingness to engage with the natural sciences.

In this chapter, Torrance's position on natural theology is examined in the context of his much wider engagement with the natural sciences, beginning with his focus on the scientific character of theology itself. It is maintained that the charge of irrationality made by W. W. Bartley against Barth[5] can also be sustained against Torrance. Despite this, however, Torrance offers a number of opportunities for a more conventional kind of natural theology that, it is argued, would restore rationality to his theological enterprise.

## *Theology as a Science*

Torrance's most significant work of theology is his *Theological Science*,[6] which is dedicated to his friend Sir Bernard Lovell, the well-known radio astronomer.

The main point made in this book, and many times elsewhere, is that the object of theology is knowledge of God, and that theology is *scientific* because it relates to its object in the way appropriate to that object. As noted by Ted Peters, and as we saw in chapter 4, this is in contrast to Pannenberg, who believes that theology will be scientific if it makes hypotheses and seeks to confirm them.[7] For Torrance, the reality that confronts us determines our knowledge of it and the way we must rationally approach it, both in theology and in the natural sciences (see also *God and Rationality*,[8] 9ff.; *The Ground and Grammar of Theology*,[9] 8). We let that reality disclose itself to us; it determines our thinking. We do not start with *a priori* conceptions and work our way toward the object. This epistemological stance commits theology, says Torrance, to dialogue with the other sciences and with philosophy (see also *Divine and Contingent* Order,[10] 1–2).

It seems to me that English is lacking a helpful linguistic nuance that is available in German. The term *Wissenschaft* is used of any academic discipline whereas *Naturwissenschaft* is specifically natural science. Indeed Torrance notes that "a scientific theology is what the Germans call *wissenschaftlich*, that is, a rigorous, disciplined, methodical and organized knowledge" (*TS*, 116). As such, scientific theology is truth seeking and dedicated to the rejection of error, and it must operate with the appropriate methods of verification. The German usage would to some degree vitiate Thomas Langford's point that Torrance's concept of "theological 'science' is so different from every other 'science' that only the most formal characteristics of similarity remain."[11] Langford notes that use of the term "science" does, however, have an apologetic value, and it helpfully contrasts Torrance with theologians who had thought being "scientific" implied being "antidogmatic."

Torrance insists (*TS*, 11) that, because theology is scientific in this way, "knowledge of God is a *rational event*." Faith is rational because it is "the behaviour of the reason in accordance with the nature of its divine Object" (*TS*, 33n2). And this is what makes theology distrustful of all speculative or *a priori* thought. However, what Torrance takes insufficient account of is that in science no observation or experiment is uninterpreted, but as human observers we approach the data with preconceptions. This is the theory-laden nature of observations, which is now widely recognized, even if neglected in earlier periods of the philosophy of science. To take a biblical example, Samuel at first interpreted the voice he heard in the night as that of Eli (1 Sam 3:2–9). That is how he understood it from within his own interpretative framework; he needed Eli to tell him that it was the voice of God. A further criticism, made by Langford, is that this makes faith too intellectualist and ignores the affective aspects of faith—probably a road Torrance does not want to go down in view of his criticism of Schleiermacher.[12]

Torrance notes that theology differs from the natural sciences because the latter can engage in controlled observation and experiment. Theology must rely on the grace of God and "allow him to determine the form our knowledge will take" (*TS*, 38). He makes a similar point in *God and Rationality*: "The object of theological knowledge is not some manipulable thing that can be subjected to experimental tests of our own contriving to force the truth out of it" (7).

Torrance writes, "Christian theology arises out of the actual knowledge of God given in and with concrete happening in space and time"

(*TS*, 26). It is concerned with "the fact of God's self-revelation," and he is concerned here of course fundamentally with the incarnation: "He [Christ] is the concrete embodiment of knowledge of God within our humanity" (*TS*, 45). That is where we have to begin. The obvious problem with this view is, how do we know this is a fact—unless, that is, we bring to bear tools of rational discourse from elsewhere; history, the sciences, and so on? As Peters notes, the existence of the object of theology, namely God, "is just what is in dispute in the modern world." Peters remarks that "to presuppose its truth and then contend that this produces knowledge seems to beg the question"—and this is his accusation against Barth and his followers such as Torrance.[13] W. W. Bartley would concur: he argues that much Protestant theology is inherently irrational.[14] We return to Bartley's criticism shortly since it is even more cogent when Torrance's approach to natural theology is taken into account.

Torrance's argument is that we are given a "profound inner experience through the Spirit of the objective reality" (*TS*, 28). That, of course, does indeed raise the same kinds of problems as it did for Barth. How do we know the experience is of a genuine reality? Torrance himself recognizes the temptation to confuse the experience with the fact, the feeling with the reality, and this he sees as the problem with much neo-Protestantism. He is surely right that the objective reality is prior, but for us it must come through our experience, and that experience must be rationally evaluated—in terms of Scripture and tradition and the discernment of the community, of course—but also with the tools of rationality common to all human discourse. This is not to give some kind of hubristic autonomy to humans, independent of God, for we can at the same time recognize, with Pannenberg and others, that all knowledge of God comes from him, and our gifts of (created) rationality stem from his grace toward us.

Torrance criticizes Schleiermacher's doctrine of the "feeling of absolute dependence," which Schleiermacher equates to "being in relation to God,"[15] as not responding to the reality of God but coming to God by way of his own subjective ideas. The mistake of modern neo-Protestantism, then, according to Torrance, is to ascribe sovereignty to inward religious experience. Echoing Bonhoeffer (whether subconsciously or not), the "God" of neo-Protestantism is the God "who meets and satisfies the needs and answers the questions of 'modern man'" (*TS*, 82). As we saw in chapter 3, Bonhoeffer too criticizes this conception of God, and complains that the "world come of age" has moved beyond this, not just in science, but in many other areas. The answer is to challenge man at his point of strength, rather than weakness, and to place Christ at the center and not the periphery of life.[16]

Torrance acknowledges that the Word comes to us "through creaturely objectivities and creaturely speech," that is, through the "inescapable media of rational communication and personal relationship" (*TS*, 39). When he speaks of theological statements, he has to acknowledge that they are, of course, "always our statements" (*TS*, 175). There is, therefore, an inevitable circularity in Torrance's thought at this point. Human experience, and thus anthropology, is coming back in as the basis for our knowledge of God, because that is the only way we can receive God's self-revelation.

Torrance insists that we must "put all our doctrines to the severest test by probing into the ground of their objectivity." We can begin "only with the fact of the prior knowledge of God and then seek to test and clarify it" (*TS*, 44). Again, the question is, how does that testing occur without the use of commonly held rational tools?

In many ways, Torrance expresses an orthodox Trinitarian and Christocentric faith that I share. Disagreement arises, first, from Torrance's insistence that there is no natural theology, in the traditional sense of utilizing only knowledge available to us all as human beings, which might provide a starting point for the exploration of these specifically Christian insights; and, second, from his ambivalent attitude toward the question of justification of Christian beliefs.

## *Theology and the Natural Sciences*

Torrance says that, because theology is itself scientific, and because theology is not concerned with "God in the abstract"—the God of the philosophers—but God as Creator, theology must interest itself in what the sciences have to say:

> Thus arising out of the very heart of theology there is an unquenchable interest in the scientific understanding of creaturely being, and for the whole fabric of worldly existence as the medium within which God has placed man and constituted him what he is in relation to Himself. . . . Theology cannot be true to itself unless it makes room for and indeed fosters knowledge of creaturely being in accordance with its creaturely and contingent nature. (*TS*, 57)

The traffic between science and theology is in fact two-way for Torrance. He writes, "Dialogue can also help natural science, in view of its recurring temptation to resolve contingence away, to remain faithful to the nature of contingent reality . . . and therefore to remain open to the realization that the universe is what it is as a whole because of its implication in a transcendent rational order, in God" (*DCO*, 84).[17]

Torrance commends Bacon's attitude to nature which "was not only allied to a deep Christian faith, but was a product of his understanding of the relation between God and creation" (*TS*, 73). In the realms of both grace and nature, "man is summoned to activity, but in the realm of nature his task is to regain and exercise the dominion over the world he lost at the fall, and which belongs to him by the bounty of the Maker." This view anticipates the more recent study by Peter Harrison, though it represents a different emphasis from that which Torrance expresses elsewhere on the contingency of the world as motivating scientific endeavor.[18]

Torrance goes on: "It is at God's command that he must occupy the earth, and it is in obedience to that command that he must engage in natural science, the aim of which is to extend the empire of man and enhance his power over nature" (*TS*, 73–74). That Baconian view now needs the corrective that man has overexploited the planet as if it existed solely for humans, ignoring the value of nature in its own right, and that anthropogenic climate change is causing damage to the environment.[19] Torrance also notes that Bacon rejected natural theology, a point we return to below.

Kant, in contrast to Bacon, believed that knowledge resulted from the nature of the questions put to the world rather than the nature of the object. This led to the dangerous temptation "to discount the thing in itself as a mythological projection" (*TS*, 89). It also had the result that "instead of reading laws of nature out of nature, man ultimately reads them into nature through the processes and structures of his active reason" (*GGT*, 26). In science, this kind of thinking inhibited progress by limiting the kinds of results that could be accepted. The barrier was broken by Einstein, Bohr, and others in physics. Torrance notes that "Einstein had to wrestle for some twenty years with Newtonian and Kantian conceptions of space and time before the theory of relativity could be formulated" (*TS*, 92). Similarly, quantum theory forced changes in the subjective structures of the mind.

Here, Torrance's view has definite merit. It does seem that general relativity, with its curved space-time, shows that Kant was wrong in supposing that Euclidean geometry is an *a priori* intuition of the human mind by which we necessarily construct our experience.[20] And quantum theory's counterintuitive experimental results also imply that the real world is impinging on the mind, rather than the mind imposing its own constructs on the world. However, it is also true that reality discloses itself in relation to the questions we ask of it, not just in "brute" fashion without our investigating it. In addition, quantum theory possesses the strange feature that we do not passively observe a system but bring about a particular state by doing the experiment.

We noted the "theory-ladenness" of experiment above. Torrance does seem to recognize this after all in referring to "the all-important interdependence of theory and experiment" (*DCO*, 40). Indeed Torrance's recognition of the importance of the breakdown of a wide variety of "dualities"—subject-object, space-time, matter-energy, nature-supernature—and their replacement by a more intimate unity and interconnectedness, for theology is seen as of major significance by Christopher Kaiser.[21] The key to this breakdown is the incarnation, and specifically the *homoousion* of the Son with the Father (e.g., *GGT*, 160–61), as also commented on by Tapio Luoma.[22] Theology thus seeks to recognize God as self-revealing object, taking account of our human limitations and mental structures but without reducing itself to them. My feeling is still, however, that Torrance gives too little attention to the "questioning" aspect in justifying theological claims. Alister McGrath makes the rather strong claim that humans are "active constructors of their own perceptual realities, not passive recipients of information."[23] However, he is surely right that the process of interpretation of revelation, however revelation is conceived but certainly including revelation in nature, "includes human perception, which simply cannot be eliminated for the sake of theological convenience."[24] I would want to emphasize the importance of rational evaluation of revelation claims on an objective basis, as well as the fact that revelational experiences (like all experiences) are conditioned by human modes of perception.

Related to this, Torrance does, however, note a big difference between science and theology, to which we have already alluded here. We can force nature to reveal itself to us by violence—so we are presumably "asking questions" of nature at least, after all. On the other hand, we cannot force God to reveal himself: when he does so it is through sheer grace. Indeed, "it is we who are questioned before Him . . . so that our knowledge of Him arises and increases out of obedient conformity to Him and the way He takes with us in revealing Himself to us" (*TS*, 97). But again, surely here too there is a subtle interplay. Can we not look at the world, at our own selves, and at what is claimed to be special revelation, and ask whether this points to God? "Seek and ye shall find," said Jesus, not "do nothing and I will reveal myself to you."

## *Natural Theology*

For Torrance, as for Barth, Jesus Christ is central, and the cross of Christ the "foundation and criterion of authentically Christian theology" (as McGrath summarizes it[25]). Torrance's concern is "the damage done by natural theology to Christology and the proclamation of the gospel." He writes, "There is no hidden God, no *Deus Absconditus*, no God behind the back of the Lord Jesus, but only the one Lord God who became incarnate in him."[26] Torrance is indeed pointing to the problem here: can we find a place for natural theology without as Christians compromising the absolute centrality of Christ? We shall see Torrance's answer in due course, and the further problems it poses.

As we have seen, Torrance argues that we cannot coerce God but must to listen to him, and that is what "theological science" does.

Natural science starts from the opposite direction, and subjects reality to rigorous and controlled experimentation. This, he says, "calls in question all natural theology." By examining nature as nature, in its sheer contingency, "we can only find nature and the limits of nature" (*TS*, 101). However, surely this fails to do justice to the role of theory in both science and theology. The natural sciences are not only concerned with experimenting on nature, but also with formulating and evaluating theories about nature. Similarly, we can "put questions," seek explanatory breadth from, or otherwise analyze or evaluate, theological claims, rather than simply accept them *de facto*. And that process would surely form at least part of what makes theology "scientific."

Natural science and theological science exhibit complementarity in a way similar to quantum systems: they offer two mutually exclusive ways of probing reality (*TS*, 102). As John Polkinghorne remarks, the notion of complementarity in quantum theory "provides no licence for the easy export of the notion to other disciplines."[27] Torrance's view here sounds similar to Stephen Jay Gould's notion of "non-overlapping magisteria" (NOMA). The natural sciences and theology should not tread on each other's toes and are indeed complementary. Nevertheless, there are areas of overlap when it comes to broader questions such as the metaphysical underpinnings of science and the use of commonly shared rational modes of inquiry—especially perhaps when the latter are applied to the data of faith. Torrance may agree in part with this, though he would very strongly circumscribe the latter point.

Torrance thinks it follows from this nonintersecting complementarity that "natural theology may offer the greatest hindrance to natural science and to scientific theology alike." Theologically, "justification by Grace alone not only sets aside natural goodness, but sets aside natural theology, for both belong to the natural life of the natural man" (*TS*, 102). Reinforcing the point, he writes:

> Natural science starts from premises that do not include God, and moves in an opposite direction to theology in accordance with the nature of its subject-matter, but "natural theology" starts from the same premises and the same phenomena as natural science and seeks to move toward God, and in so

> doing brings itself into conflict with natural science and with pure theology, proving to be a source of confusion to both if not an actual obstacle in their progress. (*TS*, 103)

Natural theology must be excised from scientific theology as a "sort of 'foreign body,'" writes Torrance (*TS*, 103), if scientific theology is to be consistent with its commitment to respond to God as he has actually revealed himself—although, as we shall see, it does come back in again in a different guise.

Torrance notes that Francis Bacon rejected natural theology because it mixed final and physical causes and produced false theology and false science (*TS*, 74). He replaced it with natural science to the benefit of both theology and science. Torrance concedes, however, that Bacon did allow a negative function to natural theology, that of confuting atheism (*TS*, 74n4) so that—even if "at best"—it may help "to remove the grounds of rational doubt" (*TS*, 103). Torrance then quotes, with apparent approval, Geddes MacGregor: "It is being more and more widely admitted that a disposition towards theistic belief is a necessary antecedent to the presentation of a reasoned case for theism" (*TS*, 104n1). It does not seem a very big step to me to go from "removing the grounds for rational doubt" to "providing positive evidence for theistic belief," which would be consistent with the Geddes quotation, even if not what Torrance himself intends.

Another significant concession Torrance makes is to assert that there is, after all, a natural knowledge of God! This is "a 'sense of the presence of God' which all men have unless they obstruct or suffocate it." The problem is, however, that "this natural knowledge cannot be worked up into a 'natural theology.'" Even in our disobedience to God, there is a form of knowledge, but "what scientific theology rejects is the attempt to treat 'natural theology' as a foundation upon which positive theology can be made to rest" (*TS*, 104).

Despite his explicit rejection of it (though with the above concessions), it seems to me that elsewhere Torrance offers opportunities for natural theology (in the sense of *praeambulum fidei*). Thus, in *Divine and Contingent Order*, Torrance notes that "the rational unity of the cosmos, spanning celestial as well as terrestrial spheres" (3), is a fundamental assumption of the natural sciences. It grounds our confidence that when we investigate the world it will disclose its rational order to us. But that rational order itself is grounded in the rationality of God; indeed, it is through the Son as divine agent that the world receives its rational order and unity (*DCO*, 24; *GGT*, 52–53). It seems to me that this can very easily be translated into an argument of "natural theology" as John Polkinghorne, Roger Trigg,[28] and others do. The rational unity of the cosmos is the datum and prerequisite of science, and thus cannot be explained by science. The fact that theism can explain it is not just a comforting thought for the believer, but may be offered to the unbeliever by way of "inference to the best explanation." This move of natural theology fulfils an apologetic task that goes beyond that of "removing the grounds of rational doubt," which Torrance concedes (*TS*, 103).

Torrance also notes, "There is a profound harmony between the rationality of the human understanding and the rationality of the universe" (*DCO*, 129). This is indeed surprising on any purely naturalistic view. For example, it is hard to see how this might be explained on the basis of "survival value," which is our endowment from the evolutionary process. How come we can understand the universe, from the smallest particle to the furthest reaches of space-time? Polkinghorne makes a similar point and uses it as a natural theological argument.[29] Although Polkinghorne commends Torrance's approach to natural theology, and resembles Torrance in recognizing it as "an integral part of the whole theological quest for understanding and by no means an isolable or merely preliminary sub-department of it,"[30] it seems to me, nevertheless, that there is quite a distance between Torrance's view and Polkinghorne's. Polkinghorne defines natural theology as "the attempt to learn something of God from the exercise of reason and the inspection of the world—in other words, from reflection on general experience rather than from specific revelatory events."[31]

Torrance's own place for natural theology is emphatically not in the apologetic realm, though he does have a place for it after all. In *Space, Time and Incarnation* (*STI*),[32] Torrance makes a significant connection between the place of geometry in physics and the place of natural theology relative to what he variously calls "positive" theology, "scientific" theology, or simply "dogmatics" (for the last, see *GGT*, 15, 49ff.). He writes:

> The fact that four-dimensional geometries are not just other ideal possibilities inventively thought up . . . but involve a profound correlation between abstract conceptual systems and physical processes, has considerable epistemological implications for theological as well as natural science. Since this gets rid of the old dualisms between material existence and absolute space and time, or between nature and supernature, it is no longer possible to operate scientifically with a separation between natural theology and revealed theology any more than between geometry and physics. In physics, this means that geometry cannot be pursued as an axiomatic deductive science detached from actual knowledge of physical processes or be developed as an independent science antecedent to physics, but must be pursued in indissoluble unity with physics. (*STI*, 69)

He goes on:

> In theology, this means that natural theology cannot be undertaken apart from actual knowledge of the living God as a prior conceptual system on its own. . . . Rather must it be undertaken in an integrated unity with positive theology in which it plays an indispensable part in our inquiry and understanding of God. In this fusion "natural" theology will suffer a dimensional change and will be made *natural* to the proper subject-matter of theology. No longer extrinsic but intrinsic to actual knowledge of God, it will function as a sort of "theological geometry" within it, in which we are concerned to articulate the inner material logic of knowledge of God as it is mediated within the organized field of space-time. (*STI*, 69–70)

This is an ingenious move, and Torrance repeats the idea elsewhere (e.g., in some detail in *GGT*, chap. 4, "The Transformation of

Natural Theology," where he cites Barth in support of a natural theology included within revealed theology). It is certainly an imaginative use of an analogy from physics, the subsuming of geometry within physics brought about by general relativity. In fact, Torrance argues strongly that a relational view of space-time and matter, as given by general relativity, is what theology needs to articulate its doctrines of incarnation and resurrection (indeed, he cites John Philoponos of Alexandria as developing such a notion; e.g., *STI*, 25; *GGT*, 54, 60ff.). He claims that the older conception of space as a receptacle, whether finite or infinite, and the dualism between space and matter, posed real problems for theology and were the source of theological error and confusion for the medieval church and Lutherans alike. Newton's view of space as an infinite receptacle was also deeply problematic, especially since space became "aligned with the infinity of God" (*STI*, 37–38; *GGT*, 24).

What is not clear to me is whether general relativity really helps here at all. It is certainly true that general relativity gives a more accurate account than did Newtonianism of the space-time structure of the universe in which God makes his self-disclosure to us, and for that reason is important to Torrance's concept of natural theology.[33] However, on any account the incarnation and resurrection are miraculous events, even if they are, as Torrance would say, "in accordance with the nature of the Creator of the universe" and therefore, in a sense, not alien to the universe.

The main point for the present is whether the relationality between space-time and matter helps much, and that seems questionable. The picture advocated by Torrance of God "making room for himself" in the incarnation, and relating that to the stretching of space, is again perhaps useful as an analogy but cannot really express what it means for God to enter our space and time while remaining transcendent, as the orthodoxy of the Fathers requires. If one adds to this philosophical doubts as to whether absolute space and time have really been done away with by Einstein, then Torrance's case is further weakened. We can measure absolute time from the big-bang singularity, and absolute space can be defined in terms of the microwave background radiation.[34] Tapio Luoma casts yet further doubt by noting that relationality for Torrance means the theological concept of relation to God rather than, as traditionally conceived, the physical relation between existents within the universe: the vertical axis is the determining factor, rather than the horizontal, to use Torrance's own terms.[35]

So it seems to me that Torrance's invocation of the importation of geometry into physics is of limited value in these areas, but also, like the principle of complementarity in quantum physics, a notion that does not easily translate to other realms of inquiry. As an analogy, it does not justify the incorporation of natural theology into positive theology to the exclusion of a traditional natural theology, which utilizes publicly available evidence and the common tools of rationality, and which may be useful as an apologetic.

Torrance's use of analogies in general is worth commenting on in slightly more detail at this point. We noted earlier the analogy between quantum complementarity and the mutual exclusivity between natural science and theology as ways of exploring the world, and now we meet that between the import of geometry into physics and the import of natural theology into dogmatic theology. Elsewhere, Torrance points to other analogies such as that supposedly between the notion of particles "containing each other" and perichoresis in the Trinity (*GTT*, 175–76). He suggested this analogy to Fritjof Capra, who found himself needing analogies from Eastern religions to express physical insights. In this case, Torrance's correcting Capra by suggesting an analogy from the Christian tradition is somewhat unfortunate: Capra was working with what is a now-defunct idea in physics, the "bootstrap theory," which has been overtaken by the theory of quarks as the fundamental building blocks of matter.[36]

A more significant analogy drawn by Torrance is that between created light and the uncreated Light that God is (*GGT*, 129–30; *Christian Theology and Scientific Culture*,[37] 75ff.). The invariance of the speed of light, which follows from Maxwell's equations, is an analogy for the constancy of God, his faithfulness toward his creation. Jesus Christ is the Light of the World and the "divine *Constant* in space and time." Torrance writes, "As the uncreated Light of God incarnate, he constitutes the ultimate pledge given to us by God of the unfaltering consistency and the steadfastness of his love toward us."

If this is stretching an analogy rather far, Torrance would seem to concur. He states:

> Owing to the vast unlikeness between created and uncreated light, any analogies drawn from the former are to be regarded as more helpful to ourselves than as appropriate to the latter. Analogies, comparisons or illustrations taken from created realities are properly employed, not to bring our understanding of the Creator within the measure of our creaturely conceptions, but rather to aid the expression and communication of what we apprehend apart from them. (*CTSC*, 75–76)

It seems to me that both the complementarity analogy and that between the correct loci of geometry and natural theology are equally between very unlike categories. These analogies serve to illustrate beliefs that already pertain on other grounds, and in that sense aid Torrance's communication of those beliefs. There is no compulsion on others to accept them.

The most important analogy of all is that which, like Barth, Torrance is at pains to reject. There is, for Torrance, no *analogia entis* or *intrinsic* likeness between Creator and creation. This "seeks to ground and justify theological statements in a movement that rises by analogical reasoning from the creaturely and the contingent to the Divine, positing unlikeness as well as likeness between man and God, thus giving it resilience as well as resistance in face of critical and sceptical attacks" (*TS*, 189). While the identifying of similarities and differences was helpful, the procedure is nevertheless wrong because "our theological statements are true only in reference, direct or indirect, to Jesus Christ" (*TS*, 190). *Analogia entis* is working in the wrong direction.

Torrance argues that "our theological statements are true through a content in the Truth which God alone gives them by His Grace" (*TS*, 195). The *analogia fidei*, in contrast to *analogia entis*, refers everything back to God, and this results in a radical questioning of the forms through which that reference is made. The Chalcedonian definition similarly uses both statements of likeness and of unlikeness "to express in an analogical manner the Christian understanding of the relation between the divine and human natures in Christ." This has been "remarkably fertile in illuminating many other theological questions, far beyond the expectations of the Chalcedonian fathers." Nevertheless, the analogical form is "not in itself important—it is in fact expendable." Torrance argues, at least consistently, that "what does matter is Christ Himself, truly divine and truly human in His one incarnate Person" (*TS*, 245). However, the use of analogies in doing anything other than elucidate truth already accepted on the basis of prior commitment to what is taken as revealed is fully acknowledged.

Torrance's approach, both to the way he conceives theology as being scientific and in the way he appropriates natural theology into dogmatic theology, does seem to lay him open to the charge of irrationality that W. W. Bartley so eloquently leveled against Barth. Of course, there has been considerable debate about what makes theories rational in science, particularly since the rise of logical positivism in the early part of the twentieth century, including the reactions to that approach. Highly influential has been Karl Popper, who, as we saw in chapter 4, prioritized the criterion of falsification for scientific theories. According to Bartley, Protestant theology is irrational because it makes itself immune from criticism by starting from an unfalsifiable premise and arguing in a circle, denying that it has to conform to standards of rationality adopted by other sciences. This seems precisely to match Torrance's approach to theology.

Bartley argues that his initial charge is obviated because in fact science is open to it as well—theology could counter with the "*tu quoque*" argument. No theory is truly falsifiable or rationally justified, because there is no ultimate commonly agreed standard of rationality or set of premises to adjudicate on whether a theory has been falsified. This would let theology off the hook, had Bartley not gone on to formulate his own nonjustificational approach, dubbed "pancritical rationalism." The pancritical rationalist refuses to commit to any position and holds everything open to criticism—not just any theory that he adopts, but also the criteria for rationality and the premises from which he starts.

I believe that Bartley goes rather too far. Yes, our beliefs, including our most cherished theological beliefs, should be open to criticism, but that ought not to preclude our being committed to them—otherwise, intellectual and moral paralysis set in. Commitment ought not to constitute a retreat so much as a launching pad for further inquiry. As Michael Polanyi puts it in *Personal Knowledge*, "The principal purpose of this book is to achieve a frame of mind in which I may hold firmly to what I believe to be true, even though I know that it may conceivably be false."[38] Torrance makes much appeal to Polanyi, but fails to see the point here about acknowledging that one's belief might be false; Bartley rightly criticizes Barth and his followers for this, but in turn fails to see that commitment is a necessary virtue.

My view is that the notion of "inference to the best explanation" is more helpful than either Torrance's or Bartley's position. Hypotheses are evaluated according to the degree to which they provide the best explanation of the evidence in question, on commonly held criteria such as simplicity and elegance. While not without its difficulties (the notion of simplicity, for example, is notoriously hard to pin down), this procedure seems in principle to be able to hold both scientific and metaphysical hypotheses as explanatory and rational. This procedure can be formalized utilizing Bayesian confirmation theory, again the subject of debate, but also in principle a tool for ensuring logical consistency in the judging of hypotheses and for evaluating their relative probabilities. Although I allude to Bayesianism a number of times in this book, the reader is referred to the literature for a full consideration of the issues.[39] The point here is that Torrance can rightly be charged with irrationality. However, as we have already begun to see, he offers insights for a natural theology of the traditional kind, which would restore rationality to theology and make the claim that theology is "scientific" rather more plausible.

All this is not to say, however, that there is not a place for natural theology within scientific theology *as well as* providing a *praeambulum fidei*. Clearly, the Christian faith has much to say about the universe as God's creation, and Torrance says much which is directly relevant to that, though perhaps what Torrance does should be called "theology of nature" rather than "natural theology." It is also important for theology to be aware of what science says about the physical universe that God has created, since, as Torrance avers, God has chosen to reveal himself within this particular space-time framework. It is also true, as Torrance interprets Athanasius saying, that "knowledge of God and knowledge of the world share the same ultimate foundations in the *Logos*, or Rationality, of God the Creator" (*GGT*, 77). However, it is my contention that natural theology, understood broadly as bringing commonly held criteria of rationality (which must be rooted in the divine rationality) to bear on publicly accessible knowledge, is useful at all levels in theology, not least for evaluating whether what is claimed to be revelation is indeed revelation. As noted above, it should also be acknowledged that no knowledge of God, whether natural or revealed, is given apart from God's will to give it—all of which makes the distinction between natural and revealed knowledge somewhat fuzzy. Old Testament scholar James Barr makes much the same point,[40] as does theologian Brian Hebblethwaite, who writes:

> The old distinction between natural and revealed theology, between what reason can achieve and what required revelation, breaks down. . . . Reason and revelation cannot be treated as different sources of knowledge. On the contrary, revelation-claims, despite being channelled through particular historical traditions, are part of the data upon which reason has to operate.[41]

Even Torrance recognizes the need for historical inquiry, though his attitude is qualified: it is not the publicly available evidence it is for Pannenberg but requires "an act of discernment beyond common historical observation" and a mode of rationality appropriate to the divine activity within it (*TS*, 325). It is at least arguable that Torrance's reservations regarding what it can achieve (which seem to stem from Ernst Troeltsch's principle of analogy) can be overcome if such inquiry is carried out without naturalistic presuppositions and allowed the freedom to evaluate the data on its merits.

Reference has been made above to the rational unity of the cosmos as providing an opportunity that Torrance offers for natural theology despite himself. There are other such opportunities, as we shall see.

But, to close this section, here is a quotation from Torrance's scientific hero, Albert Einstein, that comes as close to an argument of natural theology as could possibly be expected of someone whose God was that of Spinoza. It is an argument based on the rational order of the universe, to boot:

> You find it surprising that I think of the comprehensibility of the world (in so far as we are entitled to speak of such a world) as a miracle or an eternal mystery. But surely, *a priori*, one should expect the world to be chaotic, not to be grasped by thought in any way. One might (indeed one *should*) expect that the world evidence itself as lawful only so far as we grasp it in an orderly fashion. This would be a sort of order like the alphabetical order of words in a language. On the other hand, the kind of order created, for example, by Newton's gravitational theory is of a very different character. Even if the axioms of the theory are posited by man, the success of such a procedure supposes in the objective world a high degree of order which we are in no way entitled to expect *a priori*. Therein lies the "miracle" which becomes more and more evident as our knowledge develops.[42]

This sounds remarkably like the kind of argument employed by Polkinghorne, and Torrance was certainly aware of Einstein's appeal to the "miracle" of *Verständlichkeit* (e.g., *DCO*, 35). Einstein added, even more revealingly as Jaki puts it:

> And here is the weak point of positivists and of professional atheists, who feel happy because they think that they have not only pre-empted the world of the divine, but also of the miraculous. Curiously, we have to be resigned to recognizing the "miracle" without having any legitimate way of getting any further. I have to add the last point explicitly, lest you think that, weakened by age, I have fallen into the hands of priests.[43]

## Contingency

The idea of the contingency of the created universe is very important to Torrance (as we saw that it is for Pannenberg) and is the subject of *Divine and Contingent Order*, as well as being alluded to frequently elsewhere in his writings. Torrance thinks that the recognition of the true conception of nature as the totally free creation of God and as totally distinct from him, and given its own contingent rationality, came with the Reformation—when it was seen that nature could only be known through observation and interpretation of the creaturely processes.

Torrance sees Newton's system, via Laplace, as leading to a mechanical, deterministic universe (*DCO*, 8ff.; *GGT*, 70). Surprisingly, according to Torrance, this is reversed by Einstein's revolution in physics. This means abandoning the idealized Euclidean framework, whereupon "the universe is found to manifest itself, not as a closed deterministic system, but as a continuous open system of contingent realities and events with an inherent unifying order" (*DCO*, 11). Einstein thus gives us "a finite but unbounded universe with open, dynamic structures grounded in a depth of objectivity and intelligibility which commands and transcends our comprehension." Torrance is right insofar as a finite but unbounded universe is a possibility in general relativity, but it is not demanded by general relativity: an infinite cosmos is equally possible. His statement that "we have no option but to think of the universe as finite" (*GGT*, 101) is unwarranted, at least on the basis of general relativity alone (certain philosophical arguments might lead in that direction). Moreover, general relativity is still deterministic—whether the universe is finite and unbounded or infinite as in classical physics. Indeed, the block universe interpretation favored by Chris Isham is completely deterministic.[44]

Einstein was not happy, as Torrance correctly relates, with the Copenhagen interpretation of quantum theory. But according to Torrance this was not because he wanted a deterministic system but because he felt that science should be realistic, and quantum theory was abandoning realism (he says that Pauli corrected Born on this point [*DCO*, 44;

*GGT*, 113]). "To accuse Einstein of determinism is to make the serious mistake of confusing his concept of 'field laws' with that of 'mechanical laws'" (*DCO*, 13). Torrance does not mention Pannenberg, but he seems to be taking a similar line here in seeing the field concept as offering contingency or indeterminacy, which it doesn't, at least classically. Curiously Torrance seems to read things in the opposite way to that which one would naturally assume. The statistical approach of quantum theory leads us in a deterministic direction, and is operating still within the framework of classical mechanics, according to Torrance. At first, Torrance seems mistakenly to view the problem in quantum mechanics as to do with the observer's interfering with the system in making a measurement, and so the connections in nature remain deterministic (*DCO*, 14). But then he acknowledges the departure from classical mechanics and determinism after all in terms of wave/particle dualism and particle decay at one moment rather than another. The conclusion remains firm: "'Indeterminacy' appears to have objective ground in natural law" (*DCO*, 14).

Still, "the most significant move away from determinism, however, is found in Einstein's development of the dynamic field of space-time, in which time itself enters with space into the structure of the field. . . ." Sadly, this statement is quite false and betrays a misunderstanding of the science.[45] John Polkinghorne is a critic of Torrance for that particular error,[46] and for the idea that fields in some way constitute "a source of openness to the future." Citing Torrance (*DCO*, 77–78), that Einstein thereby introduced "non-causal connections," Polkinghorne notes that quite the opposite was the case. Indeed, noncausality was the actual reason for Einstein's opposition to quantum theory.[47]

Luoma also notes the problems with Torrance's interpretation of Einstein, making the point that it led Torrance to neglect quantum physics, a field that several other scholars have deemed very fruitful for relations between theology and science.[48] Polkinghorne makes a similar point, remarking that Torrance's heroes, Maxwell and Einstein, are "the last of the ancients rather than the first of the moderns."[49] It would seem that probability and chance are anathema to Torrance, and not how he wants to interpret indeterminacy and contingency, possibly because he sees chance as "arbitrary" (e.g., *GGT*, 58). McMullin makes the additional point that the order of Newton's universe was "in key respects a radically contingent one" because there was "no particular reason for the distribution of matter and motion in the universe." Einstein's universe is actually *more* deterministic than Newton's since the interconnectivity of matter, energy, and space-time serves strongly to *limit* contingency.[50]

Torrance is on much better ground when, referring to the universe, he argues that "the open character and endless spontaneity and surprise of its natural order" is "ultimately explicable only from beyond itself in the infinite differentiality of divine rationality and its inexhaustible source of possibility" (*DCO*, 23). Later, he says that the universe "constitutes an essentially *open* system with an ontological and intelligible reference beyond its own limits" (*DCO*, 36). Again, he says that the universe is characterized "not by closed rigid structures but by open-ordered structures, not by necessary truths of reason but by contingent truths which defy complete mathematical formalization" (*DCO*, 38). Torrance reinforces this point elsewhere when he rightly draws on Gödel's theorem, which represents the final nail in the coffin for any program of scientific reductionism (e.g., *TS*, 255).

Torrance notes with approval Michael Polanyi's claim "that all meaning lies in the higher levels of reality that are not reducible to the laws by which the ultimate particulars of the universe are controlled" (*DCO*, 20).[51] Levels of reality are open upward but not reducible downward, and do not contain their sufficient reason within themselves for their own contingent order. The universe as a whole is like this, as an open system and an intelligible whole requiring a sufficient reason beyond itself.

It is true, of course, that a number of prominent scientists espouse a reductionist metaphysics. Notable examples are Richard Dawkins, Peter Atkins, and Francis Crick. Dawkins claims that human beings are "survival machines—robot vehicles blindly programmed to preserve the selfish molecules known as genes."[52] Atkins believes that "at the deepest level, decisions are adjustments of the dispositions of atoms in the molecules inside large numbers of cells in the brain."[53] And Crick boldly announces, "The Astonishing Hypothesis is that 'You,' your joys and your sorrows, your memories and your ambitions, your sense of personal identity and free will, are in fact no more than the behavior of a vast assembly of nerve cells and their associated molecules."[54]

The counterclaim that higher scientific levels of description are not reducible to lower ones (as biology to chemistry to physics to mathematics, and supremely the reduction of mental phenomena to physical) is thus controversial. There is, nevertheless, a growing recognition that this is the case, and a growing literature on reductionism and its inverse, the phenomenon of emergence.[55] Thus it is seen that, as higher levels of complex organization of matter arise in the evolutionary process, new phenomena come into play requiring new concepts and laws to describe them, which are not reducible to the concepts and laws pertaining at the lower levels. While lower-level laws are not broken and of course do affect the higher levels, the concept of downward causation also comes into play, whereby a complex whole exercises causality and influences its parts. Of course, there are debates about whether reduction is an epistemological problem or is ontologically impossible, but perhaps in the end one should accord at least equal reality and causal efficacy to higher-level phenomena such as consciousness as to those at the lowest levels—atoms and molecules. The emphasis on the study of whole systems, rather than simply individual parts, is increasingly seen as necessary in science, and is required for the study of subjects as diverse as quantum physics (especially the phenomenon of quantum entanglement) and systems biology.[56] The relevance of emergence for theology, as well as its philosophical and scientific status, is very much a live issue for all these disciplines and for their interrelationship.

There are two ways in which the insight of Gödel's theorem strengthens the antireductionist, pro-emergentist case, as we saw in chapter 3. Remember, the theorem states that any mathematical system as complicated as (or more complicated than) arithmetic is incomplete, or else it is inconsistent. Indeed, human mathematicians can produce true statements that lie outside the scope of deduction within such a mathematical system. It follows from Gödel's theorem that physics is incomplete. There will be statements in physics that are true but unprovable. As Paul Davies puts it, "No rational system can be proved both consistent and complete. There will always remain some openness, some element of mystery, something unexplained."[57] And Stephen

Hawking has now changed his mind about the possibility of a physical theory of everything precisely because Gödel's theorem rules this out.[58]

The second help that Gödel's theorem gives is to counter the notion, propagated by proponents of "strong artificial intelligence," that the human mind is no more than a sophisticated digital computer. As Roger Penrose argues, computers operate algorithmically, that is, according to sets of rules that operate in the same way as the logical rules whereby mathematical theorems are derived by logical deduction from axioms.[59] There are therefore truths that a human being can know, but that a computer can never derive.

Torrance himself rightly sees the thermodynamics of nonequilibrium or open systems—especially as in the work of Ilya Prigogine on dissipative systems far from equilibrium—as a locus for the emergence of extra factors in which temporal becoming has a place. Prigogine's work shows how a new kind of organization spontaneously emerges out of apparently random fluctuations far from a state of equilibrium (*DCO*, 55; *GGT*, 12, 141). The importance of the work of Prigogine and his collaborators at the University of Brussels has been noted by others working at the science-religion interface, such as Polkinghorne.[60]

Torrance mistakenly thinks that the openness of the universe to the transcendent (which I believe he is correct about) is somehow dependent on its finitude. Torrance seems quite confused here about the meaning of these terms, in particular erroneously equating two quite distinct meanings of the word "open." He thinks that the universe being finite and unbounded implies that "instead of being closed from above down, the universe is to be regarded as open from below upward. The finite universe certainly has frontiers, but they are not frontiers at which it is turned back to be imprisoned in itself so much as frontiers where it is open indefinitely to what is beyond" (*DCO*, 79). However, these are technical terms. In fact, a finite universe is "closed" in general relativity, meaning that it has positive curvature. The fact that it is finite and unbounded means that it is something like the surface of a sphere in two dimensions. It might indeed be regarded as curving back on itself! An "open" universe, in contrast, has negative curvature and is spatially infinite. The two-dimensional analogy is a saddle shape. There is also the middle case of a universe with zero curvature ("flat"), which is open and infinite, and whose two-dimensional analogy is a flat plane surface. Colin Weightman has made a similar point regarding the nomenclature, drawing on a review of *Divine and Contingent Order* by Robert J. Russell.[61]

Torrance also points to the contingency of the initial conditions of the universe at the big bang: "In a finite and expanding universe in which *time* enters as an essential ingredient into its empirical reality, the questions why there are initial conditions rather than not, and why the initial conditions are what they are, cannot be avoided." Initial conditions are "boundary conditions that bear upon an intelligible ground beyond themselves, and that require this meta-empirical reference." Here again, I agree with what Torrance says, and this is precisely what is addressed in the anthropic fine-tuning discussion (the specialness of the laws of nature, especially through the constants of physics, is also addressed). This has, of course, been discussed elsewhere in much more detail, as I have pointed out elsewhere in this book.[62] Since it takes us beyond the scope of this chapter, I say no more here except to agree with Torrance in noting a certain tendency for physics, in trying to deal with the problem (especially through theories of everything or multiverses), to move back toward necessitarian ideas of the universe, thus abandoning its roots in experiment and observation that came from its inheritance in Christian theology. This may not be good for science.

Torrance notes that the contingent order of the universe derives not from science itself but from Christian theology. Nevertheless, he says, science must be pursued *acsi deus non daretur*. Science must assume principles that come from outside itself, such as contingency and order, in order to function. He says that the "intelligibility of the created universe, its intrinsic orderliness, consistency, and reliability, is the ground of our confidence in scientific inquiry" (*DCO*, 40), and, of course, for Torrance as indeed for this writer, that intelligibility is endowed by God. Given that, it is undoubtedly true that science has its autonomous domain and there is no reason to suppose that scientific questions should not receive scientific answers. To assume otherwise is the mistake of the Intelligent Design movement, which exhibits a flawed God-of-the-gaps theology. All this is in line with Bonhoeffer's view of the autonomy of the world and that we must live in the world *etsi deus non daretur* and in science do without the "working hypothesis" called "God."[63] On the other hand, it seems that natural theology can use those principles which come from outside science to point to their source in God, in the manner of *praeambula fidei*.

## Conclusion

Thomas Torrance is one of very few theologians of major stature to engage in dialogue with the natural sciences. Torrance argues that such engagement is significant for theology, which has to understand the space-time structures in which God has chosen to reveal himself, and it is important for the sciences to be reminded of the God-given lawful and contingent nature of the universe on which their pursuit depends.

It is very significant that Torrance's approach respects the integrity of both science and orthodox theology.[64] Following Francis Bacon, he commends the pursuit of science as a God-given task, not only to regain dominion over the world, but precisely because it is in the space-time realm disclosed by science that God has placed mankind and in which he reveals himself.

Torrance's most important contribution is his assertion that theology is scientific. In theology, we let the reality that confronts us determine our knowledge of it. We do not come to it with *a priori* conceptions. Theology is emphatically not a science because it shares the methods or tools of the natural sciences but only because it treats its object in the way appropriate to it.

What Torrance says about treating the object appropriately is true, but yields a minimal resemblance between theological and natural science. Torrance is also correct that we cannot manipulate the object of theology as we can the natural world, through controlled observation and experiment. However, it seems to me that it is impossible to come to any subject area without prior conceptions. These may be altered in the encounter, and Torrance indeed seems to recognize the interplay of theory and experiment in science. Torrance is right to see Kant's *a priori* conception of Euclidean geometry as part of the structure of the mind as overthrown by Einstein's general relativity with its curved space-time.

The trouble is that, if pressed too strongly, the analogy leads to questions about how we discern the true nature of what is revealed in theology—the question of justification of religious belief. The use of tools of rational discourse common to all disciplines seems to me inescapable. The danger for Torrance is that too much weight might then be given to religious consciousness in theology (which is related to the structure of the human mind), and that is not a path Torrance wishes to tread. Nevertheless, the human mind seems adapted to understand the intricacies of natural law; why not to religious insight also? When Torrance *does* recognize the human dimension (theological statements are, after all, "our statements"), it seems he is led into self-contradiction or circularity. Anthropology also seems unavoidable!

A key question, if theology is a science, is whether its claims are testable. Torrance is ambivalent about this. On the one hand he asserts that theology, like the natural sciences, seeks truth and the rejection of error, and must operate with the appropriate tools of verification. All its doctrines must be put to the severest test. The problem here is that Torrance rejects all forms of argument of a "natural theological" kind and says that justification is by God himself through grace (he sets more store by historical inquiry, though is somewhat ambivalent about what this can achieve, too). While grace is essential, Torrance's position begs the question of why some are privileged to be accorded that grace and not others. That puzzle remains on any account, but what Torrance denies us is the ability to engage with the nonbeliever on the same turf, so to speak, from the same premises of rationality.

Being a disciple of Karl Barth, Torrance is, not surprisingly, hostile to natural theology as traditionally conceived. He sees it as a hindrance to theology and science. It is a mistake, he thinks, to argue to God from premises that exclude God. However, he concedes, with Bacon, that natural theology can have a negative function of removing the grounds for doubt.

What is anathema to Torrance is to use natural theology as a foundation on which to build positive theology. Instead, Torrance employs an ingenious analogy from science—namely, the incorporation of geometry into physics through general relativity—to make a similar claim for the incorporation of natural theology into positive "scientific" theology. Torrance is keen on general relativity anyway because he believes the more relational and antidualistic conception of space-time is more suited to theology's articulation of its doctrines of incarnation and resurrection. This is doubtful, and in any case an analogy from physics does not license the transfer to theology.

At first sight, Torrance's view seems to accord well with John Polkinghorne's, particularly as Polkinghorne commends Torrance for including natural theology within positive theology. However, in contrast to Torrance, Polkinghorne does see natural theology as using reason and general experience apart from revelation. Both Polkinghorne and I believe that natural theology on its own yields only a limited view of God and needs to be filled out in detail by the insights of revelation, especially in the historical sphere, but nevertheless it is a useful apologetic tool to get people thinking about that richer source of information about God. In addition, it has been argued here that, unless one is allowed to bring to bear tools of rational criticism and evaluation common to more general scientific discourse, theology as conceived by Torrance is open to the same charge of irrationality that W. W. Bartley leveled at Barth.

Interestingly, Torrance's own observations about science open up possibilities for a more traditional natural theology, despite his intentions. Thus, the rational order of the cosmos is a fundamental assumption of science, and its fundamental harmony with the rationality of the human mind is what makes science possible. These twin rationalities are grounded upon the rationality of God, according to Torrance. This is true, but the argument he avoids is to say that *unless* it is so, the "miracle" to which Torrance's hero Einstein points is left unexplained.

While Torrance is confused about which scientific theories are endowed with what degrees of contingency (and certain other scientific tenets), he is nevertheless absolutely right to stress the importance of the contingency of the universe in Christian doctrine. Because it is the free creation of God, the universe both exists contingently and exhibits contingent processes. This doctrine was of prime importance in sparking the scientific revolution, since contingency licenses and even necessitates the experimental method if we are to find out what the universe is actually like.

For Torrance, nature possesses an open character with endless spontaneity and surprise, a view that he well substantiates by appeal to Polanyi, to Prigogine and colleagues, and to Gödel's theorem. The universe as a whole, with all its intelligible contingencies, is thus open to its transcendent ground without which it cannot make sense of itself. That seems also to be usable in a positive way in traditional natural theology, even if it does not get one very far. It can certainly be argued that theism provides the best explanation both for why the universe is ordered in the first place *and* why it is not self-sufficient and self-explanatory, but open to truths that transcend any of our formalisms.

Torrance rightly points to the initial conditions at the singularity of the big bang as being contingent. Physics is up against limits or boundaries beyond which it cannot proceed. It seems to me that there are again opportunities for natural theology here, though the arguments need to be expressed very carefully and to take account of what physicists are attempting to do about the problem. The fact that the initial conditions seem to be what is required for an interesting universe conducive to life can be used to argue for divine design and purpose behind the universe.[65] The alternatives of either a physical "theory of everything" or a multiverse seem themselves to take us away from contingency to necessitarian modes of thinking—and Torrance is right here to point science back to its roots in Christian theology.

I have made a number of criticisms of Torrance's discussion of science and theology, and in particular what he has to say about natural theology. Torrance nevertheless remains a towering figure in theology, and a most significant contributor to the ongoing dialogue between Christian theology and the natural sciences—a justly acclaimed winner of the 1978 Templeton Prize.

# Alister McGrath
## Renewing Natural Theology

Alister McGrath is one of Britain's most prolific theologians, writing books on a broad spectrum of theological topics for professional theologians, theological students, and the laity and wider public.

McGrath started his academic career as a scientist before training in theology and being ordained in the Church of England. He spent much of his career at Wycliffe Hall, Oxford, where he became principal, before moving first to Harris Manchester College, Oxford, and finally to King's College, London. He was elected professor of historical theology at Oxford in 1999 and professor of theology and education at King's in 2008.

McGrath has returned to science in his most recent writings, and in particular to natural theology. His early background makes him very well equipped to do so, and he says that his becoming a mature theologian first has been essential before coming to this point.

McGrath was brought up in Belfast where the "troubles," the strife between Catholics and Protestants, formed the backdrop that, together with his interest in science and his political leanings toward Marxism, led him to atheism. However, during his first term at Oxford, he began to realize the flimsy intellectual foundations of atheism and that Christianity had much better intellectual credentials than he had formerly realized, so, as he puts it, "By the end of November 1971, I had made my decision: I turned my back on one faith, and embraced another"

(*Dawkins' God*,[1] 6). This background as well as his immense erudition in theology has enabled him effectively to critique the writings of Richard Dawkins. While his two books countering Dawkins (*Dawkins' God* and *The Dawkins Delusion*[2]) are undoubtedly excellent, and point to multiple flaws in Dawkins, I do have a certain reservation about McGrath's approach that will become clear as this chapter progresses. Indeed, his position on natural theology leaves him still exposed on one of Dawkins's most crucial points: the importance of evidence and theology's total lack of it. McGrath's position has been emerging in his trilogy, *A Scientific Theology* (*Nature*, *Reality*, and *Theory*),[3] a summarized form of which is to be found in *The Science of God*,[4] and becomes most apparent in *The Open Secret*.[5] It is further developed in his Gifford Lectures, published as *A Fine-Tuned Universe*.[6]

Besides the two books devoted to Dawkins, McGrath has an incisive and, to my mind, brilliant chapter on Dawkins in the interim volume *The Order of Things*.[7] Here, as in *DG*, McGrath cites Richard Swinburne's approach to the probability of God as much more carefully argued than Dawkins's "sloppy analysis" (*OT*, 34). While in both cases it is not clear whether McGrath endorses Swinburne's approach, and from his more general stance I think he does not, nevertheless in *OT* he does give coverage to another theme that is discussed later on, namely "inference [or abduction] to the best explanation" (*OT*, 36–41). In this case McGrath boldly states that "Christian apologists argue that the 'best explanation' of the world is that it is the handiwork of a creator God" (*OT*, 39). I totally agree with that statement, but the confusion comes in what McGrath says elsewhere about natural theology—namely, that it can only be done legitimately from within the framework of a full-blown Trinitarian Christian dogmatics. Yet in these pages in *OT* he makes no statement that you need to presuppose the Trinitarian God in order to draw this inference. Indeed, my concern about McGrath's approach is that which he himself cites C. S. Lewis as leveling against a scientific worldview that cannot explain its own success in the realm of explanation: "that it was, in effect, obliged to presuppose its conclusions" (*OT*, 40).

## *Preparing the Ground: McGrath's First Books on Science and Religion*

McGrath's first book on science and religion, coming after twenty years' concentration on theological research, is his *The Foundations of Dialogue in Science and Religion.*[8] McGrath's own approach, developed more fully in later books, begins to be seen here—for example, his indebtedness to Thomas Torrance, and his espousal, even in this first book on the subject, of "inference to the best explanation" (*FD*, 131–38).

His second book, *Science and Religion: An Introduction*,[9] is indeed just that: an introductory text. As such it is an excellent example of the genre and gives an introduction to many of the key topics in the science and religion dialogue. It is especially useful for those undertaking courses on science and religion who have little prior background in these disciplines. There is some repetition of material from the first book.

## *The Trilogy:* A Scientific Theology

McGrath's trilogy titled *A Scientific Theology*, with individual volumes called *Nature*, *Reality*, and *Theory* (*STN*, *STR*, and *STT*, respectively), is very much a development of Thomas Torrance's approach to a "scientific theology," which McGrath signaled in *Foundations*, and the first volume is dedicated to Torrance. Indeed McGrath describes it in his own words as "a sympathetic yet critical response to the imposing and stimulating contribution made to the dialogue between theology and the natural sciences by Torrance, widely regarded as the greatest British theologian of the twentieth century" (*STN*, 77). In particular he is concerned to develop what he believes is an authentically Christian natural theology, and he wants it to be a public theology, capable of interacting with other disciplines. The extent to which he achieves this is a subject of debate in this chapter. This theology is to be realist, as McGrath understands the natural sciences to be (*STN*, 71–77, though the notion of "critical realism" is developed more fully in the second volume).

The trilogy is essentially about theological method and is preparatory to further work on natural theology and, most importantly, an ambitious multivolume systematic theology. As for Torrance, theology is a science in its own right in the sense that it should adopt methods suitable to its object (*STN*, 190). As he frequently puts it, "Ontology determines epistemology." This is not so self-evident as it may seem, since it runs counter to Enlightenment views of the primacy of universal reason and the construction of reality by the human mind (see later for further discussion). McGrath carries out his task in the light of the sweep of intellectual history from the patristic and premodern eras, through the Enlightenment (which he sees as failing in its grandiose claims), to postmodernism—and he seems to accept, at least in part, something of the latter critique of modernism.

In this endeavor the natural sciences function for McGrath as an *ancilla theologiae* (*STN*, 7, 18–20), much as philosophy has in the past, and certainly not as in any way trumping theological methods. Where I am in full agreement with McGrath, and indeed where I find Barth and Torrance so impressive, is his commitment to Christian orthodoxy. He is right to see some approaches that give more unquestioning weight to the sciences, and correspondingly less to biblical and creedal statements, as veering away from orthodoxy (for example, process theology—see *STN*, 36–41). He insists too that he is concerned only with the interface between the natural sciences and Christian theology, not "religions."

One important line of argument in *Nature* is that the concept of nature is a socially constructed notion. For McGrath the concept is "profoundly ambivalent" (*STN*, 86). Certainly nature has been interpreted in different ways. McGrath points to Wordsworth, who could draw moral lessons from nature, and Tennyson, who famously saw nature as "red in tooth and claw" (*STN*, 84–85). However, as I discuss later, it seems to me that not all interpretations are equal and some may be more rationally justified than others. Indeed, my view, as frequently reiterated in this book, is that nature—understood as the physical universe and the subject matter of the natural sciences—is more rationally interpreted as creation than, for example, as a fortuitously fine-tuned member of a self-subsisting suite of universes. My difference from McGrath here is in wanting to argue that case from a traditional natural theological perspective, rather than to base it on the prior assumption of a comprehensive Trinitarian understanding of God. But that discussion must wait till later.

McGrath notes that with the rise of modern science in the seventeenth century, nature began to be seen as mechanistic, describable mathematically, and increasingly the Newtonian universe came to be seen, though not by Newton himself, as having an autonomy of its own (e.g., *STN*, 247). He also notes the rise of the "two books" tradition—that of God's word in Scripture, which was the object of theological study, and that of God's works in nature, which was studied by the sciences. This was a major motivating force for the new kind of natural theology that started to develop during this period (*STN*, 104, 245). However, the idea of nature as a book is also important for the postmodern deconstruction of nature. As for all texts, must this not "be open to multiple readings on the part of its autonomous readers" (*STN*, 104)? Again, I challenge this point later on; after all, postmodernism is not a philosophy with which most scientists feel at all happy. The fact that nature is always approached from within a preexisting conceptual framework is certainly something we ought to be aware of when drawing inferences from it, either scientific or theological. While this constrains such endeavors, it does not make them a complete free-for-all.

McGrath notes that Derrida and Barthes believe that the meaning of a text is "a free construction of the human mind" so that, for the book of nature, "suggestions such as these radically undermine the plausibility of world-views which hold that 'nature' is an objective reality" (*STN*, 121). But that would only be the case if Derrida's and Barthes's "suggestions" had any merit or plausibility in themselves. And, of course, like so many postmodern claims, they do not. Indeed, to insist that they did would contradict postmodernism with its idea that no claims at all have universal validity.

In an interesting section on naturalism, McGrath notes Willem Drees's question: "Can one offer—independently from a naturalist view—a justification for holding a naturalist view?" (*STN*, 131). Drees, a naturalist according to McGrath, says this is impossible, which undermines the naturalist position. Naturalism is, in the end, merely a *blik*, simply a socially mediated outlook (R. M. Hare's term: such an outlook is without cognitive content, being unverifiable and unfalsifiable; see McGrath, *STN*, 132). However, there is a potential *tu quoque* here. Surely a fully christologically orthodox and Trinitarian Christian view also demands justification?

Essentially accepting the critique of nature as socially constructed, McGrath goes on to replace it by the notion of creation. He notes that Pannenberg thinks that "nature" is in fact the better concept to handle (*STN*, 135). This term is in public discourse and therefore keeps theology within that discourse. Moreover, the concept of "creation" might be the result of a "theology of nature." Notwithstanding McGrath's criticisms, I am inclined to agree with Pannenberg about this. Indeed, as will become apparent, I think that McGrath himself is really engaged in a "theology of nature" rather than "natural theology."

McGrath makes the interesting point that the doctrine of *creatio ex nihilo* is a distinctively Christian understanding. The Old Testament can be understood instead as the divine subjugation of the forces of chaos; Jewish tradition was divided on the matter, only adopting it definitively in the fifteenth century (*STN*, 156). As he later enunciates, the doctrine of creation in the New Testament, now understood christologically in terms of the *Logos*, forms an important apologetic (*STN*, 159, 260–62), notably in Paul's Areopagus address. Indeed, confusingly, he argues that Paul "presupposes some form of natural theology," using the idea of creation as a *praeparatio evangelica* (*STN*, 261), and he sees Athanasius doing much the same in *de Incarnatione Verbi* (*STN*, 253). Following a quotation from Athanasius, McGrath remarks, "The divine *logos* is embedded within the structures of the created order—including human rationality—thus allowing humanity to gain at least some access to a knowledge of God through creation, as an anticipation and preparation for the recognition of the *logos* incarnate in Christ" (*STN*, 253). This is precisely how I see natural theology myself.

McGrath notes the development of the doctrine in the patristic period up to its rigorous defense by Bonaventure and Aquinas. He affirms that the heart of the doctrine is about ontological origin over temporal beginnings—"if, indeed, it is concerned at all—with issues of chronology" (*STN*, 166). McGrath makes an important point here that is overlooked by scientists, such as Stephen Hawking, who think that a cosmological model which avoids a temporal origin negates the need for God; creationists, who insist that the Bible says the world was made in a literal six days; and more sophisticated philosophers such as William Lane Craig, who use the big bang theory to support the "kalam cosmological argument." It is also about God not being constrained by the properties of preexistent matter as in alternative cosmologies of the ancient world (e.g., that of Plato in the *Timaeus*).

McGrath believes that emphasis on the doctrine of creation does not lead to deism because, for Nicene orthodoxy, it is bound up with christology and the doctrine of redemption. God did not just "light the blue touch paper" at the beginning and retire as it were, but sustains and upholds the universe in being—and this he does through the Son, by whom the redemption and reordering of the world comes to be (*STN*, 181–91).

For McGrath, the Christian doctrine of creation implies a correspondence between the works of God and the being of God (which sounds like an *analogia entis*), and it has the following implication for natural theology: "The fundamental assumption of a responsible natural theology, to which we shall return later in this project, is that we are authorized by Scripture to seek a partial disclosure of the glory of God through the works of God in creation. God is rendered in and through creation" (*STN*, 193). He alludes to Polkinghorne's point that the rationality of the universe explored by science, and its correspondence with that of the human mind, can be explained by the rationality of the Creator (*STN*, 194–95). So, too, can the "ordering of creation" (*STN*, 218–32) be understood on the basis of the Christian doctrine of creation. As always, following Barth and Torrance, McGrath only goes from God to nature and does not use an argument from the order of nature to God being behind nature (though see later regarding what he says about "inference to the best explanation"). We return below to McGrath's important discussion of how this relates to the concept of *analogia entis*.

With regard to whether natural theology based on reason rather than revelation can form a *praeparatio evangelica*—which, as we saw in chapter 2, would seem to be a reasonable interpretation of St. Paul on the Areopagus—James Keating makes an interesting comment in his generally very positive review of the trilogy.[10] Although McGrath's work is ecumenical in its appeal and intention, there is nevertheless a sharp difference between Catholic and Reformed theology at this point. A greater confidence in reason in Catholic theology enables a more harmonious way of relating scientific and theological views of nature, with the former "a God-given first step"[11] toward an understanding completed by the acceptance of revelation. Moreover, "this confidence in reason lies behind the Catholic habit of constructing philosophical demonstrations for God's existence to move the intellect of those without faith and thereby prepare the way for the Word of God revealed in Christ. McGrath, in contrast, sees the proofs as an example of philosophical overreach and as theologically suspect."[12] Curiously, I am closer to the Catholic position here, despite an otherwise similar theological stance to McGrath. I agree with Keating, however, that "the primary culprit is a foundationalism which implies the existence of a set of universal truths with epistemic primacy over revelation."[13] As will be apparent, I think there are ways of rationally adjudicating between metaphysical worldviews—not in the manner of proof or of the kind of foundationalism criticized by McGrath, but by appeal to commonly accepted criteria of rationality. Then, even if revelation is primary, and philosophy subordinate to it, surely Keating is right to ask of the insights thus obtained, "Do they not, at least potentially, possess a binding force on all God's human creatures regardless of historical or cultural context?"[14] Universal rationality and truth are back in.

In *Reality*, McGrath sketches the rise and collapse of classical foundationalism as the basis of a universal rationality (*STR*, 20–35). He proceeds to argue that, just as nature is a constructed notion, so rationality is a "contested notion" (*STR*, 64). Appealing to Alasdair MacIntyre, McGrath argues that, because there is no universal rationality, theology is free to advance its own tradition-specific rationality, though McGrath cannot align himself with postmodernism or relativism as the alternative to Enlightenment rationality. On the contrary, the Christian tradition possesses a transtraditional rationality that is able to account for other perspectives, notably other religions. Its internal coherence and understanding of natural theology are key components of this approach (*STR*, 55ff.).

It seems to me that if Christian theology explains nature better, and explains other traditions better than either these traditions or atheism explain the same things, then that counts as evidence for the Christian tradition being true. But then McGrath's version becomes virtually indistinguishable from traditional natural theology. I come back to this later with reference to *The Open Secret*, but the point can already be made from what McGrath says in *Reality*.

Interestingly, McGrath is able to bring the realism of the natural sciences to bear so as to advance his argument—as Keating notes, a useful employment of the *ancilla theologiae*. As McGrath says, "A generally realist position unquestionably represents the working assumptions of most natural scientists—assumptions which they regard as constantly confirmed by the outcome of their engagement with the external world" (*STR*, 133). Yes indeed, and the Sokal hoax, discussed by McGrath (*STR*, 188–91), beautifully exposed the fatuousness of postmodern attempts to undermine scientific realism.

The realism that McGrath advances is not a naïve realism but a "critical realism." While commending some of the writing in the science-religion community, notably that of John Polkinghorne, McGrath comments that these writers largely ignore the mainstream discussion of critical realism in the philosophical community, where he sees Roy Bhaskar's style of critical realism as having significant advantages. The main failure of the science-religion writers on the subject is their lack of recognition of "cultural, historical and social factors shaping human perceptions of reality" (*STR*, 208). However, perhaps these are not quite so important when discussing the natural sciences and any natural theology that might appeal to them.

Andreas Losch traces the use of the terminology "critical realism" in both philosophy and the science-religion debate.[15] He notes that Bhaskar's version is a concatenation of his earlier concepts of "transcendental realism" and "critical naturalism." Bhaskar rejects "empirical realism," which he takes to mean the assignment of reality to the concrete objects of experience but not to mechanisms and structures that do not appear in experience but cause things that do: "transcendental realism" assigns reality to the latter as well. "Critical naturalism" is concerned with the extent to which the social and natural sciences share the same methods. Indeed critical naturalism recognizes significant differences based on real differences in subject matter, and can thus be seen to be of relevance to the key idea that theology is scientific because it treats its object in the way appropriate to it. Bhaskar's approach to "critical realism" also embraces the stratification of reality, another aspect that is of major importance to McGrath. As Losch points out, the idea of such a stratification is also to be found in the triumvirate of scientist-theologians Ian Barbour, Arthur Peacocke, and John Polkinghorne. Clearly this is also a strong emphasis in Michael Polanyi, who has probably influenced all the authors in question, including, Losch points out (contra McGrath), Bhaskar himself.[16]

A key argument derived from Bhaskar, which comes up time and again in McGrath (and of course Torrance before him), is that "ontology determines epistemology" (e.g., *FTU*, 214). This means that "the manner in which things may be known, and the extent of the ensuing knowledge, is influenced by how things are in themselves" (*OS*, 51), or, to put it more simply, the way an object is determines how it should be known. That is true for the sciences, and also for theology (*STR*, 121ff.). Indeed, John Polkinghorne states a similar formula for science, which he sees as also applying to theology, namely "epistemology models ontology": what we know reflects what is the case.[17] While that seems almost trivial to most scientists, it does lie in complete opposition to foundationalism's starting point of a set of indubitable and incorrigible beliefs (*OT*, xv), that is, that epistemology is prior, as well as postmodern relativism. If foundationalism's demise is also the demise of universal reason, as McGrath claims, then, as I argue later, some of the criteria for assessing statements about reality to which McGrath appeals do seem to bring back the universal. Indeed, is not the statement "ontology determines epistemology" itself meant to command universal assent? It is, after all, taken over by McGrath from a secular philosopher in Bhaskar, even if the Christian theologian Thomas Torrance had also appealed to it. Elsewhere McGrath states the belief of the American pragmatist philosopher John Dewey in "a group of universal values to which all people can have access simply by virtue of being human" (*OS*, 56), indicating an essential role for the transcendent, in contrast to the commonplace view of Dewey as a naturalist whose vision of reality is confined to the everyday world (*OS*, 56).

Dewey's view comes perilously close to the kind of statement of natural theology from which McGrath wishes to distance himself, as indeed does the notion of "critical realism" in theology. For these kinds of reason I find McGrath so tantalizing—at times thinking he is succumbing to irrationalism and at others stating the position as I see it myself. Then I wonder whether in the end the difference is more in the way the arguments are expressed than in their substance, and in the strategy one might adopt for the unbeliever.

Key passages relating to this point appear in *Reality* and *The Order of Things*, where McGrath discusses the dispute between Barth and Heinrich Scholz, which we met in chapters 2 and 4 (*STR*, 285–90; also *OT*, 108–16; *FTU*, 216). McGrath sees strength in both protagonists' positions. Barth, as would be expected, is affirmed for prioritizing the object of theology as determining what can be known and how (a view attributed to Martin Kähler, *STR*, 286; *OT*, 113). Thus, Scholz is wrong for wanting theology to lay out its axioms and deduce its further statements in the manner of mathematical logic, which McGrath sees as a foundationalist approach, but he is right to insist that theological statements be open to testing (*STR*, 287). For McGrath this will be both for their coherence and historical origins. Interestingly, McGrath would seem to side with Pannenberg at this point, who thought that Scholz was surely right, contra Barth, to insist that theological statements be free of contradiction and should be testable.[18]

In *Theory*, McGrath argues that theories are a response to reality and seek to express the orderedness revealed by reality. They cannot of course have precedence over the reality being modeled itself, from all that has been said already. Theological theories may need to develop both in order to capture better the revealed reality since at any given time a theory will be accommodated to the language and concepts available at that time, and also to take into account the apophatic aspect of the reality of God (*STT*, 50–53). In this, theology is similar to the sciences, and equally realist. For carrying out its task, McGrath accepts the picture of Neurath's boat, an image of the collapse of foundationalism since all the resources for fixing the boat are carried within it or are merely passing driftwood (*STT*, 217–21).

Responding to the concerns of Barth, McGrath discusses the important concepts of *analogia entis* and *analogia fidei* (*STT*, 108–19). There is such a thing for McGrath as a "responsible *analogia entis*" (*STT*, 118–19). This "cannot be conceived as an assertion of human epistemological autonomy, but is rather to be seen as reflecting a desire to follow through the implications of the revealed notion of the divine creation of the world in and through Christ. The capacity of the created order to model God is thus a revealed, not a natural, insight." The *analogia fidei* (the idea that the capacity of human language to talk about revelation must be given by God) is then enabled by the *analogia entis*, whereby God freely chooses how and where he will be revealed in nature. McGrath summarizes the distinction helpfully thus: "A Christian doctrine of creation affirms the capacity of any aspect of nature to serve as a medium of disclosure for the nature and purposes of God. The *analogia entis* affirms the theoretical capacity of any aspects of the created order—including events and entities—to mirror their creator; the *analogia fidei* identifies those aspects that have been authorized to act in this manner—whether or not they correspond to human preconceptions of their suitability for this purpose" (*STT*, 116). The fundamental point in all of this, it seems to me, is that all knowledge of God (even so-called natural knowledge of God) is granted to human beings by God's grace.

There is also a consideration of the key concept of abduction (or "inference to the best explanation" [*STT*, 153–65; 234]), of explanation more fully (*STT*, 133–234), and of revelation (*STT*, 138–93). In theology, abduction is primarily from the aftermath of the revelatory events in the life, death, and resurrection of Jesus back to the events themselves. This is analogous to abduction in historical natural sciences, such as cosmology and evolutionary biology (*STT*, 153–62).

A useful summary of the trilogy is given in McGrath's *The Science of God*. Very positive and sympathetic review essays are given by Elmer Colyer, who is also a significant scholar of T. F. Torrance.[19] One interesting criticism Colyer makes is that McGrath's identification of the rationality of creation (*logos*) with the rationality of God (*Logos*) seems to conflict with his simultaneous approval of Torrance's more restrained (and surely correct) view that the creation possesses a different rationality from that of God, namely a "created or contingent rationality" (see Colyer's review of *STN*, and more substantially that of *STR*). As Colyer notes, these two views would clearly have very different implications for the status and role of natural theology. Because created rationality is contingent and not self-subsistent, it points beyond itself to God, and experiment is motivated as a way to understand it. Colyer is also critical (in the *STR* review) of the little attention McGrath pays to explaining the strata of reality that theology is to engage and the theological implications of Bhaskar's critical realism. In *STT*, the theological strata are spelled out slightly more fully; they consist of what is accessible in the present, also termed the *depositum fidei*, and include, for example, Scripture, church structures, and the sacraments. However, Colyer now criticizes McGrath's abduction from these strata to the events of revelation themselves, which McGrath sees as past. This is to ignore the ongoing work of the Holy Spirit in making Christ present for the salvation of the world now (review of *STT*). But my own criticism, as we shall see later, is that, despite his protestations, McGrath is using what might be deemed "universal rationality" to justify theological claims after all.

As noted above, McGrath's ultimate aim is a multivolume systematic theology for which all the work described in this chapter is only a preparation.

## *Further Preparation:* The Order of Things

*The Order of Things* (*OT*) is a series of previously unpublished essays and sermons that forms an interim work briefly expounding and taking forward the trilogy, preparatory to the major work on natural theology in *The Open Secret* and the Gifford Lectures, and looking forward even further to the proposed multivolume dogmatics.

One point worth picking up from a very favorable review of the trilogy by Benjamin Myers, republished in *OT*, is that McGrath differs from Torrance in asserting that pre-Enlightenment natural theology made no attempt to prove the existence of God (McGrath cites Aquinas as only being concerned with internal consistency rather than arguing for God's existence in, for example, *DD*, 7–8; in *OT*, 68, they are "explanations of the explanatory dividend resulting from faith in God"). But Torrance criticized medieval natural theology precisely because it did regard natural theology "as an antecedent science or as a *praeambulum fidei*, and as such supplied the general frame of reference in which 'revealed theology' was interpreted."[20] I have already noted that McGrath includes here a very good chapter engaging with the thought of Richard Dawkins.

*OT* also contains a chapter comprising a University Sermon on natural theology that is largely concerned with the common yearning for transcendence often provoked by the natural world. Scientific understanding of the world does not dispel that longing, nor the symbolic reference intended by poetry, as Dawkins seems to think in his disparagement of Keats in *Unweaving the Rainbow*[21] (see later for additional discussion of this point). McGrath further argues, as elsewhere, that the Christian revelation can explain why science works and why there should be a correspondence between the human mind and the rationality of the cosmos.

This and a further chapter on renewing natural theology are very much setting out ideas that are developed more fully in *The Open Secret*. One of the recurring points is again that a Christian natural theology "presupposes and reinforces fundamental theological affirmations" (*OT*, 64). Furthermore it "posits that something of God may be known outside the Christian tradition" (*OT*, 64). Indeed, as noted with reference to *STR*, the ability of the Christian view to explain the existence of other perspectives is part of what makes the Christian vision "tradition-transcendent" and thus able to lay claim to offering public truth.

It seems to me that there is a certain circularity in all this. One reason is that the premise leads to a conclusion embracing the premise. McGrath even seems to agree with this: "Natural theology is caught up in a hermeneutical circle, in which it must presuppose its conclusions" (*OT*, 67). But another reason is that the second claim here actually validates the traditional approach to natural theology. This is precisely because McGrath is effectively here conceding—indeed, stating as a positive strength—that no appeal to revelation is necessary to infer something about God from the natural world. Then again, McGrath is confusing because almost in the same breath he says that we are only justified in seeing the rationality of the universe as revealing "the mind of God" if we have "prior authorization or enablement, both of which lie beyond the competency of human reason" (*OT*, 67). A major question is then whether other religious traditions than the Christian are so authorized. It seems to me that all human beings are at least entitled, through God's common grace, to infer something about God from the natural world, which is publicly available to all, even if many do not do so. Indeed, one might ask, how could they be "without excuse" (Rom 1:20) for not inferring anything about God unless they were authorized to do so in the first place?

McGrath notes helpfully that Barth's view of eighteenth-century natural theology as "an assertion of human autonomy over and against divine self-revelation" (expressed in Barth's *Protestant Theology in the Nineteenth Century*[22]—see *OT*, 71) is too simplistic. This might be true in certain instances—for example, that of the deists—but it was not so for the orthodox, where the concern was apologetic rather than dogmatic (*OT*, 72–73). In the light of anxiety concerning the reliability of the Bible, the church did not reject revelation but utilized natural theology as an apologetic bridge to the prevailing culture. This is precisely how I perceive matters today, where many are either ignorant of the Bible, or suspicious of its trustworthiness, or both.

In the chapter in *OT* on stratified levels of reality, McGrath discusses the pertinent concept of reductionism and its antithesis, emergence. Emergence could be either weak, whereby the behavior of a system at a higher level of complexity can in principle be derived from that at the lower, even if this behavior is unexpected or the derivation is impossibly difficult in practice; or strong, in which case the derivation is not possible even in principle, because novel causal powers come into play. Either way, he argues as ever that each level of reality needs to be engaged in the manner appropriate to it, so that, for example, the language of atomic physics is not best suited for the study of macroscopic aggregates of matter, especially biological systems.

McGrath's examination of levels of reality in the natural world leads him once again to his position that theology must treat its object in the manner appropriate to it, which feeds into the discussion in this volume of the Scholz-Barth debate, already discussed above. He returns to the topic of emergence and its relation to natural theology in *FTU*, as we discuss later.

A chapter in *OT* addresses the development of doctrine. McGrath rejects the "meme" approach of Richard Dawkins for the transmission of ideas and culture, a concept McGrath has (in my view rightly) also roundly criticized elsewhere (e.g., *DG* and *DD*) as unnecessary and without empirical warrant. He writes, "All human cultures possess means by which information may be transmitted within existing populations and to subsequent generations, none of which appear to be genetically determined but rather to be the outcome of cultural and technological developments such as books, traditions, institutions, and oral traditions" (*OT*, 151). The meme as an analogy of the gene is "functionally redundant." But McGrath draws an analogy for Christian doctrine from Simon Conway Morris's study of evolutionary convergence. Christian doctrine would emerge inevitably whatever the contingencies of history—for example, the Augustinian doctrine of the church would have emerged at some point as an "island of doctrinal stability," even without the Donatist controversy (*OT*, 168). The Chalcedonian definition is another "triumph of convergence over contingency" (*OT*, 162, 165). He also likens the metaphysical framework in which Christian doctrines such as the Chalcedonian definition are expressed to Stephen Jay Gould's "spandrels," accidental byproducts of evolution. While the basic architecture of the definition can be maintained, it can come to be expressed in different and more modern categories. The Chalcedonian and Trinitarian formulations represent God's self-disclosure, and the church's reflection on the "deposit of faith" will inevitably lead it, like evolutionary convergence, to them (*OT*, 227).

McGrath explores the relevance of Jean Piaget's contribution to the study of cognitive development of children to the development of doctrine. The Piagetian term "assimilation" denotes the incorporation of new insights, chiefly from the surrounding culture, into existing structures of understanding; "equilibration" means exercising restraint in such incorporation in the light of conflict with biblical or liturgical tradition; "accommodation" means making any conceptual adjustments necessary to achieve closure on the issues raised. A subsequent and ongoing process of review monitors the agreed closure "as an act of theological vigilance" (*OT*, 182). One begins to see from this how McGrath's systematic theology will be developed. A key component is the ordering of the world, including the moral order bestowed on the world by God, reflected in "natural law."

McGrath's systematic theology begins with the empirical reality of the church, likened again to von Neurath's ship (*OT*, 196). Interestingly, it is the church, rather than Scripture, that is the starting point for McGrath the evangelical, the reason being that the church both preceded and received the Scriptures. Indeed, "the Bible is the creation of the church" (*OT*, 217), and the church interprets it. Nor is McGrath's starting point, as it was for Barth, the doctrine of the Trinity, which McGrath sees as the outcome of reflection on the revelation received by the church rather than the content of that revelation. McGrath notes that his approach more resembles that of Schleiermacher in being empirically based.

The church transmits its institutions, texts, liturgy, and sacraments, but above all Jesus Christ himself embodied in these, to succeeding generations. It will also be iterative following the Reformation notion of *ecclesia semper reformanda*. McGrath homes in on Barth's starting point after one iteration, with the result that his starting point for natural theology is not too far down the road.

This approach is empirical, says McGrath, beginning with what we can observe, and proceeding "by a process involving abduction, iteration, construction, and *le bon sens* (Pierre Duhem), to build the best account of reality that we can manage" (*OT*, 204). However, it is emphatically not empirical in the way of the Boyle lectures, whose starting point was the natural world. For McGrath, as we see elsewhere in this chapter, the problem is that nature is not "a self interpreting entity" (*OT*, 207). He criticizes Locke's approach to knowledge of God as constituting a classical natural theology: Locke has a cosmological argument based on inferring the necessary existence of an eternal mind from the human capacity to think and the impossibility of this arising from the purely material. In contrast, John Dewey "broadens the concept of 'experience' beyond the mere categories of cognitive understanding, to embrace the categories of culture as much as of nature" (*OT*, 213). Then human reflection on experience, which is primary as for McGrath, leads to a more "holistic account of reality" (*OT*, 214). John Searle is also helpful in insisting on the reality of social entities, requiring a different level of explanation from more fundamental levels, such as particle physics (*OT*, 215–16).

One can see how these views can be harnessed by McGrath in support of his own starting point for systematic theology, the church, as empirical social reality. Fundamentally, it is the church through which Christianity is encountered in the world. Natural theology represented the "most systematic attempt to subvert any role for the church in finding God" (*OT*, 218). As he says many times, "That tradition is ultimately incapable of disclosing God without presupposing God" (*OT*, 218). Again, "without the trinitarian hermeneutical apparatus that is distinctive to the Christian faith, nature cannot legitimately lead us—or be assisted to lead us—to the 'God and Father of our Lord Jesus Christ'" (*OT*, 218). So McGrath's natural theology is indeed circular, though I agree with McGrath that the traditional kind of natural theology does not get one to Christ. However, cannot the empirical reality of the church be utilized as evidence for the church's claims, in the manner of a ramified natural theology?

Stanley Hauerwas is a significant theologian who has influenced McGrath. Hauerwas insists that Christianity is not simply a set of ideas but a way of life "made possible by the gracious action of the Holy Spirit, which orients its adherents to the Father through Jesus Christ" (*OT*, 223). Doing theology, as indeed being a Christian at all, is the result of inhabiting a narrative, the Christian way of life, and a way of seeing the world. McGrath quotes C. S. Lewis as he does elsewhere as saying, "I believe in Christianity as I believe that the Sun has risen—not only because I see it, but because by it, I see everything else" (*OT*, 227).[23]

In a way it seems to me that McGrath's approach makes natural theology too easy. Its conclusions are presented rather than argued for in comparison with other views, as is done in the traditional model.

## *McGrath's "New Vision for Natural Theology"*

The subtitle of McGrath's book *The Open Secret* is *A New Vision for Natural Theology*, and that is what he aims to give. He wants to present an account of natural theology that differs from the traditional one, put by William Alston thus: "the enterprise of providing support for religious beliefs by starting from premises that neither are nor presuppose any religious beliefs"[24] (*OS*, 7; see also *STN*, 241; *OT*, 67). He also cites James Barr's similar definition:

> Traditionally, "natural theology" has commonly meant something like this: that "by nature," that is, just by being human beings, men and women have a certain degree of knowledge of God and awareness of him, or at least a capacity for such awareness; and this knowledge or awareness exists anterior to the special revelation of God made through Jesus Christ, through the Church, through the Bible.[25] (*OS*, 10)

McGrath continues this enterprise in *A Fine-Tuned Universe* (*FTU*).

In many ways McGrath is following in the footsteps of Thomas Torrance, whose biographer he is. He expounds Torrance's view of natural theology as rightly done from within dogmatic theology in *STN* (283–86), and his own view is that "natural theology cannot be conceived as an autonomous theological discipline, precisely because its foundational and legitimating insight—namely, that nature is to be viewed and recognized as God's creation—is derived from divine revelation" (*STN*, 295). It is thus to be pursued "within the scope of a revealed knowledge of God, rather than as an autonomous discipline outside its bounds" (*STN*, 295).

In the sense that he is thus following Torrance, McGrath's is not a "new vision," although he undoubtedly takes Torrance's line much further. McGrath has the advantage of a scientific training that helps him avoid some of the pitfalls into which Torrance fell.

McGrath agrees with Polkinghorne that theism is "a more powerful explanatory tool than naturalism" and a Trinitarian theism "superior to a more generic theism in this regard" (*OS*, 17) under the categories of economy, scope, elegance, and fruitfulness. However, as I have pointed out when discussing Torrance, Polkinghorne does see natural theology in terms of what we can know about purely by being human, much like Alston and Barr, even though he does see it as part of, and not detached from, the overall theological enterprise. Polkinghorne also sees a revived natural theology, though in terms I would more identify with than those of McGrath.

Although McGrath notes Calvin's notion of *sensus divinitatis* (*OS*, 70, 193; *STN*, 273), he says that discernment must still take place since some inner voices ("personal demons") are to be challenged. And someone coming with a precommitment to there being no transcendent dimension to the world will see nature very differently than someone with no such precommitment (*OS*, 75).

McGrath gives examples of the discernment of God within the natural order, including that of Samuel in 1 Samuel 3. Following Torrance he concludes that there is no theologically valid distinction between the "natural" and the "supernatural" (*OS*, 77; *OT*, 70). It seems to me that discernment is indeed necessary. As I argued when critiquing Torrance's position, that will entail validating a putative revelation against the background of the Christian tradition and doctrine but also bringing to bear commonly held rational criteria. It is the latter that Torrance and McGrath seem to deny (though read ahead!).

McGrath includes a chapter by Joanna Collicutt McGrath on "Discernment and the Psychology of Perception." This is clearly important to the McGraths, and the upshot is that anthropology is coming back into theology in a serious way, indeed in a way again more conducive to a Schleiermachian (or at least Brunnerian, as McGrath acknowledges [*OS*, 109]) perspective than a Barthian one. Thus, "any account of revelation needs to give due weight to the manner in which human beings create and use conceptual schemes" (*OS*, 92). And again, "however revelation is to be understood, it involves human cognition and perception, which recognize it for what it actually is" (*OS*, 107). McGrath is right to say that this "does not involve the 'reduction' of theology to psychology" (*OS*, 109).

This is all consistent with McGrath's critical realist stance, discussed above, though some statements seem rather less consistent. McGrath states that "there is no such thing as 'objective' human perception because the perceiver operates from a given perspective" (*OS*, 98). Thomas Nagel argues that it is nevertheless possible to abstract oneself from one's own perspective to imagine that of humans in general, even if one's own perspective is inherently "subjective"—that is, it is *my* perception that can only be accessed by me—and the global perspective will therefore inevitably be incomplete.[26]

McGrath goes on to argue that, although humans have developed the capacity to understand more of the universe than can be "perceived directly through the sense organs," and have "developed technologies to exploit this fact," he thinks that "Euclidean and other sophisticated geometries give only an illusion of objectivity in the perception of space" (*OS*, 99), and technology in a similar way gives us an illusory sense of omniscience.

I disagree that the perception of objectivity in space is illusory, and this seems to me too strong a statement for a critical realist. The same applies to his statement a few pages on, that humans "are active constructors of their own perceptual realities, not passive recipients of information" (*OS*, 106). On its own that statement would seem to be tending in the direction of nonrealism. However, McGrath qualifies it somewhat by conceding that "the process of construction is influenced by real events in, and real properties of, the natural world" (*OS*, 106).

What is true is that Euclidean space is only an approximation to the Riemannian geometries of Einsteinian physics. One of the reasons most scientists are realists is that nature forces these strange, nonintuitive conceptions on us. Of course, reality is always filtered through our perceptual apparatus, but it seems to me that the human perceptual apparatus is a generally reliable guide to the objective world; Kant was wrong to say that Euclidean geometry was a structure of the mind by which we necessarily construct our experience.

One of my problems with McGrath's approach is that, of course, if one takes his line with regard to objectivity in the natural world, the same applies to what he says about revelation. There is a real danger, although it is far from McGrath's intention (I assume), of relativizing the Christian message here and, in dwelling on natural theology as done from within, of losing its universal claim on humankind. How McGrath nevertheless claims that it is universal is considered later.

## *The Ambiguity of Nature*

McGrath has a chapter with this title in *The Open Secret*. It is also reflected in what he says elsewhere, for example, in *STN* (249–57) and in his engagement with the writings of Richard Dawkins. He says that nature can be interpreted atheistically, as Dawkins does, or theistically, as Christians do, but that nature mandates neither interpretation (e.g., *DG*, 53–57; *DD*, 13). While this is true, it does not seem to me to go far enough in answering Dawkins, whose constant refrain is, "Where is the evidence?" McGrath counters Dawkins very effectively at a number of points, and although he does turn this crucial question back on Dawkins's own lack of evidence for many of his claims, he provides little by way of positive answer to it from his own Christian theistic perspective.

In *The Open Secret* McGrath cites Isaiah 45:15 ("Truly you are a God who hides yourself") in support of his thesis of the ambiguity of nature (*OS*, 116). Jesus himself "strongly endorses the notion that nature has the capacity to disclose the divine," but human beings are only capable of perceiving the divine in nature under certain conditions. However, "tantalizingly little is said about what these conditions are" (*OS*, 116).

Yet it is clear that Jesus does indeed appeal to nature "as a means of disclosing the kingdom of God," and in this James Barr would concur—though Barr sees much natural theology, in the sense of his definition given earlier, throughout Scripture. Indeed, for McGrath also, Jesus uses "a developed 'natural theology,' understood as an interpretative framework by which nature may be 'seen' in a way that connects with the transcendent" (*OS*, 119), though it is important for McGrath's position that the meaning of the parables, for example, is often "shrouded in mystery" (*OS*, 121). It is a quotation from John Dominic Crossan, that Jesus' life and preaching are characterized as "the Message of an Open Secret," which leads to McGrath's title (*OS*,

121). Nature is indeed publicly accessible, but the information about God that it conveys is not self-evident (*OS*, 125). McGrath is right that Jesus never used nature to prove the existence of God, since he and his hearers would all have taken God's existence for granted (*OS*, 123n31).

Why in the modern era can it not be part of the vocation of Christian theology to point to the features of the universe, such as its remarkable ordering and anthropic fine-tuning, and argue that commonly accepted criteria of rationality make it highly likely that there is a God behind it all? The argument will be framed in terms recognizable to philosophers or scientists and, while always debatable and probabilistic, nevertheless will be expected to be accepted as evidence in favor of Christian belief. McGrath does indeed cite such features (see later), but they function within his own antecedent Trinitarian framework.

McGrath believes that the "hidden meaning" in nature precludes nature from being interpreted "in a single way, valid for all times, places, and cultures" (*OS*, 125). Indeed, "there is no *right* interpretation of nature" (*OS*, 138). This is a large claim, sounding dangerously postmodern. So, can we interpret nature any way we please? Can we interpret a text or work of art in any way we please?

McGrath is constantly wanting to distance himself from the universal power of reason of the Enlightenment (see later for discussion). But if the meaning needs to be pointed out, that does not preclude its being the universally valid interpretation. A theistic way and an atheistic way of interpreting nature cannot both be valid, and one cannot be valid for me and another for you. If the Christian theistic way is valid at all, then it is valid for everybody, everywhere, at all times. That does not mean that it is easy to establish the validity of that view, or that there will not be debate about it, of course. Indeed some of the arguments adduced may be finely drawn. But it remains the case that if the Christian view is valid, then it is universally valid. And that point needs to be made against Dawkins: we cannot leave him thinking that his atheistic view is perfectly valid, as noted at the beginning of this section. And that is why I think Keith Ward's riposte to Dawkins[27] is in the end more compelling than McGrath's.

McGrath states, "The doctrine of creation enables us to see nature in such a way that it can act as a signpost which points to God; the doctrine of the incarnation enables us to see nature in a way that discloses God within itself" (*OS*, 133). If I am a Christian, then I will be looking at nature with the desire and expectation of finding God there, and learning more about God. But it seems to me that nature is a signpost regardless, and the Christian can point others to God through it and commend God as Creator to them with reasoned argument based on it.

I find McGrath's arguments here bewilderingly circular and confusing, if not confused. He seems to recognize what I have just said: "This does not mean that all such interpretations are of equal validity, nor that the quest for the 'best explanation' or 'most authentic account' of nature is meaningless, or lies beyond our grasp" (*OS*, 139). But then, his main point stands: "The insight that nature has the capacity to disclose God is only given from the standpoint of knowing that God" (*OS*, 139). McGrath gives great weight to "inference to the best explanation" (IBE, see later), where he names criteria that seem to be universal, even in line with the Enlightenment kind of rationality he wishes to reject. But only Christians are able to make the IBE from nature to God because they believe in God in the first place! So where is the inference if the conclusion is already the premise?

Let me give an analogy from mathematics. I am a teacher of mathematics, and I know that Pythagoras's theorem is true. My class, however, does not know this, with the possible exception of a few who do know it already. I draw a right-angled triangle on the blackboard, squares on the three sides, and then a few more lines. From the premises of Euclidean geometry, and what the whole class knows about congruent triangles, and how to calculate areas of triangles and rectangles, I prove Pythagoras's theorem. The point is that the theorem is true for everybody, not just for me. Those who didn't know it before the lesson now do, assuming they follow the logic, and those who did know it beforehand, perhaps by having seen some examples and not found any counterexamples, have their belief reinforced by a rigorous proof.

Natural theology is, or ought to be, inductive rather than deductive (McGrath is certainly right to reject the latter), but it ought also to proceed by rational argument. A Christian will believe the result of the argument, either because he knows the argument itself or, more likely, for other good reasons (to do with revelation, or his own religious experience, for example). A non-Christian will not believe the result of the argument beforehand, but may be persuaded when he hears the argument. However, there is always a way of avoiding the conclusion of an inductive or probabilistic argument; it can never be absolutely compelling, and the skeptic may reject the argument itself, or have other reasons for rejecting the conclusion not related to the argument (a bad experience of church as a child perhaps). Metaphysical argument is much looser than the logic of mathematical proof, even though I believe that there is a valid comparison to be made.

## *Critique of Enlightenment Rationality*

In chapter 7 of *The Open Secret* ("A Dead End? Enlightenment Approaches to Natural Theology"), McGrath critiques the Enlightenment approach. He notes that natural theology had become a means of demonstrating God's existence by the early eighteenth century. He cites Cotton Mather in 1715 as saying that the physico-theology of the time meant a "theology that seeks to prove the existence and attributes of God from the evidence of purpose and design in the universe" (*OS*, 146n20). I agree with McGrath that it is a mistake to use natural theology to "prove" God's existence. Proof only occurs in pure mathematics and deductive logic. But that does not mean that natural theology cannot be used rightly in inductive or probabilistic argumentation. I believe it can, and point once again to Richard Swinburne as a pioneer of a new inductive approach, utilizing the formalism of Bayesian confirmation theory.

McGrath argues that today the case for an objective natural theology is weakened by the recognition that nature "does not designate an objective autonomous reality, but essentially designates the ways in which human observers choose to see, interpret, and inhabit the world," the case being presented more fully in *STN*, as we have seen. It does seem to me, again, that this represents too much of a departure from critical realism, at least of the kind espoused by scientists such as Peacocke and Polkinghorne. Scientists generally believe that nature is objective, and our scientific theories are a response to the way the natural world impacts us, often surprisingly.

McGrath repeats his basic point: "A Christian natural theology is about seeing nature in a specific manner, which allows the observer to discern in what is seen the truth, beauty, and goodness of a trinitarian God who is already known" (*OS*, 147). But then he adds what seems to me to be a contradiction: "and which allows nature to function as a pathway towards this same God for secular culture as a whole" (*OS*, 147–48). If the latter is true, then I am of course in agreement. But that is surely "classic" natural theology!

Another statement along similar lines is the following: "It [the Christian tradition] holds that what may be known of God through the publicly accessible reality of nature, although in a fragmentary and potentially inconsistent manner, may be clarified and extended through the Christian revelation, which is *specific* to the Christian tradition" (*OS*, 249). Yes, indeed! But the problem is that McGrath seems to be denying this in so many other places. He gives with one hand but takes away with the other.

McGrath notes on the one hand the Enlightenment's "unrealistic aspirations to total objectivity" (*OS*, 155). On the other hand, while at times his approach seems to me to tend in a postmodernist direction, he nevertheless regards postmodernism as an indefensible alternative. He writes that the proper response to the Enlightenment failure is "not to abandon any attempt at critical evaluation of interpretative possibilities, but to encourage a realistic and cautious attempt to determine which of the various interpretations of nature may be regarded as the 'best explanation,' as judged by criteria such as parsimony, elegance, or explanatory power" (*OS*, 155). I agree, of course, but reiterate that those criteria are "universal," and the best explanation is the best explanation for anybody, atheist or Christian alike.

Discussing the Barth-Brunner controversy, McGrath notes that a major concern of Brunner is that Barth "allows no conceptual space for the active involvement of humanity in the process of the interpretation of nature," whereas Brunner himself is rather more open to this, though not taking it far enough (*OS*, 161, 163). Barth, of course, does not want theology to become "beholden to anthropology or psychology."

This does seem an area in which McGrath clearly differs from Barth, in view of McGrath's earlier emphasis on the process of perception. He notes that Barth offers "little in the way of clarification of how human beings arrive at the epistemologically decisive insight that *this* event or *this* person is indeed to be accepted as divine self-revelation, where others are not" (*OS*, 162), a statement with which I am in full accord. As noted above, anthropology is again of central importance in theology.

As we have seen, it is an important theme for McGrath that nature is a constructed notion (e.g., in addition to references above, *OS*, 167, and *STN*, 257). Moreover, rationality is not objective either but culturally conditioned. In the words of Richard Rorty, "rationality is what history and society make it" (quoted in *OS*, 167). Natural theology based on rationality then also becomes historically contingent, a point reinforced for McGrath by Alasdair MacIntyre, for whom the Enlightenment's ideal of a universal rationality is unattainable. Of course the same would apply to "Christian rationality," and the trouble with all this is again how perilously close to postmodernism it gets. This is where I feel most scientists would be much more objective and universalist, and where I would side even with Dawkins and Atkins.

McGrath writes, "Nature is patient of a vast variety of interpretations—including, but not limited to, Christian, Jewish, Islamic, panentheist, pantheist, atheist, and agnostic readings—while demanding none of them." Moreover, "there is no universal metacriterion which determines which of these multiple readings is to be preferred" (*OS*, 169). As noted above, it does not seem adequate when countering Richard Dawkins to tell him that his interpretation and McGrath's own are just two of many conflicting possible interpretations of nature, and indeed just culturally conditioned rather than objectively rational. This approach does not cut much ice with a hard-nosed scientific realist—and one does not have to go as far as Dawkins as a rather antediluvian positivist to share that with him. It may be that no "universal metacriterion" *determines* which reading is to be preferred, but it may be that one could decide which reading is most probably true or, in McGrath's own adopted terminology, one may be able to make an "inference to the best explanation."

This point leads McGrath to deny a sharp distinction between the "natural" and the "dogmatic" (*OS*, 169), a position I agree with, but for different reasons. It seems to me that one should apply similar criteria to evaluate putative revelations as putative natural knowledge of God.

McGrath goes on as before to advocate tradition-based rationalities, and to advocate a "renewed" natural theology on the basis of the Christian revelation. He writes:

> In other words, a specific interpretation of nature is adopted, which is believed to be (but cannot be *proved* to be) the best account possible in terms of criteria of explanatory excellence—such as the degree of empirical fit, conceptual elegance, and fecundity. Such an approach will be both internally coherent and grounded in reality, recognizing that it represents a tradition, while claiming that this tradition offers the best explanation of what may be observed in nature, culture, and human experience—including the existence of rival traditions. (*OS*, 170)

The trouble with this, once again, is that it is either circular or contradictory to what he has said already. It is circular if the criteria he names are somehow internal to the Christian revelation, for you then get back to where you started from: the Christian God. It bears a disconcertingly similar resemblance to the approach of Ludwig Feuerbach, discussed by McGrath, who started from a materialist premise that no objective basis exists in reality for the concept of God, and concluded that God must be a projection of a human longing for significance (*STN*, 204–9). It is not a refutation of Feuerbach to point to the human longing as a consequence of human createdness, as McGrath does on the grounds of the Christian doctrine of creation, if that doctrine is simply an unsubstantiated alternative starting point. Indeed this seems to be precisely what McGrath is saying when he writes, "What Feuerbach proposes as an extrasymmetric critique of Christian theology can be reformulated as its intrasystemic confirmation" (*STN*, 207). He next points to Augustine's classic statement in the *Confessions* that "you have made us for yourself and our heart is restless until it rests in you"

(*STN*, 208). McGrath then acknowledges, "Nothing can be proved from this discussion," and that the two different accounts, that of Feuerbach and that based on the Christian doctrine of creation, are "equally unverifiable and unfalsifiable" (*STN*, 209).

A better strategy here is to recognize something like Richard Swinburne's "Principle of Credulity" and "Principle of Testimony," and to argue that, with suitable qualifications, what a person describes as an experience of God is actually very likely to be an experience of God. The Principle of Credulity states in essence that what people generally perceive corresponds to what is actually the case, and the Principle of Testimony holds that we can generally rely on what other people tell us.[28]

However, the criteria McGrath points to do not seem to be internal to the Christian faith—"intrasystemic," to use McGrath's word. On the contrary they seem to be universal rational criteria (just as the Principle of Credulity claims to be), even though McGrath repeatedly says that there are no universal criteria (e.g., again, *OS*, 249). They are the kind of criteria used to adjudicate between competing scientific theories. They are generally taken to be a guide to truth, though I agree with McGrath that they will not generate proof. And if the Christian revelation does indeed provide the best explanation when compared with other rivals, as McGrath and I agree it does, then I see no difference here from what is being done in the "traditional" natural theology that McGrath repudiates—because it follows from the argument that nature does indeed provide universally acceptable evidence for the God of the Christian revelation!

McGrath rather surprisingly cites a Richard Swinburne paper in which discontent with natural theology is supposedly discussed (*OS*, 170).[29] Oddly enough, the article is in a special issue of *Faith and Philosophy*—"The Continuing Relevance of Natural Theology"—most of the contributors to which—including, of course (perhaps above all), Swinburne himself—are in favor of natural theology as traditionally conceived. However, one of the contributors, Daniel Howard-Snyder, reiterates a rather technical objection to Swinburne's approach originally attributed to Alvin Plantinga: namely, that of "dwindling probabilities." Swinburne provides an answer that seems entirely valid, at least in principle.[30] His only reference to the "discontent with natural theology" attributed to him by McGrath is in the single sentence: "It was only as a result of what I can only regard as rather bad arguments by Hume, Kant, and followers of Darwin, that natural theology went out of favour for most of the nineteenth and twentieth centuries."[31] But the paper affirms the important place of natural theology up to that time, and its continuing relevance today, both in the form of what Swinburne calls "bare" natural theology and "ramified" natural theology. The former refers to arguments for theism whereas the latter is an extremely useful category referring (mainly) to historical arguments in favor of the particulars of a religion—for Swinburne, the Christian faith.

## *McGrath's "Christian Approach to Natural Theology"*

Moving on to "A Christian Approach to Natural Theology" (*OS*, chap. 8), McGrath draws attention to the biblical narrative of the call of Samuel, briefly alluded to above. Samuel is called four times by God and attributes the voice to Eli the first three times (*OS*, 174–77). He needs Eli's help to discern that the voice, which is heard as a "natural" phenomenon, is that of God. That point is important, and I have raised the story myself in critiquing Torrance's approach to natural theology, which I feel takes too little account of the need for discernment.

McGrath writes, "The Judaeo-Christian tradition holds that nature possesses a derivative capacity to disclose something of God's wisdom, without undermining or displacing divine revelation itself" (*OS*, 184). In support of his own position, McGrath cites Emil Brunner's argument that, since God "leaves the imprint of his nature on what he does," the creation is a revelation of God. Thus "God did not leave himself without witness [*unbezeugt*] to the heathen," but only someone "who stands within the Christian revelation in Christ" can possess a "true natural knowledge of God."

McGrath gives a classic statement of the Christian doctrine of creation as "having at least as much to do with why there is anything at all as it has to do with the question of the unfolding of life in the universe" (*OS*, 186). The doctrine of creation *ex nihilo*, a rather ambiguous notion purely from Scripture but becoming much more clearly expressed in the early patristic era, ensured that God's capacity for self-expression in the material world was not compromised as in Gnostic (or indeed Platonic) views of creation using preexistent matter (*OS*, 187). This approach then creates room for the relationship of analogy between the Creator and his creation, whereby the world signifies or models God, while, in Christian thought, God remains distinct from his creation (*OS*, 188–89).

McGrath acknowledges that the church has seen the doctrine of the *imago dei* as "indicating that there is something intrinsic to human nature which enables it to discern, however dimly, the character of God in the created order" (*OS*, 190). This is reflected in the writings of the great figures of the church, such as Augustine and Aquinas. Calvin espoused a limited natural theology based on humanity's "reflecting on the external order of the world, and the internal *sensus divinitatis*" (*OS*, 193, alluded to earlier). However, likening human perception of God in the world to the condition of visual agnosia, whereby subjects can see aspects of an object but not what it is as a whole, McGrath believes that humans similarly see the parts of nature but fail to discern its meaning—"the 'big picture' which transcends its individual components" (*OS*, 198).

McGrath links natural theology with the economy of salvation. He notes with some justice the "blithe and breezy cosmic optimism" of Paley's account (*OS*, 198–99). He further notes that the Enlightenment style of natural theology was essentially deistic, appealing to God as creator of a mechanical universe that is able to run itself without the need for God's involvement beyond "lighting the blue touch paper," as it were, and retiring (see also *OT*, 73–77, and *STN*, 181–91, referred to above).

The God inferred in this way bore little resemblance to the "God of Christian orthodoxy" according to McGrath (*OS*, 200). At the same time the disorder in the world was increasingly noticed, as revealed in such natural disasters as the Lisbon earthquake and tsunami of 1755. This is a problem on any account. It has been addressed—though in very different ways, and it is arguable how successfully—by such writers as Swinburne and Polkinghorne, who are more disposed to the traditional way of conceiving natural theology (again differently from each other, but each maintaining that it is to do with what we can know about God apart from revelation).

McGrath's answer to this problem of theodicy is to invoke "the traditional understanding of the 'economy of salvation,' which undergirds a trinitarian understanding of God" (*OS*, 201). He criticizes the answer that Thomas Burnet, chaplain to William III, gave in 1681, that the Earth had been made perfect but ruined by Noah's flood (*OS*, 200–201): this is indefensible in the modern world. However, it seems to me that McGrath's own answer fares little better. McGrath appeals to Augustine to the effect that nature has in some way been "defaced, degraded, or diminished as a consequence of the fall" (*OS*, 202). He also sees Calvin's major contribution to the doctrine of creation as his "emphasis on the intrusion of disorder within the created order as a consequence of the fall" (*STN*, 174). This is both an ontological change in the structuring of the world and, more plausibly, a "noetic" degradation of the human capacity of reflection on that ordering (*STN*, 175).

In a similar way to Burnet, McGrath then argues that "it cannot be assumed that the 'nature' which is observed directly corresponds to the state of nature which might be thought to bear the imprint of the creator" (*OS*, 202–3). This seems to me to parallel Burnet's argument remarkably closely; merely substitute the sin of Adam and Eve for the sins of mankind that precipitated the flood.

While McGrath may be right, appealing to Anselm (*OS*, 203) and Calvin as noted above—that sin has damaged the human capacity to discern God in nature—it is much harder to see how nature itself has been affected. Large parts of nature have been untouched by humans, and we know for certain that earthquakes, tsunamis, animal predation, viruses, and bacteria all preceded the fall, even if we understand that to be a historical event, however demythologized. Of course, there is a sense in which nature is being disordered right now through the direct activity of human beings (global warming), but that is a different matter from McGrath's assertion—and even then, we are only considering the Earth, not the rest of the cosmos.

For McGrath it is not simply that human perception is affected by the fall, so that nature cannot be seen to display the ordered rationality and beauty with which the Creator has endowed it, and hence the rationality and beauty of the Creator himself. Nor is it just that nature possesses "seemingly disordered, ugly and evil aspects" (*OS*, 203). It really is disordered. Nature itself is fallen in some sense. "Nature, as an empirical reality, cannot be equated with its original state . . . nature, *as presently observed*, cannot be assumed to be nature, *as originally created*" (*OS*, 208). This has the consequence, for traditional natural theology, that "tensions, incoherencies, and contradictions within the realm of nature, which Christian theology classically attributes to the fall, are now, on account of the presuppositions of the traditional style of natural theology, *projected onto the concept of God*" (*OS*, 204).

McGrath is right that the disorder in the natural world also needs to be addressed by natural theology, whether in its traditional or McGrath/Torrance form. This is the ancient problem of theodicy. If we are suggesting, as in traditional natural theology, that the orderliness of the world constitutes evidence for the existence of a good God, then evil and suffering might count as evidence against that hypothesis in the building up of a cumulative case. That negative impact is lessened if good reasons can be provided why a good God would create a world in this particular way. Such attempts have been made by, for example, John Hick, Brian Hebblethwaite, and Richard Swinburne. John Polkinghorne sees the "shadow side" of creation as a necessary component of God's making a world that makes itself, which is in itself a good thing.

One of the points Swinburne raises is that if we include in our hypothesis more of the resources of Christian theology, then the prior probability of the hypothesis is weakened (this point recurs in an argument I use later to compare Swinburne's approach with that of McGrath). I do think, however, that the theodicy problem can at least be mitigated with the help of some of those resources—for example, the hope of resurrection and the incarnation whereby God takes on, and identifies with, the suffering of humanity. Indeed Swinburne has changed his mind on this point himself and now also thinks such further resources are necessary.[32] I agree with McGrath, drawing on Torrance (*STN*, 175–76; *OS*, 205–6), that the eschatological hope of God's repairing and reordering what is disordered is helpful. But if we introduce those elements, then they also need to be argued for in the public square, and I think they can be. Indeed, the evidence for the resurrection of Christ seems very strong, and that both makes claims for the general resurrection probable and vindicates the claim that Christ is indeed God incarnate. This is where Swinburne's notion of a "ramified natural theology," embracing arguments for the particularities of the Christian faith, becomes essential.[33]

What I would say at this point is that none of this stops us questioning. We still raise the "why suffering?" question, even as Christian believers, and we go on grappling with it until the eschaton—or we ought to. From the point of view of natural theology, the question is whether we can say enough for the overall case to be persuasive, or "probable" in Swinburne's terminology. Again, without repeating all the arguments—and not necessarily agreeing with every single point of Swinburne (I have concerns about his theodicy to a greater extent than other aspects of his program, with which I am in broad agreement)—I believe it can.

Meanwhile I see in McGrath something of the "positivism of revelation" of which Bonhoeffer accused Barth, as discussed in chapter 3. In McGrath, it seems, as in Barth (although McGrath wants to distance himself from Barth), that one has to accept the whole package—"a positivist doctrine of revelation which says, in effect, 'Like it or lump it!': virgin birth, Trinity, or anything else; each is an equally significant and necessary part of the whole, which must simply be swallowed as a whole or not at all. That isn't biblical."[34] One might add "eschatology" to the list.

McGrath makes the point that the God revealed in Christ must be the same as the God revealed in nature, and regards this as a critical issue for natural theology. This might seem obvious to the modern mind, which finds it hard to conceive that there might be two or more gods, but not in the second century when Gnosticism made just this distinction. Yet the distinction McGrath might be drawing is probably that between "the God of the philosophers" and "the God of the Christian revelation." Still, if rational arguments of the traditional kind lead to God as necessary being and Creator of the universe, for example, then Christ must be that same God. While this is quite a staggering claim, I do not see that there is any contradiction involved. Natural theology in the sense of providing evidence for God's existence from what we know as human beings apart from revelation does need to be supplemented by what revelation tells us about God. As Polkinghorne observes, the concept of God arising just from natural theology might well be rather etiolated, telling us something, though not nearly enough, about God. That squares with what McGrath himself writes: "Truth, beauty, and goodness may be intimated in nature; they are, however, more fully disclosed through Christ" (*OS*, 214).

As noted above I agree with McGrath's dictum, "Ontology determines epistemology." For McGrath this has the implication that "who God *is* determines how God *acts*" (*OS*, 214). As noted above, McGrath's expression echoes that of Polkinghorne concerning science—namely, "epistemology models ontology": what we know reflects what is the case.[35] In the theological case, again it does not undermine traditional natural theology since, although God reveals himself supremely in Christ, he also reveals himself in nature. McGrath's acknowledgment that his theological analysis "must be supplemented from the perspective of an understanding of human perception and cognition" also brings in anthropology, as before.

McGrath draws a parallel between his approach and the development of science somewhat resembling Torrance's analogy with geometry becoming part of physics with the advent of general relativity. McGrath says that older scientific theories tend not to be valid in their own right, but special, limiting cases of more advanced theories (*OS*, 216–17). His example of quantum mechanics is somewhat problematic here, since no one knows how to make the transition from the classical to the quantum realm. Still, is his point about theology, presumably that natural theology is in some sense a special case, or an area of limited validity, of full-blown Trinitarian theology, valid? That could be seen as a rather more positive way of presenting the issue. After all, classical (Newtonian) mechanics can get one to the moon, no mean feat! I think traditional natural theology can get one to the probable existence of God, a staging post from which to advance by taking account of revelation. So sometimes McGrath's approach can be read as compatible with traditional natural theology and other times not.

In the third part of *The Open Secret* McGrath takes the sense-making role of natural theology beyond the giving of a rational account of why things are as they are (*OS*, 223), the main emphasis also in *FTU*. Thus, as indicated earlier, natural theology also extends to the Platonic triad of truth, beauty, and goodness. Surprisingly, perhaps, he thus sees natural theology embracing natural-law ethics, since, following Hauerwas, "the ultimate basis of Christian ethics in the world is a specific way of *seeing* the world" (*OS*, 224). Mystical experiences, as described by William James and Rudolf Otto, take one beyond the merely "rational." And, following Keats, simply reducing the rainbow to "the dull catalogue of common things" neglects the emotional and imaginative engagement with the world. Of course, as we have seen, Richard Dawkins believes that "unweaving the rainbow" kills religion with its obscurantist, mystical appeal. In fact, of course, scientists, including Dawkins himself, continue to be struck with awe at the wonders of the universe, and that awe is by no means removed if we understand the physics of rainbows. Indeed, beauty has often been seen as a guide to truth in the formulation of scientific theories (as McGrath acknowledges—see, for example, *STN*, 237–40).

The ambivalence of McGrath's approach appears again in this section in *The Open Secret*: "The vision for natural theology set out in this work affirms that our experience of the rationality, beauty, or goodness of the cosmos has the potential to elicit the quest for the divine, or intimate the nature of God." Here I agree with McGrath and indeed with his further statement that "the human capacity to recognize and respond to them [rationality, beauty, and goodness] is grounded in humanity's possessing the image of God, even if in a weakened and attenuated form" (*OS*, 229). Again, however, this seems to conflict with his repeated assertion that one starts with the Trinitarian God of Christian faith and then looks at nature.

McGrath opens his chapter on natural theology and truth in *The Open Secret* by exploring the sense-making capacity of natural theology, "affirming its significance, yet contesting its finality" (*OS*, 232). The problem, of course, is that nothing can be uncontested, and that includes the finality of the Christian revelation, at least in dialogue with those of no faith or of other faiths.

But sense-making is key for McGrath, and his main thesis is that "the existence of a God such as that proposed by the Christian tradition makes sense of what may be observed of the world" (*OS*, 233). I agree, and also with his statement that while this may not prove anything, it is "at the very least consistent with the existence of a creator God." Another important word for McGrath to describe the relationship between Christian doctrine and what is seen in the natural world is "resonance" (*OS*, 233ff.). This is undoubtedly similar to Polkinghorne's use of the word "consonance." While Polkinghorne is hesitant about the kind of analytic philosophy approach of Richard Swinburne and others, it does nevertheless seem to me that his position is more favorable toward the traditional approach than McGrath's, in that, for Polkinghorne, natural theology does concern what we can learn about God apart from revelation, even if its deliveries are limited in scope. For McGrath, as ever, this has the effect of reinforcing the plausibility of the Christian worldview for those already committed to it (*OS*, 234).

McGrath notes the anthropic "coincidences" necessary for life to develop in the universe and that similar phenomena are found in chemistry, biochemistry, and evolutionary biology (*OS*, 242), a point expanded upon considerably in *FTU*, as we shall describe. He believes that his approach to natural theology is ideally adapted to engage with such phenomena because they do not offer proof of God's existence but are consistent with the Christian view of God. Yet Robin Collins, whom McGrath cites in a footnote, uses the evidence of the universe's fine-tuning as an *argument* for God's existence: it is not merely "consistent with" Christian belief. Indeed, in a more recent work on a similar topic, Collins states, "In this contribution, I will attempt to explain why, contrary to the impression one often gets, contemporary physics and cosmology are not only compatible with theism, but could arguably be thought to suggest a theistic explanation of the Universe or multiverse."[36] Note that this chapter is in a "secular" book whose main contributions are from professional cosmologists.

But then McGrath seems once again to give back with one hand what he has taken away with the other. He goes on to say that "the finely-tuned fruitfulness of the world and the intelligibility of the world, though both insights that arise from science, nevertheless call for some explanation and understanding which, by its very nature, is likely to go beyond what science itself can provide." Moreover, "this is not a repristinated version of Paley's argument from design, but a scientifically and theologically informed variant of 'inference to the best explanation' (Harman) or 'abduction to the best explanation' (Peirce)" (*OS*, 244). Here McGrath is acknowledging Gilbert Harman's original use of the expression "inference to the best explanation" in the 1960s and the American pragmatist Charles Peirce's term "abduction" coined much earlier, but having essentially the same meaning. Peter Lipton is a more recent exponent of the method.

In *FTU*, McGrath notes Peirce's own abductive argument for the existence of God, appealing to the order of the universe as best explained by the existence of a transcendent cause that has bestowed on us the cognitive powers to infer its existence. But again, all the old questions apply. Is not "inference to the best explanation" globally valid? Or does "theologically informed" actually mean "only valid if you start from the Trinitarian God in your premises in the first place"?

What, according to McGrath, are the criteria for making the IBE—that is, deciding which of competing hypotheses is explanatorily the best? The answer is that, although the subject of debate and possessing an inevitable degree of imprecision, they include "'epistemic virtues' such as simplicity, elegance, consilience, and concision" (*OS*, 236). McGrath notes the Bayesian formulation of the argument and the fact that it can transfer from the scientific to the transcendent realm. Indeed, he rightly commends Richard Swinburne's *The Existence of God* as "one of the most important twentieth-century affirmations of the explanatory capacity of theism" (*OS*, 236–37). He points to various features of the universe that need to be explained and again asserts, following Torrance, the universe's "intelligibility reflecting its contingent origins in the rationality of God" (*OS*, 237). But once again, if the rationality of God explains the intelligibility of the universe, then that very same intelligibility is evidence in support of a metaphysical hypothesis that God did indeed create the universe. And if this is the best explanation, then the explanatory power of Christian theism is the greatest of all the competing hypotheses. That much is pure logic.

On a Bayesian reckoning, the matter will then hinge on the relative prior probability of the hypothesis, which, although also only assessable with considerable imprecision, may nevertheless lead to a judgment of the relative posterior probabilities of the hypotheses. That is precisely Swinburne's program. McGrath's approach neglects the prior probabilities, which are in fact crucial, and may well be the deciding factor, even though their assessment may be difficult and controversial. McGrath thus ignores the fact that one hypothesis may render evidence more likely than another does but could effectively be ruled out because it is immensely less probable in the first place.

Another aspect of natural theology adverted to by McGrath, as indeed by other writers such as Polkinghorne, is the remarkable way in which mathematics, a construct of the human mind (though perhaps with an eternal Platonic referent or referent in the mind of God), is so effective in expressing the laws of nature uncovered by science, which has an empirical referent in the natural world. Citing the famous paper by Eugene Wigner[37] (*STN*, 209–14, *OS*, 149–50), McGrath says this fact requires explanation (*OS*, 149), even though he still apparently regards the eighteenth-century consensus about the book of nature thus witnessing to the character of God as simply historically contingent (*OS*, 153).

I agree with McGrath and Polkinghorne that this close fit of the mathematical and the physical makes sense on the grounds of "a created correspondence between the world and the mind" (*OS*, 247). As McGrath notes Torrance saying, this correspondence of the mathematical world with the physical world is an assumption of science but cannot be substantiated from science. With Torrance, I agree that this has to be established from beyond science. But again, contra McGrath and Torrance, I would want to say that because it is to be expected if the universe is God's creation and human beings are made in the image of God, it therefore provides evidence for Christian belief that can be utilized in the traditional mode of natural theology. One reason for drawing back from, or at least nuancing, McGrath's position that theology is an *a posteriori* discipline is that mathematical beauty can precede experimental verification. Witness the importance of mathematical beauty as a guide to truth, even in preference to empirical data, for Paul Dirac, and even Einstein. This signals the important interplay between theory and observation in science. While McGrath does also appear to recognize this (see, e.g., *OT*, 89ff.), like Torrance it seems to me that he significantly underplays it. Alternatively, perhaps it is simply that he draws a different conclusion from me—that there is no universal rationality and natural theology should be done with the prior assumptions of Christian dogmatics, instead of saying that both the natural world and revelation that gives rise to those assumptions need to be evaluated for their probable truth according to commonly accepted rational criteria.

Something that gets rather lost in the discussion, but is worth mentioning, is the Trinitarian nature of God that McGrath has deemed so important. However, McGrath again seems to be much closer to my own position in what he says next concerning this insight from mathematics. Indeed he acknowledges that a traditional natural theology may provide "fleeting, fragmentary glimpses of a greater reality" from these insights. These glimpses are then "clarified and consolidated from within the standpoint of the Christian tradition, which is able to affirm whatever can be known in this tantalizing manner, while clarifying it and placing it upon a firmer foundation in the divine *logos*" (*OS*, 248).

Indeed, it works both ways. In the language of the kind of natural theology that Richard Swinburne and others do, call E the evidence that mathematics is effective in describing nature. The probability that this is so if God exists, P[E|G], is likely to be high for reasons with which McGrath would concur. But this is related to the probability that God exists given that E pertains, P[G|E], through Bayes's theorem:

$$P[G|E] = P[E|G].\ P[G] \,/\, \{P[E|G].\ P[G] + P[E|{\sim}G].\ P[{\sim}G]\} \qquad (6.1)$$

If it turns out that P[G|E] > P[G], then it can be said that E constitutes evidence for the truth of G, indeed that E "confirms" G in the language of confirmation theory. As in evaluating all the evidence in the way that Swinburne does, one needs to consider the relative values, at least qualitatively, of the various terms in this equation, and this task is, as always, not a trivial one. But it is perfectly reasonable to suppose that P[E|G] > P[E|~G], on the grounds that E is utterly mysterious if there is no God. It then follows that it is indeed the case that P[G|E] > P[G].

In fact, we have reached a position where it is possible to make a direct comparison of Swinburne's and McGrath's approaches, by formulating the two in Bayesian terms.

Swinburne essentially builds a cumulative case by taking a succession of items of evidence, $E_1, E_2, \ldots, E_n$, say. He argues that each $E_i$ is to be expected on the basis of G (and, for $i > 1$, the $E_j$ from $j = 1$ to $i - 1$), so that P[E|G] is high compared with P[E|~G], where $E = E_1 \,\&\, E_2 \,\&\, \ldots \,\&\, E_n$. From Bayes's Theorem it follows that P[G|E] is much greater than the prior value P[G]. That is, of course, the probability that a "minimal" kind of theism is correct. Swinburne then goes on to claim that G entails the Trinitarian God of Christian theism T,[38] so that P[T|E] = P[G|E] (since obviously T also entails G). The probability of the correctness of other doctrines given T can then be estimated, so that one ends up with an estimate of P[C|E] where C comprises the fundamental doctrines of Christianity—especially the incarnation and resurrection. This is obviously less than P[T|E], but, according to Swinburne, still high—despite the problem of "dwindling probabilities" addressed in the paper cited already.

My purpose here is not to engage in detail with Swinburne's argument, which is sophisticated and would demand considerable space, but merely to compare it with McGrath's approach. If one does not go all the way with Swinburne, and I am inclined not to at this point, in accepting that G entails T, one could in principle argue for some value of P[T|E] < P[G|E] on the basis of the evidence (including that from revelation). Indeed Swinburne himself recognizes that his arguments here are tentative and on occasion makes the less dogmatic but still strong claim that T is the most probable among competing accounts of G.

McGrath, in contrast, starts with C. He then says that each $E_i$ is to be expected on the basis of C (and, for $i > 1$, the $E_j$ from $j = 1$ to $i - 1$). Hence once could argue, as for Swinburne, that P[E|C] is high compared with P[E|~C], where again $E = E_1 \,\&\, E_2 \,\&\, \ldots \,\&\, E_n$. From Bayes's Theorem this feeds back as before so that P[C|E] is much enhanced over its prior value P[C]. In essence, McGrath has done everything in one fell swoop—given the translation into Bayesian terms that he would not accept.

Are the two approaches equivalent then? The main difference is that Swinburne's P[G] would be much greater than McGrath's P[C] since C contains more information, or to put it differently, is more complex than G. This would feed through to comparison of the values of P[G|E] and P[C|E]. However, arguably McGrath's $P[E_i|C \,\&\, E_{i-1} \,\&\, E_{i-2} \ldots \&\, E_1]$ are greater than Swinburne's $P[E_i|G \,\&\, E_{i-1} \,\&\, E_{i-2} \ldots \&\, E_1]$, and Swinburne's steps in going from P[G|E] to P[T|E] and P[C|E] may end up with a similar final answer. At least, it seems to me, the gaps could be filled in in principle to show that the two arguments are roughly equivalent, even if the details are different.

I think the main problem with the above is that McGrath would not endorse it. Swinburne's approach is an example of the traditional kind of natural theology that McGrath repudiates. So McGrath can hardly intend that we draw this conclusion. I think that in practice the task of expressing McGrath's kind of natural theology probabilistically would be much more difficult than for Swinburne. The reason is that one is expected to grasp Christian doctrine "whole" so to speak, in one single embrace. And to apply that apologetically—that is, suggesting it to a nonbeliever—smacks of the "positivism of revelation" of which Bonhoeffer accused Barth, as I noted above. On the other hand, to apply McGrath's approach to an existing believer might well show more in the end than does Swinburne's approach. In other words, it would tell the believer more about nature in the end than the unbeliever would gain through Swinburne's approach. That is because the approaches are different, and for the believer the quantities $P[E_i|C \,\&\, E_{i-1} \,\&\, E_{i-2} \ldots \&\, E_1]$ are where the focus would lie.

From what I have said, one can see similarities and differences between McGrath, Swinburne, and indeed Polkinghorne. Swinburne would see the maximum delivery from traditional natural theology. Polkinghorne would be nearer to McGrath in also denying the existence (as Polkinghorne puts it) of an Archimedean point, yet even he would also affirm the need to bring rational criteria to bear in evaluating the unique claims of the Christian revelation. That, perhaps, is where McGrath seems most to be operating in a circle.

## *Truth, Beauty, and Goodness: Expanding the Scope of Natural Theology*

The question one wants to address to McGrath, which his approach makes problematic, is the basic one: "Is it true?" As one would expect, his answer is in the affirmative. Thus McGrath sides with J. R. R. Tolkien, C. S. Lewis, and others in affirming that other religions and pagan myths contain some truth, or hint at something that is made explicit in the Christian myth—the one true myth. That ties in with McGrath's view of tradition-transcendent rationality. But C. S. Lewis at least certainly used arguments of a traditional natural theological kind to promote the Christian faith. Indeed McGrath recognizes this when he cites Lewis as saying, "Unless all that we take to be knowledge is an illusion, we must hold that in thinking we are not reading rationality into an irrational universe but responding to a rationality with which the universe has already been saturated"[39] (*OS*, 256). Nevertheless, Lewis supplemented this with "something more elusive, and in Lewis's view more fundamental and compelling—an appeal to the imagination" (*OS*, 257). McGrath himself wants to go beyond the purely intellectual realm in his own understanding of natural theology. I agree that nature undoubtedly stirs the imagination, and imagination may well be "more compelling" on McGrath's concept of natural theology. In the classic sense of the term, my suspicion is that reasoned argument will be of more value, though I am not sure that much hangs on this.

McGrath extends the scope of natural theology (in his sense, of course, though it would also apply to the classic sense) to cover the place of beauty and of goodness in addition to that of truth. He notes, for example, that Augustine discovered late a sense of beauty "already planted deep within him" (*Confessions* 10.27.38; *OS*, 262–63). As McGrath notes, Hans Urs von Balthasar is a significant modern-day theologian who has expounded a theology of beauty, with a point of contact in human culture and creativity (*OS*, 264–65; *STN*, 237).

McGrath cites George Steiner as arguing that "there is aesthetic creation because there is *creation*"[40] (*OS*, 284), and this can be the basis for a natural theology. He also notes that C. S. Lewis argues for a point of contact in the human quest for beauty: "We possess an instinct of transcendence, stimulated by beauty—a 'desire for our own far-off country, which we find in ourselves even now'"[41] (*OS*, 287; McGrath cites another passage from this essay of Lewis, *STN*, 235, in making a similar point). All this appeal to human culture and "points of contact" would, of course, be anathema to Barth. Indeed it doesn't sound altogether different from Schleiermacher's "feeling of absolute dependence."

McGrath notes how Ruskin thought the glory of God could be encountered directly through nature (*OS*, 271), without intermediaries. Yet his concern that nature be distorted by theoretical representations led to "the overwhelming of his own capacity to perceive it" (*OS*, 273).

McGrath also notes the criterion of beauty in the development and evaluation of scientific theories (*OS*, 273), a point noted by Polkinghorne and seen in the writings of Einstein and Dirac, for example, and Polanyi, for whom beauty was essential to belief in the truth of a theory.[42] At the same time McGrath notes the vagueness of the concept in that "there is as yet little evidence that the natural sciences have identified which aesthetic properties might indicate the truth of scientific theories, or how such criteria might be incorporated within the process of theory-testing and selection" (*OS*, 275). Perhaps, however, we do not need precision in these matters for the widely accepted notion among scientists that beauty is a guide to truth in science to provide a distinct strand in a traditional-style natural theological argument as well as McGrath's style of natural theology. The former way is just how John Polkinghorne uses it. Since, as McGrath acknowledges, one would expect beauty in the "mind of God" to be reflected in the creation, this can indeed also function as an argument for God being behind the universe.

Beauty, though, goes beyond the mere beauty of scientific theories to a more imaginative and affective engagement with the aesthetics of nature, which is seen in the Romantic poets. Indeed, poets such as Goethe and Keats "held that science offered a reductionist account of nature, which threatened to diminish its intrinsic wonder" (*OS*, 281). Famously Keats referred to Newton as "unweaving the rainbow" by reducing it to its prismatic colors, as noted above. McGrath, however, thinks that Keats makes a valid point, if exaggeratedly, notwithstanding Dawkins's criticism. In seeing the parts, one may miss the aesthetic impact of the whole. Interestingly, McGrath argues that, from a Christian perspective, "an interpretation of the beauty of nature can be interpreted as a transitory intuition of what is eternal, the experience *signifying* yet not *delivering* something of immense and transformative importance, and thus creating a sense of absence, a feeling of longing, within the human soul" (*OS*, 282). Again, the notion of "feeling" recalls Schleiermacher.

McGrath also considers the third element, goodness, of the Platonic triad of truth, beauty, and goodness. He notes Iris Murdoch's moral realism (*OS*, 47–48), and her argument that moral progress involves awareness of, and submission to, the purposes of a reality that transcends us[43] (*OS*, 292). That might lead one in the direction of natural law ethics. Nevertheless, while McGrath recognizes that natural law ethics has been "remarkably resilient" (*OS*, 293), he criticizes it for being "dependent on a theory of nature which nature itself cannot supply" (*OS*, 293).

McGrath examines the history of natural law in relation to natural theology. He notes the Sophist treatment of nature as the ultimate basis of morality and Aristotle's appeal to the order of nature in determining what forms human laws should take (*OS*, 294). One of his claims, characteristic as we have seen of his whole approach, is that a viable natural theology of goodness is dependent on a Christian understanding of nature (*OS*, 293). One of the aspects of the latter is that the creation is ordered (*OS*, 293; *STN*, 218–32). Yet in Aristotle we have a pagan philosopher who of course recognizes the order apart from the Christian understanding! I would also argue that there is much in common between Old Testament law, notably the Ten Commandments, and pagan law codes, notably the code of Hammurabi. There is a sense in which human beings have access to ethical norms purely by virtue of being human. So again classic, traditional natural theology does what is required in arriving at natural law ethics, which is God-given in any case. As McGrath quotes Calvin, "The law of God is nothing else than the natural law and that conscience which God has engraved within the human mind" (*Institutes* 4.20.16; *OS*, 295). The natural law is accessible to us despite our sin. Interestingly, C. S. Lewis argues for its commonality among widely differing civilizations.[44]

McGrath notes the moral ambivalence of nature (which is clearly related to the notion of nature's "disorder" considered earlier). Thus Tennyson in *In Memoriam* famously wrote of "nature, red in tooth and claw." McGrath also points to John Ruskin's changing views of the beauty and goodness of nature (*OS*, 301). Yet "natural law" ethics does not read off from nature how humans should behave, and so is not guilty of the "naturalistic fallacy"—unlike, as McGrath rightly sees, the evolutionary ethics of such as Herbert Spencer and Julian Huxley (*OS*, 306). Rather, natural law is taken to be implanted by God in our human nature, and we are moral beings because we are rational. Hence, if this is a criticism of natural law, it certainly fails. However, I agree that natural theology needs to take account of the moral ambivalence of nature, as well as the problem of evil more generally (see above). It may be that these things count against the existence of God in the classic kind of natural theology, but could be outweighed in a cumulative argument. Richard Swinburne seems to make the stronger claim that one can provide good reasons for the existence of evil that even nullify its negative impact. Either way, the argument needs to be made, and that is not the purpose of the present chapter, where I simply point out the possibility that this can at least be done in principle, and that a number of significant proposals have been made.

As noted above, the problem of evil also needs to be addressed on McGrath's view of natural theology, and I have considered his answer unsatisfactory. Indeed it is the biggest problem for faith, and so for the credibility of his starting point. He repeats, in this section on the moral ambiguities of nature, his view that nature must now be seen as decayed. But he also cites, more promisingly in my view, John Haught's appeal to the "'self-emptying God' who 'participates fully in the world's struggle and pain'" (*OS*, 304), a view that McGrath regards as fully incarnational and Trinitarian in its vision of God. He also notes the eschatological resources of the Christian faith, something to which

Swinburne also now appeals while recognizing, unlike McGrath, that taking more of Christian dogma into account reduces the prior probability of one's hypothesis.

McGrath notes that "nature can be 'read' in ways that appear to endorse such morally questionable notions as oppression, violence, and eugenics" (*OS*, 307). That is true and is an argument against evolutionary ethics, but it does not impact natural law ethics for reasons given above. Because such behaviors run counter to natural law, which humans recognize even if they do not recognize its source, evolution shows that there is more than just evolution involved. Indeed, the existence of morality itself points to God and can be used in a traditional natural theological sense as an argument (as such diverse thinkers as Kant and C. S. Lewis have done).

McGrath believes his approach resolves the "Euthyphro dilemma." He says that "the dilemma gains its force precisely because we are asked to consider the relationship between two allegedly independent entities: what *human beings* recognise as good, and what *God* recognises as good. . . . But if these can be shown to be related to each other in any way, the force of the dilemma is lost" (*OS*, 311; *STN*, 216). Of course that relationship is for McGrath the doctrine of the *imago dei*, whereby "there is a congruence between divine notions of truth, beauty, and goodness and proper human notions of the same on account of the creaturely status of humanity" (*OS*, 312; *STN*, 216). I must admit I fail to see, true and important though this is, that it really solves the dilemma since the two poles are not human and divine conceptions of the good but God's commands and the "good" in the abstract, apart from any conception of it. And in any case the dilemma forces itself upon us when we consider what seem to be divine commands in Scripture, which are either not perceived to be good (McGrath) or just not good (my interpretation of the dilemma). The classic example is the command to sacrifice Isaac, which Kierkegaard considered in *Fear and Trembling*, but other seeming commands to kill men, women, and children seem equally problematic. Some other kind of resolution of this—for example, in the latter case in terms of the growing understanding of God by the Israelites—must surely be an alternative to really affirming that God did command the immoral.

## *McGrath's 2009 Gifford Lectures:* A Fine-Tuned Universe? The Quest for God in Science and Theology

These lectures, published more fully in book form,[45] have two parts. In the first, McGrath again outlines his vision for a Trinitarian natural theology, and in the second he focuses on examples of fine-tuning in the universe and their interpretation.

The first part takes us through the familiar themes of McGrath's approach to natural theology. He writes of the crisis of confidence in modern natural theology and his vision for renewing it. There are chapters on natural theology and the explanation of reality, and on the dynamics of a Trinitarian natural theology. The dependence on Torrance is evident; the book is dedicated to him and also, interestingly, the eminent Anglo-Catholic existentialist theologian John Macquarrie.

Whereas in *The Open Secret* McGrath broadens natural theology to include its potential of revealing the moral and aesthetic dimensions of nature, in *FTU* he concentrates on its sense-making role. The Christian doctrine of creation enables us to see that the universe is both intelligible and contingent, both features vital to the scientific enterprise yet otherwise surprising. Others, such as Polkinghorne and indeed Torrance, have also drawn attention to these features.

Again, McGrath affirms the location of natural theology within dogmatic, orthodox Trinitarian theology. His approach provides a theory-laden explanatory account of the so-called anthropic phenomena in cosmology and elsewhere (*FTU*, xi–xiv). McGrath is not sympathetic to Stephen Jay Gould's "non-overlapping magisteria" classification of science and religion but sees them as offering to each other "possibilities of cross-fertilization on account of the interpretation of their subjects and methods." Again for McGrath, nature is a social construction (*FTU*, 6), making traditional natural theology situation-specific rather than universal. He sees the recent discussion as setting out "to deduce the existence and at least something of the nature of God from an engagement with nature." That is indeed the case with William Lane Craig, whom he cites in a footnote (*FTU*, 7n28), but not Richard Swinburne, discussed above, who sees inductive rather than deductive inference as more appropriate. Certainly "demonstration" and "proof" in this context, which may be how natural theology has been seen in the past, are far too grandiose claims. McGrath is right to point out, however, that simple appeal to the Bible became problematic during the Enlightenment, so encouraging the alternative of natural theology whereby Christian faith could be based on pure reason. Where I part company again is with his assertion that "there is no compelling reason to defend a modernist vision of natural theology in a postmodern culture" (*FTU*, 14). That may be so if one is a postmodernist sympathizer, but not if one rejects postmodernism, as indeed do most scientists, and for very good reason: they see their discipline as saying something true about the real world.

Again, McGrath cites the paper by Swinburne on dwindling probabilities as indicating a negative view of traditional natural theology, whereas in fact Swinburne supports his natural theology *against* the dwindling-probabilities argument (*FTU*, 15n16). A few pages later McGrath correctly notes that "Swinburne offers an inductive and probabilistic approach, which sets out to determine whether theism offers a superior account of such regularities in nature than does its alternatives" (*FTU*, 18).

Regarding Barth, McGrath correctly notes that the initial target was "religion" (*Der Römerbrief*, 2nd ed., 1922); then it was Schleiermacher's reduction of theology to anthropology (*Die Christliche Theologie im Entwurf*, 1927); only later in CD II/1 §26 was the target "natural theology" (*FTU*, 18–19). He notes that Barth's critique of natural theology is directed against an "attempt to prove God's existence or to gain access to knowledge of God under conditions of humanity's own choosing," which certainly seems to be Barth's understanding. McGrath's own view of natural theology undertaken from within dogmatic theology is thus untouched; while natural theology does not prove God's existence for McGrath, "it is confirmed that the fundamental themes of the Christian faith offer the best explanation of what is seen" (*FTU*, 20). If this is so, as McGrath repeatedly claims, then once again my response is that "what is seen" "confirms" those fundamental Christian themes in the sense of Bayesian confirmation theory.

In the chapter on renewing natural theology, McGrath points to the classic notion of *theologia tripartia*, with its divisions into "mythical theology" (*theologia fabulosa*), "civil theology" (*theologia civilis*), and "natural theology" (*theologia naturalis*). All three were to be found in Augustine, though the first was both primary and, unlike the Greek myths, grounded in the historical reality of Jesus of Nazareth. The second meant that Christianity could be offered as a civil religion, and the third, that it could engage with the wider culture and could affirm "the intellectual vitality of faith without recourse to revelation" (*FTU*, 25). In the classical era, McGrath says, natural theology was rational and philosophical in kind; only much later did it become identified with the physico-theology of John Ray and others, culminating in Paley's famous treatise of 1802. A key change at the Enlightenment was the interpretation of "reason" as "a human faculty that 'submitted all reality to the structures of the mind'" as opposed to the classic notion of it as "'an ordering principle inherent in reality'" (*FTU*, 26, with quotations from Louis Dupré[46]). If, however, as McGrath claims, Augustine saw natural theology as not reliant on revelation, then the "classic notion" is in fact quite similar to the version that Barth criticized—though perhaps those adopting the classic notion would not agree with Barth's interpretation of it. McGrath goes on to summarize the approach already given in *OS*. Again, however, if natural theology "can play an important apologetic role . . . in providing a navigable channel from human interest in the beauty of nature or the notion of the 'transcendent' to the 'God and Father of our Lord Jesus Christ'" (*FTU*, 28), then it does sound like the classic notion once again!

Indeed, in a key passage, McGrath seems to acknowledge all that I have been saying:

> On this approach, we might *begin* by seeing natural theology as disclosing simply a creator God; as we begin to follow this through, in the light of the Christian revelation, we realize that this provisional judgement is ultimately unsustainable, and requires reworking and reconceptualization. The classic model of natural theology is therefore nothing more than a heuristic starting point, which is developed and modified as the iterative process proceeds. We might begin with a sense of

> the transcendent—a vague, impersonal, perception which we realize might be the gateway to something greater. Yet when we pass through the threshold of that gateway, we encounter a way of seeing the world which causes us to interpret that initial sense or feeling in a new way. We end with a Trinitarian vision of God, which in one sense was not included in that original perception, and yet in another sense it is. The God, who *is* Trinity, is not initially *perceived* as Trinitarian. (*FTU*, 33)

That is very much my approach. One offers the "classic" approach to a skeptic, and invites him to go further. If the argument leads anyone to a vague notion of a Creator, he can be led on to consider the specifics of the Christian revelation—the detail of who that Creator is, known from revelation. However, it does not quite tally with what McGrath says a short while later that natural theology is better seen as "a retrospective validation of belief in God" (*FTU*, 34). Indeed in the next chapter he reverts to his "Trinitarian natural theology" as opposed to "classic natural theology."

McGrath believes it is correct to designate his approach as "Trinitarian natural theology" rather than a "Trinitarian theology of nature" since it gives an account of the role of the human observer of nature. I am not convinced that this is sufficient if Trinitarianism is still the starting point, as it appears to be much of the time in McGrath, though if it works as in the long quotation just cited, then it looks as though we are only arguing about semantics.

In another place McGrath writes (*OS*, 226): "Natural theology must be able to express a richer, more expansive, and more comprehensive range of human responses to the natural order than the insight, typically encountered in the writings of Paley, that it is logically supportive of the existence of a wise and benevolent God. Rational explanation must be supplemented by adoration and worship, responding to the sense of awe in the presence of God's creation." I agree with McGrath that natural theology should consider beauty and goodness, as well as truth, but I would see worship and adoration stemming more from a theology of nature than natural theology.

In the chapter on natural theology and the explanation of reality in *FTU*, McGrath makes an interesting point about circularity of explanation, a criticism of his approach that we have made a number of times. He rightly recognizes that explanations may be self-evidencing or circular in the sense that it is both true that hypothesis A explains evidence B and that B justifies A (*FTU*, 52–53), which is precisely the point of the Bayesian formulation. However, this explanation is not circular in the sense of assuming the Trinitarian God as a Christian and inferring the same from the evidence that nature provides. In McGrath's case this seems often to be put as though only a Christian can make the inference, in which case it is circular. However, it is not circular if the hypothesis of theism is framed as a genuine hypothesis whose probability is first assessed apart from the evidence being considered and irrespective of one's own faith in God. Then, if the hypothesis explains the evidence, that in turn is genuinely evidence for the truth of the hypothesis. To quote McGrath again, "A Christian natural theology is able to explain much of what is observed in nature; that capacity in turn becomes an additional reason for asserting that the Christian tradition, whose fundamental ideas gave rise to this form of natural theology in the first place, is justified in its beliefs" (*FTU*, 56), though I would argue that the "additional" might be additional to other arguments in a cumulative chain of reasoning, rather than a prior fundamental conviction. McGrath's statement that inference to the best explanation "appears to have a significant advantage over Bayesian approaches in being able to illuminate the context of scientific discovery" (*FTU*, 57) seems paradoxical.

McGrath claims that Trinitarianism explains the trend toward unification we see in science. He is worried also that classic natural theology only gives an attenuated view of God, to be filled out by what can be known of God from revelation. In again discussing St. Paul's sermon on the Areopagus (*FTU*, 64), he almost implies that Paul himself is vulnerable to the charge of simply providing extra information about God to that which the Athenians already had from their own vague awareness of divinity. But if that is so, I do not feel I am in bad company for adopting a similar approach! However, I should note that McGrath is aware of my drawing this conclusion and nuances his reflection on Paul by stating that "Paul *names* this unknown divinity, before expanding it into a fully orbed Christian vision of God, such as that set out in his letters." McGrath concludes, "The transition is thus between an *intimated* 'unknown God' and a *disclosed* 'God and Father of our Lord Jesus Christ' (Romans 15:6)" (*FTU*, 64).

It also seems that Calvin is doing something similar, according to McGrath, leading his readers from "a natural or intuitive perception of God to a more biblically grounded understanding of God, which extends and clarifies what can be known through nature." Again, I am not worried to be in such company! And how the specifics of Trinitarianism relate to natural theology in McGrath remains somewhat obscure (the trend to unification in science may reflect the unity of the persons in the Trinity, but is perhaps a rather tenuous link). Certainly Trinitarian doctrine gives a role in creation to the members of the Trinity, as, for example, in Irenaeus's "two hands" expression for the Son and Spirit (*FTU*, 78). The *Logos* may be the rational principle behind the universe, the agent of creation and its sustainer. And the Holy Spirit may indeed guide the interpreters of the two books of nature and Scripture (*FTU*, 72). The *imago dei* may give some insight into the structure of the human mind, as in Augustine's thought (though his mental metaphors also seem rather abstract and stretched in relating to the Trinity; indeed, McGrath thinks they are based on the mistaken science of his day [*FTU*, 105]). More significantly, the correlation of this image with the *Logos* may help explain the capacity of the human mind to discern nature's rational structure (*FTU*, 75). Most of all, the doctrine of the Trinity is vital to an understanding of the whole economy of salvation, running through creation, fall, and redemption to consummation. However, it seems to me that the impact specifically on *natural theology*, as opposed to the doctrine of creation and these wider doctrines, is very limited, and McGrath does not satisfactorily spell it out. Although McGrath points to natural theology being an enterprise of "a fallen humanity reflecting on a fallen nature" (*FTU*, 78), McGrath's view of the fall of nature is problematic (as noted above). However, again as already noted, the problem of "natural evil" is a serious one for classic natural theology and might be regarded as counterevidence in the total cumulative case for theism. McGrath cites

Ruskin as counterbalancing the picture of nature as all "sunshine, and fresh breezes, and bleating lambs" (*FTU*, 81) with "the carcase of a ewe, drowned in the last flood" which "lies nearly bare to the bone." This is the "shadowy side" of nature, says McGrath (*FTU*, 82), echoing a phrase of Polkinghorne. As I say, this shadowy side of nature remains a problem since there never was a time when nature was different—"unfallen" in a state of pristine harmony.

A novel feature of McGrath's book is his appeal to St. Augustine on creation. The chapter in which he expounds this point opens with the familiar quote from C. S. Lewis about the sun rising (*FTU*, 95, and see above). But then McGrath tells us, significantly, that he has chosen Augustine specifically because that theologian developed his theological system in the light of Scripture and the Christian tradition long before the emergence of modern science (*FTU*, 97).

A brief discussion follows of prediction as an epistemic virtue in science. However, whether this is merely psychological, and there is thus no real difference between prediction and retrodiction as confirmatory, is debatable, as McGrath is aware from his citation of key papers both here (*FTU*, 98) and earlier (*FTU*, 59–60). Nevertheless, McGrath shows how Augustine's approach has "merits which he himself could not have known or anticipated at the time of writing" (*FTU*, 98). Since McGrath does not seem to endorse confirmation theory in the style of the philosophers he quotes or, in the theological sphere, of Richard Swinburne, he presumably means Augustine offers confirmation only to those already operating from within Trinitarian Christianity.

In particular in this context, McGrath quotes Augustine's commentary on Genesis, *The Literal Meaning of Genesis*. For Augustine, the universe is a created entity and contingent, and time is a part of the created order, in contrast to the view of most neo-Platonists that the world is eternal. But, writes McGrath, "Augustine does not limit God's creative action to the primordial act of origination." No, he also sets "the direction of the subsequent unfolding and development of the causalities which were embedded within the created order by that act of creation" (*FTU*, 100).

As McGrath notes, Augustine appeals to Ecclesiasticus 18:1 as stating that God created all things together. However, a better translation is "all things commonly," as the RSV and NRSV have it—"He who lives forever created the whole universe"—rendering Augustine's point rather less soundly based on Scripture (and the Apocrypha at that).

Notwithstanding the above qualification, I agree with McGrath that Augustine's view of the unfolding of embedded causalities is a helpful one. These are the "*rationes seminales*" or seedlike principles that are present from the cosmic beginning, in each of which is contained the potential for the later development of a specific living kind. "In the earth from the beginning, in what I might call the roots of time, God created what was to be in times to come," as St. Augustine himself puts it (*The Literal Meaning of Genesis* 5.4.11). And "there was present from the beginning in all living bodies a natural power, and I might say, there were interwoven with these bodies the seminal principles of animals later to appear" (*The Literal Meaning of Genesis* 3.14.23). This is not, of course, evolution as now understood, but nevertheless one can see some resemblance between these very early fifth-century statements and Darwin's words at the end of *Origin of Species*: "To my mind it accords better with what we know of the laws impressed on matter by the Creator, that the production and extinction of the past and present inhabitants of the world should have been due to secondary causes, like those determining the birth and death of the individual."[47] See also, "there is grandeur in this view of life, with its several powers, having been originally breathed into a few forms or into one; and that, while this planet has gone cycling on according to the fixed law of gravity, from so simple a beginning endless forms most beautiful and most wonderful have been, and are being, evolved."[48]

Elsewhere Augustine also refers to all the members of adults being contained within the causal principles of infants (*City of God* 22.14), and in *The Literal Meaning of Genesis* he is using the same idea for the generation of all living beings, as did Darwin so many centuries later. As McGrath acknowledges, Augustine's views were at least "partly shaped by his knowledge of the natural science of his day" (*FTU*, 101). Thus he interprets Genesis 1:12 as asserting that the earth "received the power or capacity to produce things by itself," in McGrath's paraphrase (*FTU*, 102), but bringing to mind Charles Kingsley's similar phraseology about Darwin's *Origin*. As I say, this isn't evolution, because, on the basis of the science of his day, Augustine believed in the fixity of species: "A bean does not come from a grain of wheat" and "A man does not come from a beast" (*The Literal Meaning of Genesis* 9.17.32). Nevertheless, Augustine's concept of *rationes seminales* provides the theological lens through which, in part 2 of *FTU*, McGrath explores how "the cosmos appears to have come into existence with the potentiality for human existence" (*FTU*, 106).

In part 2 of *FTU*, McGrath explores the particularities of fine-tuning, having prepared the way earlier with a chapter on counterfactuals as related to anthropic thinking (*FTU*, 83–93)—the fine-tunings arise from asking "What if?" questions—for example, what if the constants of physics were ever so slightly different from what they are? He gives an account of the development of the big bang theory and then a standard but clear account of the cosmological fine-tunings (*FTU*, 111–26), expounded initially by Brandon Carter, who coined the term "anthropic principle," and described in detail in the classic text of John Barrow and Frank Tipler.[49] The examples he gives are drawn from Martin Rees's book *Just Six Numbers*.[50] McGrath notes that some have suggested that Barrow's and Tipler's book is possibly "the greatest work of natural theology since William Paley," affirming "'science and religion' as a legitimate, proper, and even necessary adjunct to scientific reflection" (*FTU*, 117). Contra Paley's "theological misadventures," the question why things are the way they are, and why there is anything at all, remain legitimately on the table (*FTU*, 118). Indeed the "origin and character" of the laws that gave rise to the universe we know are matters "of major apologetic importance" (*FTU*, 118). McGrath agrees with Barrow that this kind of design argument, as opposed to Paley's, is "much harder to explain without reference to God" (*FTU*, 118).

However, one must bear in mind again at this point McGrath's approach to natural theology "from within," as opposed to my own, which I utilize in the cosmological sphere in *God, the Multiverse, and Everything*. Indeed, for McGrath, anthropic fine-tunings are "resonant" (McGrath's word) or "consonant" (Polkinghorne) with the Christian vision of God—that is, with "an *existing* way of thinking" (italics in original), but do not furnish deductive proof (*FTU*, 121). As I point out elsewhere in this chapter, "deductive proof" is not the result in Swinburne's approach nor mine either, as McGrath seems to think (and Swinburne is at pains to point this out), though it is to show that the fine-tuning provides "confirmation" (or good *inductive* evidence), in the sense of Bayesian confirmation theory, for divine design of the universe. Where McGrath says (*FTU*, 40–41) that "an argument that proves unable to compel assent by demonstrating the existence of God as a necessary inference can nevertheless still be the best explanation of what is observed," of course I agree. That is precisely what Swinburne and I aim to show. McGrath's view of Swinburne seems to be slightly off-balance here. He writes (*FTU*, 41–42), "Swinburne, while rightly stressing the potential importance of deductive arguments for the existence of God as first cause, nevertheless additionally adduces the essentially inductive argument that God may be held to constitute the best and simplest explanation of what is observed in the world." No, the latter is Swinburne's whole approach; inductive arguments are central and not "additions" to deductive arguments. Indeed he contends, "I shall argue that (neither separately nor in conjunction) are any of the arguments that I consider for or against the existence of God good deductive arguments."[51] Rather, Swinburne's arguments are good inductive arguments—that is, they make it more probable that God exists when they are taken into account than if not.

McGrath notes that the multiverse hypothesis has proved attractive, although "perhaps unwisely," to some atheist physicists such as Steven Weinberg and Leonard Susskind, at least in part because "it appears to avoid any inference of design or divinity" (*FTU*, 124). The notion is indeed highly speculative and, as Robin Collins and others point out, far from incompatible with theism anyway. Collins, Don Page, Arthur Peacocke, and other Christian theists are happy, indeed—especially the latter two—positively enthusiastic about it.[52] My own reservations are expressed in *God, the Multiverse, and Everything*, and have not changed with more recent developments such as Susskind's "string theory landscape" idea.[53]

As McGrath notes, Augustine's conception of *rationes seminales*, which he has already introduced, is at least "consonant" with the fine-tunings embedded in nature (*FTU*, 125). Augustine could be regarded as remarkably prescient in seeing in broad outline, not of course in detail, how causal potentialities embedded in nature could be brought to fruition under God's guidance over an unspecified period of time, which we now know to be billions of years. And that obviously applies both to cosmological evolution and the subsequent unfolding of the conditions for life on Earth and indeed the evolution of life itself.

Further chapters in part 2 of *FTU* deal in some detail with other kinds of anthropic properties, from the biological and chemical sciences. However, there is a frequent, if not inevitable, reference back to the cosmological fine-tunings as making possible everything that happens subsequently. The further fine-tunings indicate that the universe is certainly biocentric and they include the following:

1. *The conditions necessary for the origin of life* (*FTU*, 127–42). Appealing to the work of Harvard biological chemist Lawrence Henderson (1878–1942), McGrath notes the ultimate teleology of life originating from dead matter in the first place (*FTU*, 128). Henderson makes the point that Darwinian evolution does not explain but relies on the essential chemical preconditions for life being in place before it can get going. This point is correct, and it is not God-of-the-gaps, of course, but an obvious statement of fact, ignored by Richard Dawkins no doubt because it is immensely inconvenient to his Darwin-explains-everything thesis. In particular, going back to cosmological arguments, as Fred Hoyle pointed out, the conditions inside stars need to be just right for carbon to be made in the first place. Hoyle predicted a resonance in the $^{12}C$ nucleus and an absence of a resonance in the $^{16}O$ nucleus on the basis that both nuclei are necessary for life, so not only must $^{12}C$ form but it must not all be destroyed in making $^{16}O$ (*FTU*, 132–34). McGrath remarks, "The unique chemistry of carbon is the ultimate foundation of the capacity of nature to tune itself" (*FTU*, 139). He also notes that the fundamental properties of the chemical elements are "exploited *but not created* by biological processes" (*FTU*, 141), and they have to be as they are in order for the metabolic pathways involved in living organisms to be made possible in the first place. This is all certainly consistent with Augustine's *rationes seminales*.

2. *The curious chemical properties of water*. The application of this concept to natural theology goes back at least to William Whewell's *Bridgewater Treatise* "on the power, wisdom, and goodness of God,

as manifested in the creation." As McGrath notes, Whewell pointed to such properties as the insulating capacity of snow and ice, and the expansion of water on freezing, as "selected with a beneficent design" (Whewell, quoted in *FTU*, 145). McGrath points to many further properties such as the density maximum at 4° C, the fact that ice floats on water, and various solvent properties, as unique in combination and crucial for the development of life (*FTU*, 146). They represent, as McGrath puts it, "a possible instance of an anthropic phenomenon" (*FTU*, 152) in addition to the fine-tunings of the fundamental constants that enabled such elements as carbon, nitrogen, and oxygen to form in the first place through stellar nucleosynthesis.

3. *The constraints imposed on evolution by chemical catalysts.* McGrath notes that in addition to the lighter elements referred to above, life depends on the light metal ions sodium, magnesium, potassium, and calcium, and, as is increasingly recognized, "first row transition metal ions," such as manganese, iron, nickel, and copper (*FTU*, 156). For example, manganese is a catalyst in photosynthesis. Indeed the process depends critically on the quantum mechanical properties of the excited states of manganese electrons (*FTU*, 159). Many other examples would merit close attention. For McGrath all this "serves to emphasise—though not explain—the remarkable fine-tuning of biological processes" (*FTU*, 164). He continues: "This point is not negated by suggesting that evolution can fine-tune itself. Chemical reality constrains evolution; these processes can occur only because the chemistry of certain metals, predetermined by quantum mechanical parameters, permits them to do so" (*FTU*, 164). It is also significant that the transition metals are generally thought to be manufactured, not in the cores of stars, but through neutron-capture processes that occur in supernova explosions (iron is perhaps the most notable example). We know that supernovae are necessary to make the chemical elements formed by nucleosynthesis available for the making of planets—and ultimately life. We see that they are also necessary for the manufacture of further critical elements whose quantum mechanical properties are also essential for biological processes.

4. *The origins of complexity and the mechanism of evolution.* McGrath notes Charles Kingsley's celebrated reformulation of natural

theology as pointing to a God much wiser than the one who simply made all things, who instead chose to "make all things make themselves" (*FTU*, 168). Kingsley, and Frederick Temple likewise, thus "affirmed God's continuing presence and action within the slowly evolving natural order" (*FTU*, 168), as opposed to the static account of Paley and his predecessors of God's activity in creation. McGrath cites John Hedley Brooke in this context (*FTU*, 168n4), though Brooke attributes to Aubrey Moore an even more immanentist view of divine participation in the evolutionary process, based on the incarnation.[54] Brooke makes a similar point elsewhere in his writings.[55] McGrath now notes that Kingsley's approach whereby God "made all things make themselves" is easily mapped onto Augustine's concept of *rationes seminales* (*FTU*, 168–69).

In this light, then, the emergence of adaptation to environment through natural selection may be seen as "nature fine-tuning itself" (*FTU*, 176). The critical question then becomes: "Is evolvability itself fine-tuned? In other words, is the capacity for Darwinian evolution, which many hold to be essential to any definition of life, itself an anthropic phenomenon?" (*FTU*, 180). Again, this query takes one back to fundamental parameters of chemistry and physics, and above all the organic chemistry of carbon, which enables the formation of long-chain molecules—and so, once again, to the dependence of the existence of carbon in the first place on the fine-tuning of the laws of nuclear physics operating in stars.

5. *The directionality of evolution.* The question here is whether there can be teleology in evolution (*FTU*, 184), a prospect that has been anathema to a number of biologists, including Jacques Monod and Stephen Jay Gould. However, others have argued that there is. Thus, Francisco Ayala contends that "teleological explanation is fundamental to modern biology," and evolutionary biology as a whole is teleological (*FTU*, 186–87). McGrath notes that the idea that the fundamental unit of selection is the gene, which began with George G. Williams and reached its apogee with Dawkins's *The Selfish Gene*, is now in decline, with multilevel approaches gaining the intellectual high ground (*FTU*, 188–89).

Gould famously insisted that "almost every interesting event of life's history falls into the realm of contingency,"[56] and "we are the accidental result of an unplanned process . . . the fragile result of an enormous concatenation of improbabilities, not the predictable product of any definite process"[57] (both passages cited at *FTU*, 189). Gould utilized the metaphor of replaying life's tape and getting a completely different result. However, as McGrath correctly points out, Leigh van Valen and, more recently, Simon Conway Morris, have provided a massive challenge to this with the notion of evolutionary "convergence." Time and again evolution finds its way to the same solution to particular needs, so that, for example, the C-4 mechanism of photosynthesis has evolved independently at least thirty-one times in the last 8 million years (and there are two further distinct mechanisms); and the eye has arisen some twenty times in independent branches of the evolutionary tree. Conway Morris thinks that something like human beings would arise inevitably once the process of evolution started. McGrath concludes that "a form of teleology may indeed be inferred *a posteriori*, as the 'best explanation' of what is observed" (*FTU*, 195). And he notes Charles Peirce's statement about final causation: "The general result may be brought about at one time in one way, and at another time in another way. Final causation does not determine in what particular way it is to be brought about, but that the result shall have a general character"[58] (cited in *FTU*, 197). I would see this as a possible way to think about divine action in general: God can bring about his purposes through different routes in a way analogous to Peter Geach's supreme chess grandmaster who always wins the game, whatever the opponent does.[59]

For McGrath this all again fits neatly with Augustine's concept of *rationes seminales* (*FTU*, 199–201). However, McGrath reiterates the caveat that is fundamental to his whole approach, citing Newman's remark, "I believe in design because I believe in God; not in God because I believe in design" (*FTU*, 196). Again, McGrath asks whether the evolutionary process is consonant or resonant with divine providence and the achievement of purpose by God, rather than concluding that we discern purpose through examining evolution, which points us to God.

McGrath concludes with a chapter on "emergent creation" and

natural theology. Here he draws further attention to emergent properties in nature, a matter of considerable discussion in the science-religion arena at the present time. He notes that the "classical" natural theology pertaining from John Ray to William Paley assumed a young universe as a naïve literalist view of Scripture would indicate, which of course study of the geological record and biological evolution began to challenge (*FTU*, 204–5). In addition to these we now have the emergence of novel properties and laws as increasing complexity arises within nature and reveals a multileveled hierarchy of sciences (*FTU*, 205ff.). For example, the chemical and biological properties of salt cannot be predicted from our present knowledge of the properties of sodium and chlorine, and social behavior cannot be predicted from the behavior of individual animals in isolation (*FTU*, 206).

The phenomenon of emergence naturally draws us back to the stratification of reality and Bhaskar's critical realism (*FTU*, 209–16), which we have discussed already. It is this multilayered reality with which natural theology engages, according to McGrath (*FTU*, 210). In Augustine and Charles Kingsley (both of whom cited John 5:17 in support), McGrath sees God at work not only in his original action in embedding the potentialities for what is to come but also in the continuing process of their realization (*FTU*, 211).

This book concentrates on modern scientific foci for natural theology, but at the end McGrath raises the quest for beauty, "the human longing for something unattainable," and morality, as other areas for natural theological engagement (*FTU*, 216, 219, but explored in more detail in *OS* as described above). In summary he regards primordial creation and emergent potentiality now seen in the modern discourse as nascent in Augustine and a legitimate and necessary expansion of traditional Christian notions of creation, rather than their subversion (*FTU*, 216).

McGrath sees Trinitarianism as a theory-laden way of viewing and hence interpreting nature, and his purpose is not to defend it but to explore its explanatory possibilities, particularly its capacity for "colligation" (the connecting and unifying of facts; the term comes from William Whewell). As I say elsewhere in this chapter, the Trinitarian aspect tends to get somewhat lost, in comparison with other (very different) theologians such as Pannenberg and Colin Gunton.[60] Yet I do agree that a hypothesis that explains and brings together a diverse set of facts finds support from those facts. Unlike McGrath I see natural theology as then going the other way, from nature to God, and the argument being formalized in terms of Bayesian confirmation theory.

## *Conclusion*

There is a great deal that is valuable in McGrath's prolific writings in establishing the credentials of theology as "scientific" and in what he says about natural theology. We have seen that at times McGrath comes very close to the position I myself adopt of utilizing data from the natural sciences, such as anthropic fine-tuning, to provide support for Christian belief in the way traditional natural theology has done. McGrath has been especially helpful in drawing attention to a much wider range of special features of the universe than the cosmological fine-tunings—for example, the chemistry of water and the role of certain metals in catalysis. His appropriation of Augustine's notion of *rationes seminales* is also most apposite.

McGrath also uses the kind of language appropriate to the endeavor of natural theology, notably "inference to the best explanation." His application of critical realism to theology as well as science and his identification of the multilayered structure of reality is also helpful. I agree with the fundamental claim that any science must approach its object in the manner appropriate to that object.

Where I have found a stumbling block in McGrath is in his insistence, which seems to run counter to some of the above considerations, that natural theology is about what we can learn about God from nature if we have a prior commitment to a full Nicene-Chalcedonian Christian theology. The results from McGrath's approach may in the end be very similar to those obtained by the more traditional approach, as propounded in modern form by Richard Swinburne and others, but seem to me to be not quite so helpful apologetically. Nevertheless, McGrath remains one of the most significant theologians to engage with the natural sciences in the world today, and one whose fundamental theological outlook I share.

CHAPTER SEVEN

# Conclusion
## The Way Forward for Natural Theology

IN THIS CHAPTER I come back to my initial question: Does the natural world provide any *praeparatio evangelica* for the gospel, or does nature only tell us about the God who is already known in Jesus Christ? What have we learned from the theologians studied, and are there important lessons or qualifications to make about natural theology, even if we reject Barth's sharp rebuke? We summarize some of the points gleaned from our study of the individual theologians before coming to our overall conclusions.

### *Barth*

Barth's theology is impressively Christocentric. God's revelation is to be found in Jesus Christ as attested in Holy Scripture. The idea that God can be known outside his gracious revelation in Christ is anathema, and natural theology represents a hubristic attempt to do this unaided by God's grace. Theology must not be reduced to anthropology, as happened in so much of nineteenth-century theology, but must remain true to its function of responding to its object, this self-revelation of God in Christ, in the manner appropriate to it.

I agree that Christ is the supreme revelation of God and that theology's chief task is to reflect on that revelation. There is certainly a danger if theology only focuses on nature and is completely subverted to naturalistic presuppositions. That way might well lead, for example, to some less than orthodox views of the person of Christ—not human and divine, but some kind of exemplar of what is achievable for all humans. I think there is a tendency for that in the science and religion dialogue, particularly if theology is made to conform to what are perceived (perhaps falsely) to be scientific ideas of rationality.

However, if God is the author of nature, then we should expect to discover *something* of him through nature. This approach is not hubris and is not denying God's grace, but is a consequence of God's common grace to all mankind, enabling the Christian, including the theologian, to connect to the outsider. It also accords with Scripture which, contra Barth, contains natural theology.

Barth also denies to us the means for rationally evaluating what is purported to be revelation. Barth says that only faith awakened by God can lead anyone to an acceptance of God's revelation in Christ as reliable knowledge, but it seems to me that historical-critical study can help furnish grounds for belief, provided it is not engaged with too narrow a conception (such as that of Troeltsch's principle of analogy) of what might be found. This is particularly the case when it comes to evidence for the supreme miracle of the resurrection of Christ. My faith awakened by God leads me to put my trust in Christ, and to lead my life in fellowship with him and obedient to his will as far as I am enabled by his Spirit, but I neither take the initial step of faith, nor continue the journey, in complete absence of any rational justification for doing so.

If we do allow rational evaluation of purported revelation, and if we see God's common grace in nature, then, as Barr, Hebblethwaite, and others would say, the distinction between natural and revealed knowledge of God becomes blurred, and we would be open to engaging in the "ramified" kind of natural theology that Swinburne espouses.

## *Bonhoeffer*

I agree with Bonhoeffer's criticism of Barth that the latter offers a positivism of revelation, and that this is fine for the church, but not for the outsider. Although Bonhoeffer seemed to take Barth's line on natural theology in many places, particularly in his earlier writings, he nevertheless offers a number of interesting and creative possibilities for the reintroduction of some kind of natural theology.

First, Bonhoeffer, in contrast to Barth, engages with the natural sciences in a number of places. For example, in *Creation and Fall* he affirms the materiality of the human person as even more strongly expressed in Scripture than in Darwin or Feuerbach. He also refers to mathematics, noting that its status as "eternal" and providing ultimate truth has been undermined by the discovery of paradoxes in its axiomatic formulation. Truth and eternity stem only from God. I argued that this point could be developed into a natural theological argument, even if it does not get us very far.

Bonhoeffer substitutes the term "orders of preservation," and later, in the *Ethics*, "divine mandates," for the traditional "orders of creation" (marriage, the family, etc.), which indicates that these orders are not to be considered autonomous and independent of God's revelation, but provisional—God's means of preserving the world from descending into chaos. The orders are upheld by God and receive their meaning solely through Christ, to whom they are directed. Ostensibly anti–natural theological, this move nevertheless opens up significant possibilities *for* natural theology. I have connected it with Bonhoeffer's other significant concept from the *Ethics*, that of "penultimate" in contrast to "ultimate" things. The penultimate precedes, and exists for the sake of, the ultimate, which is the word of grace. Penultimate works, such as freeing slaves, can be said to prepare for grace. There is a place for "natural life" in the penultimate, and Bonhoeffer develops what looks very much like a natural law ethic.

I have suggested that this point is easily extendable to natural theology. If people are more receptive to the gospel when well-fed and liberated from slavery, they may also be more receptive if they are given good reasons for believing in God the Creator, before being told about God the Redeemer.

In *Letters and Papers from Prison*, Bonhoeffer again engages with the sciences in a significant way. In particular he reads Carl Friedrich von Weizsäcker's book *The World View of Physics*. From this he gleans two main lessons. The first is that thinking of God as filling in gaps in the scientific account for which we have no current explanation is a big mistake. We should find God in what we know, not in what we do not know. The second idea is that an infinite universe is self-subsistent and could exist as if there were no God. I happen to disagree about this latter point, although the analogous notion today of a multiverse tends to be used that way by scientists who wish to avoid the need for God. However, these two points can be seen as components of a single point, namely that science can go about its business perfectly happily without reference to God.

Bonhoeffer extends this idea to other areas of human endeavor. God is also not a gap to meet our existential despair. In "a world come of age," God meets us and makes demands on us "at our strongest point," in our health and well-being and what we know from science. This puts Christ back at the center, not the periphery of life, and it becomes the task of the Christian to share in the sufferings of Christ in the world.

That line of thought does not seem to get us very far toward natural theology, except to say that some forms of it are completely mistaken. Although we saw in chapter 1 that Paley is more sophisticated than he is often credited for, the older physico-theology can be seen in many ways to exhibit a God-of-the-gaps mentality if naïvely construed as arguing for separate creation of individual organisms or structures within the natural world. The modern Intelligent Design movement is without excuse in this regard.

Bonhoeffer's critique of Barth's "positivism of revelation" potentially leads in a more positive direction for natural theology, implying that one cannot simply present Christian doctrine as a whole for immediate consumption. That would be fine for the church, but not for the outsider. Bonhoeffer finds a place for the mysteries of the faith to be protected within the secret discipline of the church, which would seem to leave room for the "liberal question" to be answered in its own terms. Indeed he writes, "We must move out again into the open air of intellectual discussion with the world," away from the entrenchment behind "the faith of the church" encouraged by Barth and the Confessing Church.

Another place where a more positive direction for natural theology would seem to be indicated in Bonhoeffer is his acceptance as a Lutheran of the doctrine of *finitum capax infiniti*. This goes right back to his *Habilitationsschrift* (*Act and Being*). Despite everything, God is accessible, whereas for Barth, who adopted the Reformed doctrine of *incapax finiti*, God is remote. It is interesting that Torrance—like Barth, also in the Reformed tradition—likewise adopts the *incapax* and similarly makes God inaccessible.

## *Pannenberg*

The theology of Wolfhart Pannenberg takes us into seemingly very different territory, and with very different concerns from those who carved out their theology in the fiery context of two world wars and the intervening period of political turmoil. Pannenberg also presents us with more directly hopeful avenues for natural theology. Contra Barth's authoritarian approach on the one hand and McGrath's on the other, Pannenberg favors the Enlightenment style of rationality. He does, however, temper that with a concern for Christian orthodoxy in a way I find appealing, and he gives no quarter to relativism. Christian belief cannot be true for me and not true for all.

Pannenberg's overriding concern is God's revelation in history. Nevertheless, he engages in a serious way with the natural sciences and affirms that the Christian faith must make its claims in dialogue with science. He also claims that history and theology are sciences in their own right. He agrees with Heinrich Scholz against Barth that theology must not make internally contradictory claims and must be open to testing. Theology cannot make itself immune to criticism and retain a place among fields suitable for university study.

In the historical sphere Pannenberg rejects Ernst Troeltsch's "principle of analogy," whereby unique events in history are ruled out by fiat. Indeed, the sciences of cosmology and biology also deal with a unique history—that of the unfolding cosmos and the subsequent development of life on Earth—so history cannot be unscientific for that reason.

Pannenberg is clear that the resurrection of Christ is such a unique event, and that evidence for it is public evidence and ought normatively to be persuasive. The resurrection is, however, only confirmed absolutely in the eschaton, which it anticipates. This is consistent with my view, and that of Richard Swinburne, that the resurrection is probable. It is not certain on current data—nothing is certain in any sphere of human activity—but we have enough to go on to base our lives on it. That would also be the view of John Polkinghorne, who cites Polanyi's dictum that "I may hold firmly to what I believe to be true, even though I know that it may conceivably be false," which we met in chapter 5.

Unlike Barth, Pannenberg believes that there is natural knowledge of God and that the gospel fills out that knowledge in a radical way, though he says that this knowledge is not the same as a natural theology that argues for God philosophically. While he seems ambivalent at this point, Pannenberg nevertheless affirms that the traditional philosophical arguments have a place in making God-talk intelligible and in witnessing to human aspiration toward the infinite. Where he sees the debate as "not decisively closed," I would see it as very much open. Some of Pannenberg's own arguments are very positive for it, in particular his affirmation that Christian doctrine makes truth claims that are open to confirmation at the bars of human experience and reason.

Pannenberg sees science as disclosing the contingency of the world, which is entirely in accord with the biblical picture of God's activity. He sees the big bang and anthropic fine-tuning as favoring the universe being God's creation, against, for example, the steady-state theory or an infinite universe. These cosmological developments also restore the centrality of humanity to the universe, which had been lost with the Copernican revolution. Moreover, creation is not something just at the beginning, nor is it unchanging conservation, but it is continuing creation, as God continually does new things in the history of the universe and of the world. Pannenberg, like Paul Davies, sees laws of nature coming into existence with the universe and its evolution, and new laws coming into play as new stages in the process latch on to earlier ones. The laws describe regular patterns that can be seen as God's faithfulness in creation. At the same time, like Bonhoeffer, Pannenberg repudiates the God of the gaps who would account for the lacunae in current scientific understanding of natural processes.

A weak point is the way in which Pannenberg thinks that field theory might explain the activity of the Holy Spirit. More suitable loci for this would be physically indeterminate or inherently unpredictable theories of physics such as quantum theory and chaos theory. Pannenberg does, however, recognize that physical systems, although exhibiting regularities, are not closed or isolated, and he sees unique events such as miracles as therefore not violating natural law.

Pannenberg is the boldest of my interlocutors in this study for having claimed that theology should affect scientific theory appraisal, and that theology makes predictions in the scientific sphere. He says that the processes of nature cannot be understood properly without reference to God, who as all-determining reality gives meaning and unity to everything other than God. Philip Hefner and Nancey Murphy see Pannenberg's theology as providing a Lakatosian "scientific research programme," which means, however, that theology should predict novel facts; Pannenberg seems to go along with this. This move may not be altogether wise, though his actual suggested predictions are framed in rather general terms: that physics might come up with a new form of field theory, or anthropology find a more constructive place for religion. I have suggested that a scientific prediction Pannenberg might approve of would be that research on multiverses would prove ultimately fruitless—though again, any prediction from theology might present a hostage to fortune.

Pannenberg's view that theological theories are explanatory, and that doctrinal statements are "hypotheses" is, however, entirely reasonable. Pannenberg writes of a theory as "'proved' when it is able to explain the facts at hand." I think "proved" is too strong a word here, but the idea is sound. Theology is explanatory, a notion that fits very easily into the "inference to the best explanation" or Swinburnian confirmation theory type of model, which enables theology to show its strength against competing metaphysical alternatives.

## *Torrance*

Like Pannenberg, Torrance is a major theologian who has engaged extensively with the natural sciences. He also thinks theology is a science, but in the same sense as Barth—that is, that theology deals with its object in the way appropriate to it. We let the object speak to us and do not approach it with preconceptions. However, theology is emphatically not a science in the sense that it shares the methods or tools of the natural sciences. Like Barth, Torrance wants to avoid theology being reduced to human religious consciousness—to anthropology.

A major problem for Torrance, as for Barth, is the justification of religious belief. Torrance rejects any argument of the traditional natural theological sort and argues that justification comes from God himself, through grace. I would see God's common grace at work in making his revelation in the creation available to all ("he did not leave himself without witness"), but I would also agree with Pannenberg that the evidence for the resurrection is publicly available and in that sense also constitutes "common grace."

Torrance reintroduces natural theology by redefining it. It no longer concerns what we can know about God apart from his special revelation in Christ and Scripture, but is incorporated into positive, dogmatic theology. He likens it to the way in which Einstein integrated geometry, which had formerly been a completely separate, pure mathematical discipline, into physics. I am happy to see natural theology as part of theology proper in the sense that it is an area of inquiry in which theologians engage, but would still see it in traditional terms as about what we can know of God apart from revelation. In this way natural theology functions apologetically as a *praeparatio evangelica*. Torrance's view of natural theology makes it more like a theology of nature than what has been traditionally considered to be natural theology.

I have argued that Torrance's rejection of traditional natural theology, and repudiation of arguments for religious claims from reason and evidence, ultimately renders his theological program irrational, in the same way that W. W. Bartley showed Barth's theology to be irrational. Theology cannot immunize itself from rational criticism but must be open to the cold winds of scrutiny in the public sphere.

However, despite the above, Torrance's actual engagement with the natural sciences offers opportunities for the more traditional kind of natural theology, even though Torrance would repudiate going from the world to God, insisting instead on his own strict theological method of only going from God to the world. Torrance argues that the rationality of the Creator, who reveals himself in Christ, grounds the rational order of the cosmos and its fundamental harmony with the workings of the human mind. If that is so, then the rational harmony and order of the cosmos provide rational grounds for believing they are the product of a Creator God.

The sciences are also predicated on the contingency of the universe, and it is because it is contingent that the methods of empirical and experimental science are required for its investigation. Torrance mistakenly and paradoxically sees contingency more in Einstein's general theory of relativity than in quantum theory, which is ontologically indeterminate. That is unfortunate, though his basic point about contingency is valid. Theologically, the doctrine of creation affirms that God freely creates a universe that is therefore contingent both in its existence and its constitutive processes. Again, the argument also works the other way: the contingency of the universe, to which science attests, provides rational grounds for believing that it is the free creation of God.

Torrance points to the open-ended structure of the universe, including both the multilayered nature of reality and the fact that, because of Gödel's theorem in mathematics, the universe cannot explain itself. As we have seen when discussing Bonhoeffer, Gödel's theorem is also usable in a natural theological way. Theism can explain the universe. God is the necessary self-subsistent, self-explanatory ground of the contingent, non-self-subsistent, and non-self-explanatory universe. The alternatives seem to be theism or no explanation at all, and surely theism is preferable to saying we just cannot explain this and that's all there is to it.

Like Pannenberg, Torrance points to the contingency of the universe's initial conditions, arguing that physics is up against limits beyond which it cannot proceed. Again, this is all grist to the mill of modern natural theology. If God can explain the fine-tuned initial conditions, then the fine-tunings are rational grounds for believing in God. In each case in which I have made this remark, I am in a way echoing Aquinas's refrain, "And this we call God." However, I have phrased it rather less definitively, and in each case it should be acknowledged that the data may also provide rational grounds (or, equivalently, evidence broadly conceived) for hypotheses other than God—chance, multiverse, "brute fact," physical "theory of everything," and so on. The rational approach is to compare the explanations, and as I have repeatedly suggested throughout this book, I believe that Bayesian confirmation theory provides the best tool for carrying out the comparison. Even if these alternatives do the explanatory work, which is doubtful, they may still lose out when compared for such criteria as elegance and simplicity.

Torrance is thus open to the charge of irrationality as was Barth, but nevertheless offers considerable scope for the engagement of theology with the natural sciences and for natural theology of the traditional kind.

## *McGrath*

In many ways McGrath resembles Torrance, whose biographer he is, though he also differs from Torrance in significant ways.

Like Pannenberg and Torrance, McGrath engages extensively with the natural sciences, especially in his most recent turn. He sees them comprising an *ancilla theologiae*, much as philosophy has in the past. Like Torrance, McGrath sees theology as scientific in responding to its object appropriately ("ontology determines epistemology"), and natural theology as undertaken from within Trinitarian-Chalcedonian orthodoxy. One advantage McGrath enjoys over the other theologians considered in this study is his early training as a research scientist, which makes him much less likely to commit the kind of scientific infelicity we have seen in Pannenberg and Torrance.

There is often an ambivalence in McGrath. On the one hand, natural theology only tells us something about the God we already know in the Christian revelation, and therefore seems circular and apologetically problematic. McGrath and Torrance would both seem open to the charge of "positivism of revelation" that Bonhoeffer leveled at Barth. On the other hand, McGrath concedes that Scripture passages such as Paul's Areopagus sermon in Acts 17 do seem to indicate some, albeit primitive knowledge of God as given in the creation and commonly available: Scripture authorizes us to see some partial disclosure of God in creation. Despite himself, McGrath gives even more positive opportunities for traditional natural theology than Torrance!

McGrath opposes Enlightenment rationalism, with its notion of universal reason, and foundationalism, with its starting point of incorrigible beliefs. In opposition to foundationalism, McGrath utilizes three key concepts from modern philosophy:

1. *Roy Bhaskar's notion of "critical realism."* This concept underpins McGrath's talk of levels of reality being handled by appropriate methodologies, in both science and theology, and the problems posed by human perception, which, though important, I believe McGrath overstates.
2. *The notion of "abduction"* (Charles Peirce) or, as it is alternatively termed, "inference to the best explanation" (Gilbert Harman, Peter Lipton, and others).
3. *Alasdair MacIntyre's notion of tradition-specific rationality*, which McGrath then extends to "tradition-transcendent rationality."

I have argued that all three of these moves bring one back to a universal rationalism, especially because they stem from essentially secular philosophy, even if McGrath is at pains to distance himself from such a notion. Indeed one could say that, not only is McGrath utilizing the natural sciences as an *ancilla theologiae*, but philosophy, too, as did the ancients.

Surely "critical realism" as a philosophical position, and the inference McGrath draws from it—"ontology determines epistemology"—are meant to command universal assent. I have argued that, as in the case of Torrance, if one accepts McGrath's view that Christian theology is explanatory, then what is explained is evidence for the truth of Christian claims. I showed this to be the case, utilizing Swinburne's formalism in chapter 6. The criteria McGrath cites for inference to the best explanation are of the same kind that Polkinghorne and Swinburne cite—for example, elegance, parsimony, and explanatory power. McGrath's claims that theism is explanatorily superior to naturalism, and Trinitarian theism more superior yet, sound indistinguishable from the claims of the traditional kind of natural theology he rejects. Moreover, if Christian doctrines are "tradition-transcendent" and can explain the beliefs of other religions—if indeed they provide the "best" explanation on generally accepted rational criteria—then that sounds just like a universal claim on every individual.

Another direction in which McGrath takes us is to extend the reach of natural theology beyond just providing a rational explanation for why things are as they are. It embraces the Platonic triad of truth, beauty, and goodness. All three are undoubtedly important, though in this book I have had to concentrate on the first, only giving brief attention to the others in chapter 6.

A significant theological resource for McGrath is St. Augustine's work *The Literal Meaning of Genesis*, and in particular Augustine's notion of *rationes seminales*, seedlike principles embedded in the initial creation and giving the potential for subsequent development. This is not evolution, but is certainly compatible with it. It is also compatible with cosmological insights into the way the universe was apparently set up at the big bang—that is, with the potentiality eventually to produce galaxies, stars, planets, and life.

McGrath helpfully gives examples of the cosmological fine-tuning, though is again constrained by his own version of natural theology in not turning it into a full-blooded apologetic argument. He also gives very helpful examples of other kinds of anthropic properties, from the biological and chemical sciences—the latter bringing in his own scientific training. Thus he notes Darwinian evolution's reliance on the preexisting chemical conditions for life to exist in the first place, the intriguingly unique properties of water, the constraints imposed on evolution by chemical catalysts, the origins of complexity and the capacity as Kingsley put it for things "to make themselves," and the directionality/teleology of evolution, including insights from Conway Morris's notion of "convergence."

All this is consistent with Augustine's *rationes seminales*. Moreover, it all leads back to the fundamental cosmological conditions required for an interesting universe to develop in the first place. Although McGrath reiterates his position, citing Newman—that he sees design because he believes in God and not the other way round—once again it seems to me that all these anthropic properties could be harnessed into a more traditional kind of natural theological argument.

## *Natural Theology Vindicated?*

It seems to me that taking seriously the concerns of the theologians considered in this book has not, after all, required a wholesale rejection of natural theology as traditionally conceived. On the contrary, sound reasons exist for continuing to pursue it, while remaining aware that it can only be a limited and subsidiary part of the overall theological enterprise.

Here is a summary of the lessons learned:

1. Fundamentally, the danger of neglecting natural theology is to run the risk of isolating theology from other areas of intellectual inquiry and of rendering one's theology incorrigible and irrational. We ought not to mimic the defunct logical positivism of the Vienna Circle with a take-it-or-leave-it "positivism of revelation." That might be fine for the church, but not for the outsider. Instead, the evidences and reasons for belief should be publicly accessible.

2. On the other hand, the danger of too much of a concentration on natural theology is to run the risk of neglecting or even compromising fundamental Christian doctrines. Christian theology is fundamentally about God's revelation of himself in Christ and exploring that from a position of *fides quaerens intellectum.*

3. Natural theology should not make theology reductionist. Theology cannot, for example, be reduced to anthropology, religious consciousness, or indeed to natural science.

4. Natural theology should not invoke a God of the gaps.

5. In Bonhoeffer's terms, natural theology can be seen as a "penultimate" task, akin to the notion of *praeparatio evangelica*, which all along has been suggested as the correct role for it.

6. The scope of natural theology, as it seeks to utilize insights from the natural sciences, can be significantly widened. All of the following are amenable to theistic explanation and can be built into a cumulative case for theism:

- The rational order of the universe
- The openness of that order to human comprehension
- The incompleteness of mathematics

- The contingency of nature
- The emergence and nonreducibility of higher levels of structure and complexity
- Fine-tuning in cosmology
- The right preexisting chemical conditions for the origin of life
- The chemical properties of water
- The remarkable properties of chemical catalysts
- Convergence (teleology?) in evolution

7. Natural theology can also be widened ("ramified," in Swinburne's terminology) to include the use of reason and evidence in evaluating what is purported to be revelation (otherwise one has "revelation positivism"), without of course reducing revelation to natural theology. In building a cumulative case for Christian theism, and in order to provide the "best explanation," evidence from history—and especially the evidence surrounding the life, death, and resurrection of Christ—will be most relevant to this.

8. Natural theology can be even further widened to include a consideration of beauty and goodness, as well as truth (i.e., the whole Platonic triad).

9. Natural theology is intimately connected to a theology of nature. If Christian doctrine explains aspects of nature such as those listed in point 6 above, then those aspects of nature provide evidential support for the Christian doctrines. Traditionally the doctrines in question have concerned the existence of God and aspects of the doctrine of creation. A moot point is whether the doctrine of the Trinity should be a prior assumption (Torrance, McGrath), or whether argument should proceed first from nature to theism, and then toward Trinitarian doctrine in the manner of Swinburne.

10. Natural theology will not involve deduction but abduction ("inference to the best explanation"). It will take account of uncertainties and will be "critically realist." I have argued that this approach is very much in line with the probabilistic approach of Richard Swinburne.

This last point leads me to a final consideration of Swinburne's approach. I have often indicated my preference for the kind of Bayesian methodology that Swinburne has pioneered but have never fully justified it. The subject of Bayesian confirmation theory does of course need a full treatment in its own right, and the reader is referred to the literature for this. Here, I just make a few remarks to describe the method, and give some of the reasons why I think it is such a powerful tool for natural theology.

Briefly, Bayesian confirmation theory is a way of formulating a comparison of competing hypotheses for explaining any particular evidence in mathematical terms. We met the basic equation, Bayes's theorem, in chapter 6, equation (6.1). Since the denominator in (6.1) is simply and expansion of P[E] we can rewrite the equation as follows for two hypotheses $H_1$ and $H_2$, which are candidates to explain evidence E:

$$P[H_1|E] = P[E|H_1].\ P[H_1]\ /\ P[E] \qquad (7.1)$$

and

$$P[H_2|E] = P[E|H_2].\ P[H_2]\ /\ P[E] \qquad (7.2)$$

The simplest way to compare the probabilities of the two hypotheses is to divide equation (7.1) by equation (7.2):

$$\frac{P[H_1|E]}{P[H_2|E]} = \frac{P[E|H_1]\ .\ P[H_1]}{P[E|H_2]\ \ P[H_2]} \qquad (7.3)$$

In these equations, $P[H_1]$ and $P[H_2]$ are the *prior probabilities*, the probabilities that the hypotheses might be true before the evidence is taken into account (strictly these and all the other probabilities should also be conditioned on *background knowledge*, commonly held knowledge such as the rules of logic); $P[E|H_1]$ and $P[E|H_2]$ are the *likelihoods* of the hypotheses, the probabilities that the evidence would arise, given that the hypotheses were true; and $P[H_1|E]$ and $P[H_2|E]$ are the *posterior probabilities*, the probabilities of the hypotheses revised in the light of the evidence. Equation (7.3) tells us that the ratio of the posterior probabilities is equal to the ratio of the likelihoods times the ratio of the prior probabilities.

As noted in chapter 6, estimating the probabilities to go into this equation is by no means trivial, and the best one can hope for is a broad, qualitative comparison. Most controversial is the estimation of the prior probabilities. However, the criteria for making the comparisons are precisely those that McGrath notes in his treatment of "inference to the best explanation" (IBE). For this reason, Bayesian confirmation theory may be regarded as simply a formal way of expressing IBE. Moreover, in any application of IBE, it is not good enough only to ask how well a hypothesis explains the evidence: it is also necessary to have some idea of how initially plausible the hypothesis is apart from the evidence, which in Bayesian terms means estimating the prior probability.

A key debate among philosophers is the nature of the probabilities that go into the equations. Some think they are subjective judgments.[1] Others, most notably Richard Swinburne, think they are objective, although Swinburne concedes that we can only obtain estimates, usually of a comparative nature—that is, that such and such a probability is much larger or smaller than another. While Swinburne may be somewhat overconfident in the objectivity of the judgments he makes, the problem with the subjective, or personalist, view is arguably worse, in that we end up being irrational after all: my judgment is just as good or bad as yours, and all that the Bayesian framework really achieves is to aid me to make my judgments internally consistent with each other. Consistency in my judgments is indeed useful, and I may even derive results that surprise me, but this is not very helpful in persuading others.

I have broadly followed Swinburne in this debate, especially in *God, the Multiverse, and Everything*, and have noted that scientists in their own disciplines have utilized the same assessment criteria, most especially simplicity, and found them in practice to be successful in guiding them toward truth. This pragmatic success leads me to suggest that scientists ought to find arguments framed in this way persuasive.

I believe, therefore, that the Bayesian framework best captures the logic involved in the evaluation of scientific hypotheses. The alternative framework of a Lakatosian scientific research program, advocated by Nancey Murphy and Philip Hefner, who see Pannenberg open to this, also seems to model the scientific method well, and represents an improvement to Karl Popper's falsificationism. However, Bayesians regard Lakatos's methodology as rather too vague in specifying when falsifications outweigh the predictions of novel facts in a progressive research program, or vice versa in a degenerating one.

For theology, it is a distinct drawback of the Lakatosian method that, to be counted as a scientific research program, it should predict novel facts. That generally seems a virtue in science, but it is difficult to see how theology does this, and the examples given by Murphy seem rather vague. However, although a matter of debate within the philosophy of science, it seems not unreasonable to suppose that if a hypothesis H explains evidence E, it does not matter when E was obtained. If H is formulated prior to the discovery of E and predicts E, that certainly has great psychological value. On the other hand, the probabilities entering Bayes's theorem if the discovery of E preceded the formulating of H, and H explains E, would be the same. General relativity explains the previously known precession of the orbit of Mercury, but if the precession had been discovered after it was predicted by general relativity, all the probabilities would be the same and we would be in the same position.

The conclusion of this study is, therefore, that natural theology should retain a place in the theological endeavor as a vital tool for connecting theology to other areas of human inquiry. It provides reasons to present to a skeptic as to why it is worth considering theism in the first place, *and* why it is worth going on to consider the particularities of Christian belief, especially if those particularities are given some backing in the form of a "ramified" natural theology as Swinburne has suggested. But this intellectual quest is not enough. God's self-revelation must be faced head on, and, though it does give us much deeper knowledge of a God who is already known, but rather vaguely, through natural theology, God's revelation does much more than that. At some stage, the boat has to be pushed out, the journey of *fides quaerens intellectum* embarked upon, and the living God who is revealed as both Creator and Redeemer encountered. As for Barth, the overriding goal, therefore, is still to present God's supreme revelation of himself in Jesus Christ:

> Who being the brightness of his glory, and the express image of his person, and upholding all things by the word of his power, when he had by himself purged our sins, sat down on the right hand of the Majesty on high. (Heb 1:3)

# Notes

*Chapter 1*

1. John Macquarrie in *The Blackwell Encyclopedia of Modern Christian Thought*, ed. Alister McGrath (Oxford: Blackwell, 1993), 402.
2. David Hume, *Dialogues Concerning Natural Religion* (London: Routledge, 1991).
3. Ibid., part 2.
4. Ibid., part 5.
5. Ibid., part 6.
6. Ibid., part 7.
7. William Paley, *Natural Theology, or Evidence of the Existence and Attributes of the Deity, Collected from the Appearances of Nature* (1802; Oxford: Oxford University Press, 2006).
8. William Whewell, *Astronomy and General Physics Considered with Reference to Natural Theology* (London: William Pickering, 1833), vi.
9. John Hedley Brooke, *Science and Religion: Some Historical Perspectives* (Cambridge: Cambridge University Press, 1991), 210.
10. Charles Darwin, *The Origin of Species by Means of Natural Selection, or the Preservation of Favoured Races in the Struggle for Life*, ed. J. W. Burrow (1859; London: Penguin, 1968), 50.
11. Paley, *Natural Theology*, 16.
12. Paley, *Natural Theology*, 9.
13. Rodney D. Holder, *God, the Multiverse, and Everything: Modern Cosmology and the Argument from Design* (Aldershot, UK: Ashgate, 2004), 43–47.
14. Paley, *Natural Theology*, 12.
15. Richard Dawkins, *The Blind Watchmaker* (London: Penguin, 1988), 5.
16. Darwin, *Origin of Species*, 458.
17. Ibid., 459–60.
18. Paley, *Natural Theology*, 207.
19. Holder, *God, the Multiverse, and Everything*, 36.
20. Paley, *Natural Theology*, 238.
21. John Polkinghorne, *Theology in the Context of Science* (London: SPCK, 2008), 75.

22. Quoted in Adrian Desmond and James Moore, *Darwin* (London: Penguin, 1992), 479.
23. Polkinghorne, *Theology in the Context of Science*, 77.
24. John Hick, *Evil and the God of Love* (London: Macmillan, 1966), 289ff.
25. Dietrich Bonhoeffer, *Letters and Papers from Prison*, ed. Eberhard Bethge, enlarged ed., (London: SCM Press, 1971), 361.
26. E.g., John Polkinghorne, "Where Is Natural Theology Today?" *Science and Christian Belief* 18 (2006): 169–79.
27. Ibid., 177.
28. John Polkinghorne, "The New Natural Theology," *Studies in World Christianity* 1, no. 1 (1995): 41–50.
29. See especially Richard Swinburne, *The Existence of God*, rev. ed. (Oxford: Oxford University Press, 1991).
30. Holder, *God, the Multiverse, and Everything.*
31. Richard Swinburne, "The Argument to God from Fine-tuning Reassessed," in *God and Design: The Teleological Argument and Modern Science*, ed. Neil A. Manson (London: Routledge, 2003), 105–23.
32. I have argued in *God, the Multiverse, and Everything* (98) that Swinburne's mind-body dualism somewhat weakens his version of the argument to God from fine-tuning.
33. Quoted by Karl Barth in *Church Dogmatics* II/1 (Edinburgh: T & T Clark, 1957), 79. Barth acknowledges that he is doing what is condemned in a canon of the Council, arguing that the Catholic view partitions God and that we need to know God as one—Creator, Redeemer, and Reconciler. The quotation is also in Roger Trigg, *Rationality and Religion: Does Faith Need Reason?* (Oxford: Blackwell, 1998), 177.

*Chapter 2*

1. The standard biography is Eberhard Busch, *Karl Barth: His Life from Letters and Autobiographical Fragments*, trans. John Bowden, 2nd rev. ed. (London: SCM Press, 1976).
2. John Webster, "Introducing Barth," in *The Cambridge Companion to Karl Barth*, ed. John Webster (Cambridge: Cambridge University Press, 2000), 1–16, quote appears on 2.
3. Busch, *Karl Barth*, 45.
4. Ibid., 206.
5. Ibid., 210.
6. Ibid., 255.
7. Ibid., 257.
8. Thomas F. Torrance, *Karl Barth: Biblical and Evangelical Theologian* (Edinburgh: T & T Clark, 1990), ix, 1.
9. Webster, "Introducing Barth," 1.
10. Karl Barth, *Church Dogmatics*, II/1 (Edinburgh: T & T Clark, 1957), 168 (hereafter cited as *CD*, II/1).
11. See also original German edition, Barth, *Kirchliche Dogmatik*, II/1 (Zollikon–Zürich: Evangelischer Verlag, 1940), 196.

12. Alister E. McGrath, *A Fine-Tuned Universe: The Quest for God in Science and Theology* (Louisville, KY: Westminster John Knox Press, 2009), 18–19.
13. Karl Barth, *Church Dogmatics*, I/2 (Edinburgh: T & T Clark, 1956), 280 (hereafter cited as *CD*, I/2).
14. On p. 299, Barth states, "We begin by stating that religion is unbelief." The whole section is titled "Religion as Unbelief."
15. Gotthold Ephraim Lessing, "On the Proof of the Spirit and of Power," in *Lessing's Theological Writings*, selections in translation with an introductory essay by Henry Chadwick (London: A. and C. Black, 1956), 51–56, quote appears on 55.
16. Barth, "Lessing," in *Protestant Theology in the Nineteenth Century*, trans. John Bowden, new ed., (London: SCM, 2001), 248 (hereafter cited as *PT*).
17. See Rodney D. Holder, "Hume on Miracles: Bayesian Interpretation, Multiple Testimony, and the Existence of God," *British Journal for the Philosophy of Science* 49, no. 1 (1998): 49–65.
18. Karl Barth, *Church Dogmatics*, III/1 (Edinburgh: T & T Clark, 1958), ix (hereafter cited as *CD* III/1).
19. Barth adduces Heb 11:3 in support; ibid., 4.
20. Karl Barth, *Dogmatics in Outline* (London: SCM Press, 1949), 50 (hereafter cited as *DO*).
21. Wolfhart Pannenberg, *Towards a Theology of Nature: Essays on Science and Faith* (Louisville, KY: Westminster/John Knox Press, 1993), 32.
22. Wolfhart Pannenberg, "Heilsgeschehen und Geschichte," in *Grundfragen Systematischer Theologie: Gesammelte Aufsätze* (Göttingen: Vandenhoeck and Ruprecht, 1967), 22–78, quote appears on 22; English translation: George Kehm, trans., "Redemptive Event and History," in *Basic Questions in Theology*, vol. 1 (London: SCM Press, 1970), 15–80, quote appears on 15–16.
23. Richard Dawkins, *The Selfish Gene*, new ed. (Oxford: Oxford University Press, 1989), 198.
24. John C. McDowell, "A Response to Rodney Holder on Barth on Natural Theology," *Themelios* 27, no. 2 (2002): 32–44, quote appears on 38.
25. Kathryn Tanner, "Creation and Providence," in Webster, *Cambridge Companion to Karl Barth*, 111.
26. Arthur Peacocke, *Intimations of Reality: Critical Realism in Science and Theology* (Notre Dame, IN: University of Notre Dame Press, 1984).
27. Ingolf U. Dalferth, "Karl Barth's Eschatological Realism," in *Karl Barth: Centenary* Essays, ed. S. W. Sykes (Cambridge: Cambridge University Press, 1989), 14–45, quote appears on 22.
28. The traditional doctrine of timelessness is critiqued in, for example, Richard Swinburne, *The Coherence of Theism*, rev. ed. (Oxford: Oxford University Press, 1993), 223–29.
29. Richard Roberts notes the ambiguity in Barth concerning time and eternity. See Roberts, *A Theology on Its Way? Essays on Karl Barth* (Edinburgh: T & T Clark, 1991), 1–58.
30. Swinburne, *Coherence of Theism*, 225.
31. William Nicholls, *The Pelican Guide to Modern Theology*, vol. 1 (Harmondsworth: Penguin, 1969), 94.

32. See John Calvin, *Institutes of the Christian Religion*, trans. Henry Beveridge (Grand Rapids: Wm. B. Eerdmans, 1989), I.iii.1.
33. Ibid., I.v.1.
34. Ibid.
35. James Barr, *Biblical Faith and Natural Theology: The Gifford Lectures for 1991 Delivered in the University of Edinburgh* (Oxford: Clarendon Press, 1993), 8–9, 109–11.
36. Alister McGrath, *A Scientific Theology: Nature* (Edinburgh: T & T Clark, 2001), 279.
37. Barr, *Biblical Faith and Natural Theology*, 110.
38. Calvin, *Institutes*, I.iii.1.
39. Barr, *Biblical Faith and Natural Theology*, 109.
40. Ibid., 109–10.
41. H. Richard Niebuhr, *Schleiermacher on Christ and Religion* (London: SCM, 1965), 11, quoted in Barr, *Biblical Faith and Natural Theology*, 105.
42. Avery Dulles, *Models of Revelation*, 2nd ed. (Maryknoll, NY: Orbis Books, 1992), 97.
43. Emil Brunner, "Nature and Grace," in *Natural Theology*, Emil Brunner and Karl Barth, trans. Peter Fraenkel, with an introduction by John Baillie (London: Geoffrey Bles/Centenary Press, 1946), 15–64; Barth's response "No!" is included in the same volume.
44. Ibid., 25.
45. Ibid., 31–32.
46. Karl Barth, "No!" in Brunner and Barth, *Natural Theology*, 65–128.
47. Joan E. O'Donovan, "Man in the Image of God: The Disagreement between Barth and Brunner Reconsidered," *Scottish Journal of Theology* 39 (1986): 433–59, quote appears on 434.
48. Brunner, "Nature and Grace," 59.
49. Ibid., 23.
50. Ibid., 56.
51. Barth, "No!" 89.
52. See discussion by John Baillie in Introduction to Emil Brunner, *Gott und Mensch: Vier Untersuchungen über das personhafte Sein* (Tübingen, 1930); English translation: David Cairns, trans., *God and Man: Four Essays on the Nature of Personality* (London: SCM, 1936), 24–25.
53. Brunner, *God and Man*, 116.
54. Karl Barth, *Church Dogmatics*, I/1 (Edinburgh: T & T Clark, 1936), 273 (hereafter cited as *CD* I/1).
55. Barth, "No!" 121.
56. Torrance, *Karl Barth*, 143, 183.
57. Karl Barth, *The Humanity of God* (Richmond, VA: John Knox Press, 1960), 14 (hereafter cited as *HG*).
58. An English text of the article and Barth's reply can be found in *The Beginnings of Dialectical Theology*, ed. James M. Robinson (Richmond, VA: John Knox Press, 1968), 165ff. (hereafter cited as *BDT*); quote appears on 166.
59. McDowell, "Response to Rodney Holder," 43.
60. Barr, *Biblical Faith and Natural Theology*, 10n10.

61. Ibid., 111.
62. Ibid., 112.
63. Ibid.
64. Ibid., 113, citing Christof Gestrich.
65. Ibid., 116.
66. Ibid., 115.
67. Owen Geoffrey Rees, "The Barmen Declaration (May 1934)," *Studies in Church History* 12 (Oxford, 1975): 405–33, quotes appear on 408, 412.
68. Dietrich Bonhoeffer, *Ethics* (London: Collins, 1964), 55.
69. Hugo Hahn cited in Jonathan R. C. Wright, "The German Protestant Church and the Nazi Party in the Period of the Seizure of Power 1932–3," *Studies in Church History* 14 (Oxford, 1977): 393–418, quote appears on 416.
70. Karl Barth, *The Knowledge of God and the Service of God according to the Teaching of the Reformation*, Gifford Lectures Delivered in 1937 and 1938 (Eugene, OR: Wipf & Stock, 2005), 8–9.
71. Barr, *Biblical Faith and Natural Theology*, 19–20.
72. Ibid., 20.
73. Ibid., 24.
74. Ibid., 25.
75. Ibid., 32.
76. See also *Kirchliche Dogmatik*, II/1, 136.
77. Barr, *Biblical Faith and Natural Theology*, 32n21.
78. Ibid., 24.
79. Ibid., 38.
80. Ibid., 36–37.
81. Ibid., 42.
82. Ibid., 49.
83. Douglas A. Campbell, "Natural Theology in Paul? Reading Romans 1.19–20," *International Journal of Systematic Theology* 1, no. 3 (1999): 231–52.
84. Barr, *Biblical Faith and Natural Theology*, 54–80.
85. Ibid., 83.
86. Ibid., 84.
87. John J. Collins, "The Biblical Precedent for Natural Theology," *Journal of the American Academy of Religion* 45, no. 1 supplement (1977): B:35–67. Quoted in Barr, *Biblical Faith and Natural Theology*, 91–92.
88. Richard Swinburne, *The Existence of God*, 2nd ed. (Oxford: Oxford University Press, 2004), 145–47.
89. Torrance, *Karl Barth*, 143.
90. Swinburne, *Existence of God*, 7.
91. Dietrich Bonhoeffer, *Letters and Papers from Prison*, ed. Eberhard Bethge, enlarged ed., (London: SCM Press, 1971), 286.
92. David Jenkins, *Guide to the Debate about God* (Cambridge: Lutterworth Press, 1966), 81.
93. Ibid.
94. John Bowden, *Karl Barth* (London: SCM Press, 1971), 111.
95. Roger Trigg, *Rationality and Religion: Does Faith Need Reason?* (Oxford: Blackwell, 1998), 177.

96. Torrance, *Karl Barth*, 226.
97. Heinrich Scholz, "Wie ist eine evangelische Theologie als Wissenschaft möglich?" *Zwischen den Zeiten* 9, Heft 1 (München: Chr. Kaiser Verlag, 1931), 8–35. Reprinted in Gerhard Sauter, ed., *Theologie als Wissenschaft* (München: Chr. Kaiser Verlag, 1971), 221–64.
98. McDowell, "Response to Rodney Holder."
99. Rodney D. Holder, *God, the Multiverse, and Everything: Modern Cosmology and the Argument from Design* (Aldershot, UK: Ashgate, 2004), 69; John Earman, *Bayes or Bust? A Critical Examination of Bayesian Confirmation Theory* (Cambridge, MA: MIT Press, 1992), 153–54.
100. Alister McGrath, *A Scientific Theology: Nature* (Edinburgh: T & T Clark, 2001), 302.
101. Thomas F. Torrance, *The Ground and Grammar of Theology* (Belfast: Christian Journals, 1980), 94.
102. McGrath, *Scientific Theology: Nature*, 300, 302.
103. Roberts, *Theology on Its Way?* 79.
104. Christoph Schwöbel, "Theology," in Webster, *Cambridge Companion*, 32.

*Chapter 3*

1. A helpful introduction to Bonhoeffer is Stephen Plant, *Dietrich Bonhoeffer* (London: Continuum, 2004). This book includes a chapter on *Creation and Fall*. A more detailed exploration of Bonhoeffer's theology is to be found in John W. de Gruchy, ed., *The Cambridge Companion to Dietrich Bonhoeffer* (Cambridge: Cambridge University Press, 1999). The classic biography is Eberhard Bethge, *Dietrich Bonhoeffer: Theologian, Christian, Contemporary* (London: Collins, 1970).
2. Dietrich Bonhoeffer, *Creation and Fall: A Theological Exposition of Genesis 1–3*; trans. and ed. Martin Rüter and Ilse Tödt; English edition, ed. John W. de Gruchy, trans. D. S. Bax (Minneapolis: Fortress Press, 1997) (hereafter cited as *CF*).
3. Dietrich Bonhoeffer, *Ethics*, ed. Eberhard Bethge, trans. Neville Horton Smith (1st German ed., 1949; London: Collins, 1964) (hereafter cited as *Ethics*).
4. Dietrich Bonhoeffer, *Letters and Papers from Prison*, ed. Eberhard Bethge, enlarged ed., (London: SCM Press, 1971) (hereafter cited as *LPP*).
5. Carl Friedrich von Weizsäcker, *The World View of Physics*, trans. of *Zum Weltbild der Physik* by Marjorie Grene (1st German ed., 1943; London: Routledge, 1952).
6. Martin Kuske, *The Old Testament as the Book of Christ*, trans. S. T. Kimbrough Jr. (Philadelphia: Westminster Press, 1976).
7. Clifford J. Green, *Bonhoeffer: The Sociality of Christ and Humanity* (Missoula, MT: Scholars Press, 1972), 201; also Kuske, *Old Testament as the Book of Christ*, 5–6.
8. Dietrich Bonhoeffer, *Life Together*, trans. John W. Doberstein (London: SCM Press, 1954). Bonhoeffer's method is analyzed in detail in Kuske, *Old Testament as the Book of Christ.*
9. Bethge, *Dietrich Bonhoeffer*, 162, 437.

10. Ibid., 163–64, 793.
11. See, for example, Ernst Feil, *The Theology of Dietrich Bonhoeffer*, trans. Martin Rumscheidt (Philadelphia: Fortress Press, 1985), 72–74; André Dumas, *Dietrich Bonhoeffer: Theologian of Reality* (London: SCM, 1971), 145ff.; and Green, *Bonhoeffer*, 241.
12. See, for example, Keith Clements, "Ecumenical Witness for Peace," in de Gruchy, *Cambridge Companion*, 163–64; also Green, *Bonhoeffer*, 201, and Bethge, *Dietrich Bonhoeffer*, 161.
13. Emil Brunner, *Gott und Mensch: Vier Untersuchungen über das personhafte Sein* (Tübingen, 1930); English translation: David Cairns, trans., *God and Man: Four Essays on the Nature of Personality* (London: SCM, 1936), 60–61.
14. See Green, *Bonhoeffer*, 236, 248.
15. Wolfhart Pannenberg, *Systematic Theology*, vol. 1, trans. Geoffrey W. Bromiley (Edinburgh: T & T Clark, 1991), 2.
16. See John Polkinghorne, "The New Natural Theology," *Studies in World Christianity*, 1 no. 1 (1995): 41–50.
17. See, for example, Rodney D. Holder, *God, the Multiverse, and Everything: Modern Cosmology and the Argument from Design* (Aldershot, UK: Ashgate, 2004).
18. Roger Penrose, *The Emperor's New Mind: Concerning Computers, Minds, and The Laws of Physics* (Oxford: Oxford University Press, 1989).
19. J. R. Lucas, "Minds, Machines and Gödel," *Philosophy* 36 (1961): 120–24.
20. Roger Penrose, *Shadows of the Mind: A Search for the Missing Science of Consciousness* (Oxford: Oxford University Press, 1994).
21. Stephen W. Hawking, "Gödel and the End of Physics," public lecture, Dirac Centennial Celebration, Cambridge (July 20, 2002); available at http://www.damtp.cam.ac.uk/strtst/dirac/hawking/.
22. Dietrich Bonhoeffer, *No Rusty Swords*, ed. Edwin H. Robertson, trans. Robertson and John Bowden (London: Collins, 1965), appendix 1.
23. Origen, *On First Principles*, book 4, chap. 3.
24. Green, *Bonhoeffer*, 238.
25. Charles Marsh, *Reclaiming Dietrich Bonhoeffer: The Promise of His Theology* (Oxford: Oxford University Press, 1994), 94.
26. Bethge, *Dietrich Bonhoeffer*, 131, 163; also Clifford Green, "Human Sociality and Christian Community," in de Gruchy, *Cambridge Companion*, 131n13.
27. Darwin, of course, saw man as descending from animals; Feuerbach's emphasis on the material, at least in his later years, was summarized in his well-known saying, "Man ist was er isst" ("One is what he eats"), though this is a gross oversimplification of his philosophy as a whole.
28. Brunner, *Gott und Mensch*, 154.
29. The recommendation of Brunner in the seminar is to be found in Eberhard Bethge, ed., *Gesammelte Schriften of Dietrich Bonhoeffer*, vol. 5 (Munich: Chr. Kaiser Verlag, 1972), 342.
30. See, for example, Warren S. Brown, Nancey C. Murphy, H. Newton Maloney, eds., *Whatever Happened to the Soul? Scientific and Theological Portraits of Human Nature* (Minneapolis: Fortress Press, 1998); also Murphy's more

recent book, *Bodies and Souls, or Spirited Bodies?* (Cambridge: Cambridge University Press, 2006).

31. A significant modern-day dualist would be Richard Swinburne. See Swinburne, *The Evolution of the Soul*, rev. ed. (Oxford: Oxford University Press, 1997).
32. Green, *Bonhoeffer*, 283n3.
33. Dumas, *Dietrich Bonhoeffer*, 151.
34. See Plant, *Dietrich Bonhoeffer*, 49–52.
35. Gerhard von Rad, *Genesis*, rev. ed. (London: SCM Press, 1971), 84.
36. Dumas, *Dietrich Bonhoeffer*, 150.
37. Plant, *Dietrich Bonhoeffer*, 89.
38. As noted by Dumas, *Dietrich Bonhoeffer*, 154.
39. Augustine seemed to think that we were all in Adam in a literal sense (see, for example, *City of God* 13.14), and he famously misunderstood Rom 5:12 to refer to Adam "in whom all men sinned."
40. Pannenberg, *Systematic Theology*, 1:26ff.
41. See Green, *Bonhoeffer*, 48.
42. Feil, *Theology of Dietrich Bonhoeffer*, 144.
43. J. A. T. Robinson, *Honest to God* (London: SCM Press, 1963).
44. Eberhard Bethge, *Bonhoeffer: Exile and Martyr*, ed. John W. de Gruchy (London: Collins, 1975), 15.
45. Feil, *Theology of Dietrich Bonhoeffer*, 145.
46. Weizsäcker, *World View of Physics*.
47. Carl Friedrich von Weizsäcker, *Der Garten des Menschlichen* (Munich: Carl Hanser, 1992), 471.
48. Ibid., 460–61.
49. Charles A. Coulson, *Science and Christian Belief* (1955; London: Collins, 1958).
50. Ibid., 35.
51. Charles A. Coulson, *Science and the Idea of God: The Eleventh Arthur Stanley Eddington Memorial Lecture 21 April 1958* (Cambridge: Cambridge University Press, 1958), 16.
52. Henry Drummond, *The Lowell Lectures on the Ascent of Man* (London: Hodder and Stoughton, 1894), 426–27.
53. John Polkinghorne, *Science and Christian Belief: Theological Reflections of a Bottom-up Thinker* (London: SPCK, 1994), 156.
54. Weizsäcker, *World View of Physics*, 151–57.
55. Ibid., 153.
56. For a postulated finite model, see J.-P. Luminet, "A Cosmic Hall of Mirrors," *Physics World* 18, no. 9 (2005): 23–28.
57. Weizsäcker, *World View of Physics*, 179.
58. E.g., Martin Rees, *Just Six Numbers: The Deep Forces That Shape the Universe* (London: Weidenfeld and Nicolson, 1999); Rees, *Our Cosmic Habitat* (London: Weidenfeld and Nicolson, 2001); Leonard Susskind, *The Cosmic Landscape: String Theory and the Illusion of Intelligent Design* (New York: Little, Brown, 2006).
59. Peter Bussey, "Physical Infinities: A Substitute for God." *Science and Christian Belief* 18, no. 2 (2006): 133–50.

60. See Holder, *God, the Multiverse, and Everything.*
61. Richard H. Bube, "Man Come of Age?" *Journal of the American Scientific Affiliation* 30, no. 2 (1978): 81–87.
62. Dietrich Bonhoeffer, *Act and Being*, trans. Bernard Noble (1st German ed., 1931; London: Collins, 1962), 47 (hereafter cited as *AB*).
63. Dietrich Bonhoeffer, *The Cost of Discipleship* (1st German ed. as *Nachfolge*, 1937; London: SCM Press, 1959), 79.
64. Peter Selby, "Christianity in a World Come of Age," in de Gruchy, *Cambridge Companion*, 226–45, quote appears on 237.
65. Ibid., 231.
66. Andreas Pangritz, *Karl Barth in the Theology of Dietrich Bonhoeffer* (1989; Grand Rapids: Wm. B. Eerdmans, 2000), 73.
67. Ibid., 75.
68. Bethge, *Dietrich Bonhoeffer*, 134.
69. Pangritz, *Karl Barth in the Theology of Dietrich Bonhoeffer*, 77ff.
70. Rudolf Bultmann, "The New Testament and Mythology," in *Kerygma and Myth*, ed. H. W. Bartsch (1st German ed., 1941; London: SPCK, 1953), 1–16, quote appears on 5.
71. Karl Barth, *Church Dogmatics*, I/1 and I/2 (1st German eds., 1932 and 1938; Edinburgh: T & T Clark, 1936 and 1956).
72. Karl Barth, *The Epistle to the Romans*, trans. Edwyn C. Hoskyns (1st German ed., 1919; Oxford: Oxford University Press, 1933).
73. Pangritz, *Karl Barth in the Theology of Dietrich Bonhoeffer*, 84–85.
74. Karl Barth, "The Word of God and the Task of the Ministry," in *The Word of God and the Word of Man*, trans. Douglas Horton (delivered in German, 1922; London: Hodder and Stoughton, 1928), 183–217.
75. Ibid., 202.
76. Barth, *Epistle to the Romans*, 143–44.
77. Karl Barth, *Anselm: Fides Quarens Intellectum. Anselm's Proof of the Existence of God in the Context of His Theological Scheme*, trans. Ian W. Robertson (1st German ed., 1931; London: SCM Press, 1960), 16.
78. Richard Dawkins, *The God Delusion* (2006; London: Transworld, 2007).
79. Bethge, *Dietrich Bonhoeffer*, 776.
80. Alister E. McGrath, *The Twilight of Atheism: The Rise and Fall of Disbelief in the Modern World* (London: Rider, 2004).
81. In Eberhard Bethge, ed., *Gesammelte Schriften of Dietrich Bonhoeffer*, vol. 5, 339.
82. Pangritz, *Karl Barth in the Theology of Dietrich Bonhoeffer*, 106–14.
83. Barth, *Church Dogmatics*, I/2, 172–200.
84. Dietrich Bonhoeffer, *Christology*, ed. Edwin H. Robertson, trans. John Bowden (London: Collins, 1971), 109.

*Chapter 4*

1. E.g., Richard Dawkins, *The God Delusion* (2006; London: Transworld, 2007).
2. Wolfhart Pannenberg, *Systematic Theology*, vol. 2, trans. Geoffrey W. Bromiley (Edinburgh: T & T Clark, 1994), 59–60. Soon after the magisterial three-volume work called *Systematische Theologie* started to appear in 1988–1993, the

English version followed: Wolfhart Pannenberg, *Systematic Theology*, trans. Geoffrey W. Bromiley (Edinburgh: T & T Clark, 1991–1998) (hereafter cited as *ST* 1–3).

3. Wolfhart Pannenberg, *Toward a Theology of Nature: Essays on Science and Faith* (Louisville, KY: Westminster/John Knox Press, 1993), 16 (hereafter cited as *TTN*).
4. E.g., Pannenberg, *ST*, 1:213–14.
5. Useful summary articles are to be found in Stanley Grenz, "Pannenberg, Wolfhart," in *The Oxford Companion to Christian Thought*, ed. Adrian Hastings, Alistair Mason, and Hugh Pyper (Oxford: Oxford University Press, 2000), 509–10; and Alister E. McGrath, "Pannenberg, Wolfhart," in *The Blackwell Encyclopedia of Modern Christian Thought*, ed. Alister E. McGrath (Oxford: Blackwell, 1993), 420–22.
6. Autobiographical essay in Carl E. Braaten and Philip Clayton, *The Theology of Wolfhart Pannenberg: Twelve American Critiques, with an Autobiographical Essay and Response* (Minneapolis: Augsburg, 1988).
7. Wolfhart Pannenberg, ed., with Rolf Rendtorff, Trotz Rendtorff, and Ulrich Wilckens, *Offenbarung als Geschichte* (1st German ed., 1961; English translation: D. Granskou, trans., *Revelation as History* [New York: Macmillan, 1968]; hereafter cited as *RaH*).
8. Wolfhart Pannenberg, *Jesus—God and Man*, new ed. (1st German ed., 1964; English translation: 1968; London: SCM, 2002) (hereafter cited as *JGM*).
9. Wolfhart Pannenberg, *Theology and the Philosophy of Science*, trans. Francis McDonagh (1st German ed., 1973; London: Darton, Longman & Todd, 1976) (hereafter cited as *TPS*).
10. Wolfhart Pannenberg, *Anthropology in Theological Perspective*, trans. Matthew J. O'Connell (1st German ed., 1983; Philadelphia: Westminster, 1985).
11. Dietrich Bonhoeffer, *Letters and Papers from Prison*, ed. Eberhard Bethge, enlarged ed., (London: SCM Press, 1971), 328–29.
12. See William Hasker, "Is Christianity Probable? Swinburne's Apologetic Programme," *Religious Studies* 38, no. 3 (2002): 253–64; and the reply, Richard Swinburne, "Response to My Commentators," *Religious Studies* 38, no. 3 (2002): 301–15.
13. See Bonhoeffer, *Letters and Papers from Prison*, 280, 286, 329.
14. Thomas Forsyth Torrance, *Theological Science* (Edinburgh: T & T Clark, 1969).
15. Wentzel van Huyssteen, *Theology and the Justification of Faith: Constructing Theories in Systematic Theology* (Grand Rapids: Wm. B. Eerdmans, 1989), 17–19, quotation appears on 19.
16. A helpful review of this topic is in ibid., chap. 6, "Theology as the Science of God: Wolfhart Pannenberg," 71–100.
17. There are perhaps other reasons for considering it to be more at home in the seminary, e.g., the central role of worship and prayer for the practice of theology and the formation of a theologian (Barth would agree with this point).
18. Daniel Dennett, *Breaking the Spell: Religion as a Natural Phenomenon* (London: Allen Lane, 2006).
19. Richard Swinburne, *An Introduction to Confirmation Theory* (London:

Methuen, 1973); Swinburne, *Epistemic Justification* (Oxford: Oxford University Press, 2001); and Swinburne, *The Existence of God*, 2nd ed. (Oxford: Oxford University Press, 2004).

20. Van Huyssteen, *Theology and the Justification of Faith*, 88, also reads Pannenberg as arguing that it is primarily in "integrating and giving meaning to available data" that both scientific and theological hypotheses are tested.
21. Ibid., 94.
22. Richard Swinburne, *The Coherence of Theism*, rev. ed. (Oxford: Oxford University Press, 1993); and Swinburne, *Existence of God.*
23. Philip Hefner, "The Role of Science in Pannenberg's Theological Thinking," in Braaten and Clayton, *Theology of Wolfhart Pannenberg*, 266–86, especially 281ff..
24. See, for example, in addition to Swinburne's books, Colin Howson and Peter Urbach, *Scientific Reasoning: The Bayesian Approach* (Chicago: Open Court, 1993).
25. Nancey Murphy, *Theology in the Age of Scientific Reasoning* (Ithaca, NY: Cornell University Press, 1990), 19–50.
26. Ibid., 174–211; and Murphy, "A Lakatosian Reconstruction of Pannenberg's Program: Responses to Sponheim, van Huyssteen, and Eaves," in *Beginning with the End: God, Science, and Wolfhart Pannenberg*, ed. Carol Rausch Albright and Joel Haugen (Chicago: Open Court, 1997), 409–26.
27. Pannenberg, *Jesus—God and Man*; see especially the careful treatment of 1 Cor 15, 83ff.
28. Hefner, "Role of Science in Pannenberg's Theological Thinking," 284–86.
29. Murphy, *Theology in the Age of Scientific Reasoning*, 178n4.
30. N. T. Wright, *The Resurrection of the Son of God* (London: SPCK, 2003), 17.
31. See chap. 3. A multiverse is usually conceived in terms of separate regions of an infinite universe, which I argued, contra Bonhoeffer, is *not* self-subsistent; see also Rodney D. Holder, *God, the Multiverse, and Everything: Modern Cosmology and the Argument from Design* (Aldershot, UK: Ashgate, 2004).
32. Karl Barth, *Church Dogmatics*, I/2 (Edinburgh: T & T Clark, 1956).
33. Karl Barth, *Church Dogmatics*, II/1 (Edinburgh: T & T Clark, 1957).
34. Immanuel Kant, *Critique of Pure Reason*, Everyman's Library ed., trans. J. M. D. Meicklejohn (1st German ed., 1781; first English ed., 1934; London: J. M. Dent & Sons; 1991), 39.
35. Friedrich Schleiermacher, *On Religion: Speeches to Its Cultured Despisers*, trans. and ed. Richard Crouter, 2nd ed., (1st German ed., 1799; Cambridge: Cambridge University Press, 1996), 108ff.
36. E.g., Caroline Franks Davis, *The Evidential Force of Religious Experience* (Oxford: Oxford University Press, 1989); and William Alston, *Perceiving God: The Epistemology of Religious Experience* (Ithaca, NY: Cornell University Press, 1991).
37. Van Huyssteen, *Theology and the Justification of Faith*, 75.
38. James B. Pritchard, *Ancient Near Eastern Texts Relating to the Old Testament*, 3rd ed. (Princeton, NJ: Princeton University Press, 1969), 4ff.
39. Karl Barth, *Church Dogmatics*, III/3 (Edinburgh: T & T Clark, 1960).
40. As Pannenberg notes, William Temple also criticizes Whitehead. See Temple,

*Nature, Man and God* (London: Macmillan, 1935), esp. 257–60. Temple argues that Whitehead's wholly immanent God lacks explanatory power.

41. Keith Ward sees the universe as an expression of ideas in the mind of God, yet avoids the universe therefore being necessary. God knows all possibilities necessarily, but which possibilities are instantiated is a matter of contingency. God wills to bring about the good, but goods are incommensurate and not all goods can be simultaneously realized. Hence a choice has to be made. See Keith Ward, *Religion and Creation* (Oxford: Oxford University Press, 1996).
42. St. Augustine, *The Literal Meaning of Genesis*, in *Ancient Christian Writers*, vol. 1, 4.12.22ff, translated and annotated by John Hammond Taylor (New York: Paulist Press, 1982).
43. Clement of Alexandria, *The Stromata, or Miscellanies*, 6.16, in *Ante-Nicene Fathers*, vol. 2, ed. Alexander Roberts and John Donaldson (Peabody, MA: Hendrickson, 1994), 513 [Gnostic Exposition of the Decalogue, *The Fourth Commandment*].
44. St. Augustine, *The City of God*, 11.6, in *Nicene and Post-Nicene Fathers*, ed. Philip Schaff, First Series, vol 2 (Peabody, MA: Hendrickson, 1994), 208.
45. Ernan McMullin, "How Should Cosmology Relate to Theology?" in *The Sciences and Theology in the Twentieth Century*, ed. A. R. Peacocke (Stocksfield: Oriel, 1981), 17–57; Pannenberg, "Theological Questions to Scientists," is at 3–16.
46. J. R. Lucas, *Freedom and Grace: Essays* (London: SPCK, 1976), 39.
47. Holder, *God, the Multiverse, and Everything.*
48. Paul Davies, *The Goldilocks Enigma: Why Is the Universe Just Right for Life?* (London: Allen Lane, 2006), 149–50.
49. E.g., John Polkinghorne, *Belief in God in an Age of Science* (New Haven, CT: Yale University Press, 1998), 51ff.
50. Bonhoeffer, *Letters and Papers from Prison*, 311–12.
51. Charles A. Coulson, *Science and Christian Belief* (London: Collins, 1958), 31ff.
52. Davies, *Goldilocks Enigma*, 266ff.
53. Hermann Bondi, *Cosmology* (Cambridge: Cambridge University Press, 1961), 12.
54. Holder, *God, the Multiverse, and Everything.*
55. Martin Rees, *Just Six Numbers: The Deep Forces that Shape the Universe* (London: Weidenfeld & Nicolson, 1999), 150.
56. Leonard Susskind, *The Cosmic Landscape: String Theory and the Illusion of Intelligent Design* (New York: Little Brown & Co., 2006).
57. Peter Bussey, "Physical Infinities: A Substitute for God," *Science and Christian Belief* 18, no. 2 (2006): 133–50.
58. John Polkinghorne, *Science and Christian Belief: Theological Reflections of a Bottom-up Thinker* (London: SPCK, 1994), 73.
59. Murphy, *Theology in an Age of Scientific Reasoning*, 199.
60. Hefner, "Role of Science in Pannenberg's Theological Thinking," 273.
61. Ibid.
62. John Polkinghorne, "Wolfhart Pannenberg's Engagement with the Natural Sciences," *Zygon* 34 (1999): 151–58.

63. Ibid., 153.
64. Charles E. Gutenson, *Reconsidering the Doctrine of God* (New York: T & T Clark, 2005), 197.
65. Polkinghorne, *Belief in God in an Age of Science*, 51ff.
66. See, for example, Philip Clayton, *Mind and Emergence: from Quantum to Consciousness* (Oxford: Oxford University Press, 2004).
67. Hefner, "Role of Science in Pannenberg's Theological Thinking," 275ff.

*Chapter 5*

1. Alister E. McGrath, *T. F. Torrance: An Intellectual Biography* (Edinburgh: T & T Clark, 1999).
2. Ibid., 57–58.
3. Thomas F. Torrance, *Karl Barth: Biblical and Evangelical Theologian* (Edinburgh: T & T Clark, 1990).
4. McGrath, *T. F. Torrance*, 54.
5. W. W. Bartley III, *The Retreat to Commitment*, 2nd ed. (La Salle, IL: Open Court, 1984).
6. Thomas F. Torrance, *Theological Science* (Edinburgh: T & T Clark, 1969; paperback edition, 1996) (hereafter cited as *TS*).
7. Ted Peters, *Science, Theology, and Ethics* (Aldershot, UK: Ashgate, 2003), 26.
8. Thomas F. Torrance, *God and Rationality* (Edinburgh: T & T Clark, 1971; paperback edition, 1997) (hereafter cited as *GR*).
9. Thomas F. Torrance, *The Ground and Grammar of Theology* (Belfast: Christian Journals, 1980) (hereafter cited as *GGT*).
10. Thomas F. Torrance, *Divine and Contingent Order*, rev. ed. (1981; Edinburgh: T & T Clark, 1998) (hereafter cited as *DCO*).
11. Thomas A. Langford, "T. F. Torrance's *Theological Science*: A Reaction," *Scottish Journal of Theology* 25, no. 2 (1972): 155–70.
12. Ibid.
13. Peters, *Science, Theology, and Ethics*, 28.
14. Bartley, *Retreat to Commitment.*
15. Friedrich Schleiermacher, *The Christian Faith*, ed. H. R. Mackintosh and J. S. Stewart (Edinburgh: T & T Clark, 1928), 12ff.
16. Dietrich Bonhoeffer, *Letters and Papers from Prison*, rev. ed. (London: SCM Press, 1971), 311–12, 325–28.
17. Note that Torrance uses the term "contingence" instead of the more usual "contingency."
18. Peter Harrison, *The Fall of Man and the Foundations of Science* (Cambridge: Cambridge University Press, 2008).
19. The impact of Bacon on the exploitation of nature is examined in Richard Bauckham, *God and the Crisis of Freedom: Biblical and Contemporary Perspectives* (Louisville, KY: Westminster John Knox Press, 2002), 159–68.
20. Achtemeier makes the interesting point that Newton himself regarded geometry as stemming from the practical art of measuring rather than the self-evident principles of reason. See Mark Achtemeier, "Natural Science and Christian Faith in the Thought of Thomas Torrance," in *The Promise of Trinitarian*

*Theology: Theologians in Dialogue with Thomas F. Torrance*, ed. Elmer M. Colyer (Oxford: Rowman and Littlefield, 2001), 269–302; quote appears on 299–300.

21. Christopher B. Kaiser, "Humanity in an Intelligible Cosmos: Non-Duality in Albert Einstein and Thomas Torrance," in Colyer, *Promise of Trinitarian Theology*, 239–67.
22. Tapio Luoma, *Incarnation and Physics: Natural Science in the Theology of Thomas F. Torrance* (Oxford: Oxford University Press, 2002), 90ff.
23. Alister E. McGrath, *The Open Secret: A New Vision for Natural Theology* (Oxford: Blackwell, 2008), 106.
24. Ibid., 108.
25. McGrath, *T. F. Torrance*, 75.
26. Ibid., 74.
27. John Polkinghorne, *Quantum Theory: A Very Short Introduction* (Oxford: Oxford University Press, 2002), 37.
28. Roger Trigg, *Rationality and Religion* (Oxford: Blackwell, 1998).
29. See, for example, John Polkinghorne, "The New Natural Theology," *Studies in World Christianity* 1, no. 1 (1995): 41–50; Polkinghorne, "Where Is Natural Theology Today?" *Science and Christian Belief* 18, no. 2 (2006): 169–79.
30. John Polkinghorne, *Science and Christian Belief* (London: SPCK, 1994), 3.
31. Polkinghorne, "Where Is Natural Theology Today?," 169.
32. Thomas F. Torrance, *Space, Time and Incarnation* (Edinburgh: T & T Clark, 1969; paperback edition, 1997).
33. Achtemeier, "Natural Science and Christian Faith in the Thought of Thomas Torrance," 269–302.
34. Peter E. Hodgson, *Theology and Modern Physics* (Aldershot, UK: Ashgate, 2005), 104; see also Colin Weightman, *Theology in a Polanyian Universe: The Theology of Thomas Torrance* (New York: Lang, 1994), 191.
35. Luoma, *Incarnation and Physics*, 56–57.
36. See, for example, John D. Barrow, *The World within the World* (Oxford: Oxford University Press, 1988), 174–77.
37. Thomas F. Torrance, *Christian Theology and Scientific Culture* (Belfast: Christian Journals, 1980) (hereafter cited as *CTSC*).
38. Michael Polanyi, *Personal Knowledge: Towards a Post-Critical Philosophy* (Chicago: University of Chicago Press, 1974), 214; cited in John Polkinghorne, *Faith, Science and Understanding* (London: SPCK, 2000), 33–34.
39. See, for example, Richard Swinburne, *Epistemic Justification* (Oxford: Oxford University Press, 2001).
40. James Barr, *Biblical Faith and Natural Theology* (Oxford: Oxford University Press, 1993).
41. Brian Hebblethwaite, *The Problems of Theology* (Cambridge: Cambridge University Press, 1980), 79.
42. Albert Einstein, letter to Maurice Solovine, March 30, 1952, quoted in Stanley Jaki, "Theological Aspects of Creative Science," in *Creation, Christ and Culture: Studies in Honour of T. F. Torrance*, ed. Richard W. A. McKinney (Edinburgh: T & T Clark, 1976), 164.

43. Ibid.
44. C. J. Isham and J. C. Polkinghorne, "The Debate over the Block Universe," in *Quantum Cosmology and the Laws of Nature: Scientific Perspectives on Divine Action*, ed. Robert John Russell, Nancey Murphy, and C. J. Isham, 2nd ed., (Vatican City State: Vatican Observatory Publications, 1996), 139–48.
45. A number of authors have pointed this out, e.g., Achtemeier, "Natural Science and Christian Faith in the Thought of Thomas Torrance," 295.
46. John Polkinghorne, *Reason and Reality: The Relationship between Science and Theology* (London: SPCK, 1991), 93.
47. Polkinghorne, *Faith, Science and Understanding*, 175.
48. Luoma, *Incarnation and Physics*, 111.
49. John Polkinghorne, *Belief in God in an Age of Science* (New Haven, CT: Yale University Press, 1998), 81.
50. Ernan McMullin, "How Should Cosmology Relate to Theology?" in *The Sciences and Theology in the Twentieth Century*, ed. A. R. Peacocke (Stocksfield: Oriel, 1981), 17–57, 56n50.
51. Quoting Michael Polanyi, *Scientific Thought and Social Reality*, ed. F. Schwartz (New York: International Universities Press, 1974), 136–37.
52. Richard Dawkins, *The Selfish Gene* (Oxford: Oxford University Press, 1989), v.
53. P. W. Atkins, *The Creation* (Oxford: W. H. Freeman & Co., 1981), 35–37.
54. Francis Crick, *The Astonishing Hypothesis: The Scientific Search for the Soul* (London: Simon and Schuster, 1994), 3.
55. See, for example, Nancey Murphy and William R. Stoeger, SJ, eds., *Evolution and Emergence: Systems, Organisms, Persons* (Oxford: Oxford University Press, 2007); Philip Clayton and Paul Davies, eds., *The Re-Emergence of Emergence: The Emergentist Hypothesis from Science to Religion* (Oxford: Oxford University Press, 2006).
56. Denis Noble, *The Music of Life: Biology beyond the Genome* (Oxford: Oxford University Press, 2006).
57. Paul Davies, *The Mind of God* (London: Simon and Schuster, 1992), 167.
58. Stephen W. Hawking, "Gödel and the End of Physics," public lecture, Dirac Centennial Celebration, Cambridge, July 20, 2002; http://www.damtp.cam.ac.uk/dirac/dirac/hawking/.
59. Roger Penrose, *The Emperor's New Mind: Concerning Computers, Minds and the Laws of Physics* (Oxford: Oxford University Press, 1989). Penrose has responded to critics of his position in Roger Penrose, *Shadows of the Mind* (Oxford: Oxford University Press, 1994).
60. Polkinghorne, *Reason and Reality*, 38.
61. Weightman, *Theology in a Polanyian Universe*, 190.
62. See, for example, Rodney D. Holder, *God, the Multiverse, and Everything: Modern Cosmology and the Argument from Design* (Aldershot, UK: Ashgate, 2004).
63. Bonhoeffer, *Letters and Papers from Prison*, 325, 360.
64. Achtemeier, "Natural Science and Christian Faith in the Thought of Thomas Torrance," 292.
65. See, for example, Holder, *God, the Multiverse, and Everything*.

*Chapter 6*

1. Alister E. McGrath, *Dawkins' God: Genes, Memes, and the Meaning of Life* (Oxford: Blackwell, 2005) (hereafter cited as *DG*).
2. Alister E. McGrath with Joanna Collicutt McGrath, *The Dawkins Delusion: Atheist Fundamentalism and the Denial of the Divine* (London: SPCK, 2007) (hereafter cited as *DD*).
3. Alister E. McGrath, *A Scientific Theology*, vol. 1, *Nature* (Edinburgh: T & T Clark, 2001); Alister E. McGrath, *A Scientific Theology*, vol. 2, *Reality* (Grand Rapids: William B. Eerdmans, 2002); Alister E. McGrath, *A Scientific Theology*, vol. 3, *Theory* (Grand Rapids: William B. Eerdmans, 2003) (hereafter cited as *STN*, *STR*, and *STT*, respectively).
4. Alister E. McGrath, *The Science of God* (London: T & T Clark International, 2004) (hereafter cited as *SG*).
5. Alister E. McGrath, *The Open Secret: A New Vision for Natural Theology* (Oxford: Blackwell, 2008) (hereafter cited as *OS*).
6. Alister E. McGrath, *A Fine-Tuned Universe: The Quest for God in Science and Theology*, The 2009 Gifford Lectures (Louisville, KY: Westminster John Knox Press, 2009) (hereafter cited as *FTU*).
7. Alister E. McGrath, *The Order of Things* (Oxford: Blackwell, 2006) (hereafter cited as *OT*).
8. Alister E. McGrath, *The Foundations of Dialogue in Science and Religion* (Oxford: Blackwell, 1998) (hereafter cited as *FD*).
9. Alister E. McGrath, *Science and Religion: An Introduction* (Oxford: Blackwell, 1999).
10. James F. Keating, "The Natural Sciences as *Ancillae Theologiae Novae*: Alister E. McGrath's *A Scientific Theology*," *The Thomist* 69 (2005): 127–52.
11. Ibid., 136.
12. Ibid.
13. Ibid., 151.
14. Ibid.
15. Andreas Losch, "On the Origins of Critical Realism," *Theology and Science* 7, no. 1 (2009): 85–106.
16. Ibid., 97.
17. John Polkinghorne, *Science and Christian Belief: Theological Reflections of a Bottom-up Thinker* (London: SPCK, 1994), 156.
18. Wolfhart Pannenberg, *Theology and the Philosophy of Science*, trans. Francis McDonagh (German ed., 1973; Philadelphia: Westminster Press, 1976), 269–75. See discussion in chap. 4.
19. Elmer M. Colyer, *Pro Ecclesia* 12, no. 2 (2003): 226–31; Elmer M. Colyer, *Pro Ecclesia* 12, no. 4 (2003): 492–97; Elmer M. Colyer, *Pro Ecclesia* 13, no. 2 (2004): 233–40; review essays of Alister E. McGrath, *Nature*, *Reality*, and *Theory*, respectively.
20. Thomas F. Torrance, *God and Rationality*, paperback ed. (1971; Edinburgh: T & T Clark, 1997), 133.
21. Richard Dawkins, *Unweaving the Rainbow: Science, Delusion and the Appetite for Wonder* (London: Penguin, 1998).

22. Karl Barth, *Protestant Theology in the Nineteenth Century*, trans. John Bowden, new ed., (London: SCM, 2001).
23. The quotation is from C. S. Lewis, "Is Theology Poetry?" in *Essay Collection and Other Short Pieces* (London: Harper Collins, 2000), 10–21, quote appears on 21.
24. William Alston, *Perceiving God: The Epistemology of Religious Experience* (Ithaca, NY: Cornell University Press, 1991), 289.
25. James Barr, *Biblical Faith and Natural Theology* (Oxford: Oxford University Press, 1993), 1.
26. Thomas Nagel, *The View from Nowhere* (New York: Oxford University Press, 1989, 13–27).
27. Especially in Keith Ward, *Why There Almost Certainly Is a God: Doubting Dawkins* (Oxford: Lion Hudson, 2008).
28. These principles are developed in Richard Swinburne, *Epistemic Justification* (Oxford: Oxford University Press, 2001), 123–27, 141–49; and in Swinburne, *The Existence of God*, 2nd ed. (Oxford: Oxford University Press, 2004), 303–15; 322–24.
29. Richard Swinburne, "Natural Theology, Its 'Dwindling Probabilities' and 'Lack of Rapport,'" *Faith and Philosophy* 21, no. 4 (2004): 533–46.
30. Swinburne's argument against Plantinga on this point is also in Richard Swinburne, *The Resurrection of God Incarnate* (Oxford: Oxford University Press, 2003), 215–16n4.
31. Swinburne, "Natural Theology, Its 'Dwindling Probabilities' and 'Lack of Rapport,'" 536.
32. Richard Swinburne, *Providence and the Problem of Evil* (Oxford: Oxford University Press, 1998), xi.
33. Swinburne, "Natural Theology, Its 'Dwindling Probabilities' and 'Lack of Rapport,'" 533ff.
34. Dietrich Bonhoeffer, *Letters and Papers from Prison*, ed. Eberhard Bethge (London: SCM Press, 1971), 286.
35. Polkinghorne, *Science and Christian Belief*, 156.
36. Robin Collins, "The Multiverse Hypothesis: A Theistic Perspective," in *Universe or Multiverse?* ed. Bernard Carr (Cambridge: Cambridge University Press, 2007). The older chapter cited by McGrath is Robin Collins, "A Scientific Argument for the Existence of God: The Fine-Tuning Design Argument," in *Reason for the Hope Within*, ed. Michael J. Murray (Grand Rapids: Eerdmans, 1999), 47–75.
37. Eugene Wigner, "The Unreasonable Effectiveness of Mathematics in the Natural Sciences," *Communications in Pure and Applied Mathematics* 13 (1960): 1–14.
38. Richard Swinburne, *The Christian God* (Oxford: Oxford University Press, 1994), chap. 8; see also Swinburne (2004), *Existence of God*, Additional Note 1.
39. C. S. Lewis, *Christian Reflections* (Grand Rapids: Eerdmans, 1967), 65.
40. George Steiner, *Real Presences: Is There Anything in What We Say?* (London: Faber, 1991), 67.
41. C. S. Lewis, "The Weight of Glory," in *Screwtape Proposes a Toast, and Other Pieces* (London: Fontana, 1965), 94–110.

42. Michael Polanyi, *Personal Knowledge: Towards a Post-Critical Philosophy* (Chicago: University of Chicago Press, 1974), 133.
43. Iris Murdoch, *The Sovereignty of Good* (London: Routledge, 1970), 37.
44. C. S. Lewis, *The Abolition of Man* (London: Collins, 1978), 49–59.
45. McGrath, *Fine-Tuned Universe.*
46. Louis Dupré, *The Enlightenment and the Intellectual Foundations of Modern Culture* (New Haven, CT: Yale University Press, 2004), 12–17.
47. Charles Darwin, *The Origin of Species by Means of Natural Selection, or the Preservation of Favoured Races in the Struggle for Life*, ed. J. W. Burrow (1859; London: Penguin, 1968), 458.
48. Ibid., 459–60.
49. J. D. Barrow and F. J. Tipler, *The Anthropic Cosmological Principle* (Oxford: Oxford University Press, 1986).
50. M. J. Rees, *Just Six Numbers: The Deep Forces that Shape the Universe* (London: Weidenfeld & Nicolson, 1999).
51. Swinburne, *Existence of God*, 13.
52. A. R. Peacocke, *Theology for a Scientific Age*, 2nd enlarged ed. (London: SCM Press, 1993), 107–9; Don N. Page, "Predictions and Tests of Multiverse Theories," in Carr, *Universe or Multiverse?* 411–29; Robin Collins, "The Multiverse Hypothesis: A Theistic Perspective," in Carr, *Universe or Multiverse?* 459–80.
53. Leonard Susskind, *The Cosmic Landscape: String Theory and the Illusion of Intelligent Design* (New York: Little, Brown and Company, 2006).
54. John Hedley Brooke, "Darwin and Victorian Christianity," in *The Cambridge Companion to Darwin*, ed. Jonathan Hodge and Gregory Radick (Cambridge: Cambridge University Press, 2003), 192–213, esp. 206–7.
55. John Hedley Brooke, *Science and Religion: Some Historical Perspectives* (Cambridge: Cambridge University Press, 1991), 313–14; and in Brooke and Geoffrey Cantor, *Reconstructing Nature: The Engagement of Science and Religion* (Edinburgh: T & T Clark, 1998), 165.
56. Stephen J. Gould, *Wonderful Life: The Burgess Shale and the Nature of History* (New York: W. W. Norton, 1989), 290.
57. Ibid., 101–2.
58. Charles S. Peirce, *Collected Papers of Charles Sanders Peirce*, ed. Charles Hartshorne and Paul Weiss, 8 vols. (Cambridge, MA: Harvard University Press, 1960), 1:211.
59. Peter Geach, *Providence and Evil* (Cambridge: Cambridge University Press, 1977), 58.
60. Colin E. Gunton, *The Triune Creator: A Historical and Systematic Study* (Edinburgh: Edinburgh University Press, 1998).

### *Chapter 7*

1. E.g., John Earman, and Colin Howson and Peter Urbach. See John Earman, *Bayes or Bust? A Critical Examination of Bayesian Confirmation Theory* (Cambridge, MA: MIT Press, 1992); and Colin Howson and Peter Urbach, *Scientific Reasoning: The Bayesian Approach*, 2nd ed. (Chicago: Open Court, 1992).

# Index